Sanitation in Urban Britain, 1560–1700

Popular belief holds that throwing the contents of a chamber pot into the street was a common occurrence during the early modern period. This book challenges this deeply entrenched stereotypical image as the majority of urban inhabitants and their local governors alike valued clean outdoor public spaces, vesting interest in keeping the areas in which they lived and worked clean.

Taking an extensive tour of over thirty towns and cities across early modern Britain, focusing on Edinburgh and York as in-depth case studies, this book sheds light on the complex relationship between how governors organized street cleaning, managed waste disposal and regulated the cleanliness of the outdoor environment, top-down, and how typical urban inhabitants self-regulated their neighbourhoods, bottom-up. The urban-rural manure trade, sanitation infrastructure, waste-disposal technology, plague epidemics, contemporary understandings of malodours and miasmatic disease transmission and urban agriculture are also analysed.

This book will enable undergraduates, postgraduates and established academics to deepen their understanding of daily life and sensory experiences in the early modern British town. This innovative work will appeal to social, cultural and legal historians as well as researchers of history of medicine and public health.

Leona J. Skelton is Post-Doctoral Research Assistant in the History Department at University of Bristol, UK.

Perspectives in Economic and Social History
Series Editors: Andrew August
Jari Eloranta

Forthcoming Titles

Sanitation in Urban Britain, 1560–1700

Leona J. Skelton

Routledge
Taylor & Francis Group

LONDON AND NEW YORK

First published 2016 by Routledge

2 Park Square, Milton Park, Abingdon, Oxfordshire OX14 4RN
52 Vanderbilt Avenue, New York, NY 10017

Routledge is an imprint of the Taylor & Francis Group, an informa business

First issued in paperback 2020

British Library Cataloguing in Publication Data
A catalogue record for this book is available from the British Library

Library of Congress Cataloging in Publication Data
Skelton, Leona J., author.
Sanitation in urban Britain, 1560-1700 / Leona J. Skelton.
1. Sanitation--Great Britain--History--16th century. 2. Sanitation--Great
Britain--History--17th century. 3. Public health--Great Britain--History--
16th century. 4. Public health--Great Britain--History--17th century.
I. Title.
RA485.S536 2016
363.720941--dc23
2015029600

ISBN: 978-1-84893-592-1 (hbk)
ISBN: 978-0-367-66856-3 (pbk)

Typeset in Times New Roman
by Saxon Graphics Ltd, Derby

Dedicated to the memory of Prof. Christopher W. Brooks
(1948–2014)

*My brilliant PhD supervisor who died before he could see this
work in print*

Contents

Figures

Acknowledgements

Many people have assisted me in the important task of writing an early modern history of British sanitation. I owe the biggest debt to my MA and PhD supervisors, Prof. Christopher Brooks and Dr Adrian Green, who helped me to conceptualize the project and to develop my arguments cogently between 2007 and 2012 at Durham University. They both exceeded the call of duty substantially, sharing very willingly far more of their time, insight and experience than necessary. Their respective expertise in legal history and in architectural and landscape history underpins this book substantially. Sadly, in August 2014, Chris Brooks died unexpectedly, before he could see the project in print, but this book which he urged me to write is dedicated to him with immense respect and as an expression of my appreciation for all that he did for me. It was a huge priviledge to have been taken under his academic wing.

I also owe a huge thank you to Prof. Maureen Meikle, who helped me a great deal as I transcribed many Scots manuscript archives during my doctorate. As my external doctoral supervisor, her expertise in relation to the broader Scottish and comparative Anglo-Scottish contexts of the project proved invaluable. Maureen supervised my undergraduate dissertation, 'Pursuing Improvement: Public hygiene in Scottish burghs, 1500–1700', at the University of Sunderland, which won the Royal Historical Society/*History Scotland* prize in 2007 for the best undergraduate dissertation on Scottish History. Maureen sparked and fuelled my passion for early modern British history as an undergraduate and has kindly mentored and supported me throughout my early academic career, and for that I am and always will be grateful.

I would like to thank the Durham University Doctoral Fellowship Scheme for awarding me such a generous scholarship, without which I could not have completed this project in its original format as my PhD thesis. The thesis itself stood very much on the shoulders of my interdisciplinary MA in Seventeenth-Century Studies, which was very fortunately and generously funded by the Arts and Humanities Research Council. I count myself as extremely lucky to have been given the opportunity to complete my MA and PhD with the much-appreciated cushioning of full financial support.

The archivists who showed me the way through a vast array of English and Scottish archive collections during the research stage of the project were hugely helpful. Their knowledge of the manuscript collections was first-rate. If not for their advice and support, I could not have harvested such a large volume of rich, original research. Though she is now enjoying her well-deserved retirement from her position as Assistant Keeper of the Archives and Special Collections at Durham University Library, I would particularly like to thank Miss Margaret McCollum for equipping me with my palaeographical skills as a masters student, for giving me the confidence to handle original documents and for offering kind support throughout my doctoral research too.

I have benefited from much praise, constructive criticism and encouragement, in relation to my research into this topic, from far more scholars than I have the space below to acknowledge. In particular, I would like to thank Prof. Richard Oram (University of Stirling), Prof. Elizabeth Ewan (Guelph University), Prof. Roey Sweet (Leicester University), Prof. Guy Geltner (University of Amsterdam) and Prof. David Moon (University of York). I also thank this book's two anonymous reviewers for suggesting improvements to the manuscript. Thank you to everyone for enabling me to write the book for which I searched high and low as an undergraduate, but never found.

Conventions

I have endeavoured to make my transcriptions of the original documents as clear as possible. In some cases this has necessitated changing the original spelling to a more modern format, but the words themselves have not been changed. The now obsolete thorn, represented by the letter 'y' has been changed to a 'th' and the obsolete yogh has been changed to a 'y' in all cases. The interchangeable letters, 'i' and 'y' and 'u' and 'v', respectively, have been swapped where appropriate. The superfluous 'i' before the 's' in Scots plural words has also been removed in all transcriptions. All dates have been modernized. For example, a date which was recorded as 04/02/1582, shortly before New Year's Day which was celebrated on 25th March, has been written as 04/02/1583. Currency is in English pounds (li), shillings (s) and pence (d) followed by 'Scots' in the case of pounds Scots. A Scottish merk was worth 13s 4d.

English and Scots glossary

English

Besom   A broom made from a bundle of twigs tied around a central pole

Dunghill   A heap of manure, usually piled on a forefront for storage before eventual removal by the householder, a scavenger or local farmer

Dungmixon   A heap of manure, or a dunghill, a term which was used most commonly in Bristol

Forefront   The area between the front of one's property and the crown of the street for which householders tended to be responsible in terms of cleaning and paving

House of Office   Toilet, usually a simple wooden seat suspended above a deep pit

Midding/midden   A large pile of dung and/or household waste, usually piled on a forefront for storage before eventual removal by the householder, a scavenger or a local farmer

Midding Stead   A temporary holding dump at the edge of a town in which large quantities of dung could be stored until they were transported to the surrounding countryside

Privy   Toilet, usually a simple wooden seat suspended above a deep pit

Soo   Bucket

Shule   Shovel

Tipstave   Officer of a court

Scots

Backland   A long narrow plot of land, situated behind residential and business properties on a burgh's main streets, upon which livestock could be kept, horses stabled and crops grown. They were similar to English burgage plots

Band   Bound – livestock in band was securely retained within cruives on backlands rather than roaming through the streets out of band

Besom   A broom made from a bundle of twigs tied around a central pole

Burgh   A town

Burgh Muir   Common pasture possessed by, but usually outside of, a burgh upon which urban inhabitants could graze their livestock – especially cattle

Calsay   Causeway/thoroughfare

To Clenye   To clean

Closs Glass   Glass fitted close to the window frames

Cobill   A cistern for the reception of drainage

Cruives   Pig pens – usually on backlands

To dicht   To clean or tidy

Fleschour/flesher   Butcher

Fuilyie/failyie   Excrement, dung, sweepings of the street, rubbish, waste

Furrier   Cleaner and/or processor of animal skins and/or furs

Gavel   End wall of a property

Haill   The whole or every

Ilk   Each

Jaques   Privy

Jaw holl   Vertical pipe or shoot, usually made of lead, for the drainage of liquid waste descending from inside a property down into a sewer

Kine   Cattle

Laithe   Low

Nolt   Cattle

Provost   Principal urban official in a burgh – similar to an English mayor

To Red   To clear/clean

Red   Waste material, typically building debris or rubble

Rubbish/rubbidge   Unwanted material to be removed from properties, often the by-products from demolition and construction

To Set   To sell (i.e. to set the gait dichtings meant to sell the contract for collecting the burgh's muck)

Shield   Privy

Stanchions   Stanchions/brackets

Swine   Pigs

Syre   Sewer

Tallow   Hard animal fat, which was melted down to produce candles

Tirles   Tiles

To waird   To imprison

Walker/walkster   Fuller of cloth, male/female

Watergait   An open drain into which liquid waste could be deposited. They were also intended to prevent flooding by facilitating the drainage of rain water

Weshe   Stale urine

Wynd   A close or lane

Introduction

The 'chamber pot in the window': myth or reality?

Between 1560 and 1700, the area of local government which today is known as public hygiene was, then as now, crucial to successful cohabitation in urban settlements. Throughout this period, townspeople across Britain developed more sophisticated and efficient methods of disposing of waste, they suppressed and regulated insanitary nuisances increasingly rigorously and they cleaned the streets more frequently, often using innovative and imaginative methods. Most twenty-first-century British people take for granted teams of street cleaners, weekly rubbish collections and the underground sewerage network to which their flushing toilet is connected. Today, these systems are maintained largely behind the scenes, and their effective functioning requires minimal effort from householders. But even now lapses in adequate public hygiene provision can occur, during strike action by local council waste-collection operatives, for example. It is true that maintaining an acceptable standard of outdoor cleanliness was far more a part of inhabitants' daily lives, far more hands-on and far more beholden to householders' compliance and efforts than it is in a modern-day context. This element of urban life required significant amounts of physical labour – shovelling, sweeping, scouring, carrying and hauling – which was often performed by paid servants and labourers on householders' behalves. Pre-industrial British towns lacked flushing toilets and comprehensive networks of underground sewers; waste disposal was largely householders' responsibility and it often involed dealing with the bulky byproduct of manure from urban agricultural activity or horse-drawn transportation in which many engaged heavily on or near to their properties. On the other hand, certain elements of the sanitation infrastructure required minimal effort from householders. For example, many townspeople could take for granted the efficient functioning of the civic-funded main street open sewers which drained their streets and the maintenance of some public areas such as marketplaces and gates which were repaired and swept by civic employees.

Images of sixteenth- and seventeenth-century urban dwellers throwing their rubbish, dirty water and the contents of their chamber pots out of windows and doors down into the streets below, day after day, are deeply entrenched in the current, popular historical imagination. It is widely implied, moreover, that contemporaries disposed of their waste in this way without expressing any concern for the sanitary standard of the outdoor public spaces in which they lived and worked. The period 1560 to 1700 in particular, and the whole pre-modern period more generally, is misunderstood as an epoch during which, apparently, urban inhabitants did not value maintaining a clean environment in their wards and neighbourhoods, and in their streets, market places and other outdoor public areas. Regrettably, the stereotypical image of a maidservant leaning out of an upstairs window, thoughtlessly clutching an upturned chamber pot in her hands as a shower of filth descends upon the heads of those passing by on the street below, has become almost synonymous with the early modern period itself. Typically, a popular writer and journalist, Richard Girling, asserts that pre-modern town dwellers 'scent-marked the future' by 'swilling everything into the street'.[1] Describing the entire early modern period (1500–1800), Girling elaborates, 'in terms of hygiene, medieval England would stretch well into the nineteenth century, where it would find Charles Dickens waiting for it'.[2] And in 2011, the popular historian Dan Snow presented a three-part BBC television series entitled 'Filthy Cities' in which medieval, early modern and nineteenth-century cities were portrayed as places populated by people who acquiesced in muck and made no efforts to improve sanitation.[3] But those who write for the public do not work alone in disseminating the 'chamber pot in the window' myth. Less than four decades ago, Lawrence Stone asserted that there was an 'almost total ignorance of … public hygiene' in early modern England.[4] In the same decade, the social historian Frederick Emmison wrote a history of everyday, domestic life in Essex villages, in which he concluded that Elizabethan environmental regulation systems were ineffective, that 'manor courts grappled in a ceaseless struggle with the problems of foul drainage and filthy dumps' and that the environment was consequently filthy.[5] Christopher Smout's comment in 1969 that Scottish urban communities were 'lucky if the burgh employed a man with a horse and cart to shift the middens' was written in a similar vein.[6] And, according to Peter Clark and Paul Slack, writing in 1976, while an early modern town's main thoroughfares 'might occasionally be kept paved and relatively clean by rudimentary improvement schemes, most streets were little more than open sewers'.[7] James Thomas came to a similar conclusion several decades earlier, in 1933, in his *Town Government in the Sixteenth Century*, in which he argued that sanitation infrastructures were inadequate and that environmental concern was low.[8]

As recently as 2007, Emily Cockayne published a monograph presenting a highly selective, and unrepresentative, list of the worst examples of sensory experiences in early modern London, Oxford, Bath and Manchester.[9] It is significant that Cockayne's *Hubbub* is based on far more edited and printed collections of the manuscript sources, and on proportionately far fewer of the original manuscript archival series themselves. Edited collections of primary documents tend to contain disproportionately more of the most noteworthy, worst and unusual extracts from the extensive archival manuscripts. When writing about such a complex issue as attitudes towards dirt and cleanliness, Cockayne's methodology inevitably leads to an unbalanced, unrepresentative and inaccurate depiction of early modern urban street scenes, featuring, for example, 'the festering stew that littered urban streets', wandering swine which 'poked their filthy snouts into grain sacks and discarded entrails, and grubbed through stinking dunghills' and paving stones 'coated with dirt and mire', thus reinforcing the 'chamber pot in the window' myth.[10] Cockayne's tone is consistently patronising towards our forebears, the people who laid the foundations in the long term for modern-day urban planning in what were very difficult technological, demographic and economic circumstances. The book's chapter headings – Ugly, Itchy, Mouldy, Noisy, Grotty, Busy, Dirty and Gloomy – which evoke the fairytale of *Snow White and the Seven Dwarfs*, are incongruous in the context of a serious analysis of historic sanitation. Indeed, as Bernard Capp rightly asserts in relation to *Hubbub*, 'this is a survey rather than a history', and he also observes that Cockayne 'does not explore in any depth the balance between progress and deterioration, or how far contemporary perceptions changed on what was acceptable or desirable'.[11] While *Hubbub* uses a plethora of descriptive examples with which to emphasize very effectively and vividly the failures of seventeenth-century urban sanitation systems, and the often overlooked sensory experiences of those failures, it fails to penetrate in any significant depth local governors' and inhabitants' attitudes towards this area of daily life and contemporaries' aspirations towards creating a cleaner urban landscape. Indeed, all of the above contributions towards the 'chamber pot in the window' myth, some of which were written in academic books which are still read widely today, fail to do justice to the increasingly complex, sophisticated and positive action taken by urban dwellers and their local governors to improve the sanitary condition of their outdoor environment and thereby their daily life quality. Indeed, as Mark Jenner observes, 'historians have too often depicted the inhabitants of pre-industrial cities as wallowing cheerfully in grime from which they were finally rescued by nineteenth-century sanitary intervention'; such assumptions, he argues, 'beautifully exemplify the abiding condescension of posterity'.[12]

Of course, a minority of urban inhabitants did throw waste into the streets and certain individuals created a whole array of other insanitary nuisances in their neighbourhoods throughout the period 1560 to 1700 – including leaving dunghills unremoved for longer than was permitted, allowing livestock to roam freely, throwing human waste out of windows, sullying wells and rivers and blocking open sewers with solid waste. But the majority of urban dwellers valued their townscapes and endeavoured to protect collective standards of outdoor cleanliness against their less fastidious neighbours whose insanitary activities threatened to undermine them. However filthy early modern urban streets seem through modern-day eyes, it is profoundly unjust to assume that the people who lived and worked in them were necessarily indifferent to the cleanliness of their immediate outdoor environment. Urban governors and the overwhelming majority of neighbours perceived the wilful creation of insanitary, and especially malodorous, nuisances in their townscapes as unambiguously unacceptable and they invested significant time, money and energy into suppressing them. Significant evidence of contemporaries' concern over the cleanliness of the outdoor urban landscape survives in the form of petitions to local councils, treasurers' accounts, local court presentments for contravening sanitation bylaws and the minutes of insanitary nuisance court cases which clearly originated from one neighbour's perceived need to suppress the insanitary activities of another. Across Britain, typical urban inhabitants were quick to complain to civic officials and to their local courts when their neighbours disposed of waste or conducted noxious crafts in ways which offended them and they were not afraid to petition their councils when dirty conditions reduced their life quality. Indeed, there is much evidence to suggest that the majority of urban neighbours acted as an informal, but remarkably coherent and effective, institution in their collective and individual efforts to regulate their micro-scale environment largely in harmony with official top-down regulation from formal governing institutions.

The term 'waste' was not used by contemporaries in relation to rubbish and other unwanted materials, though they did use the term 'rubbidge' or 'rubbish' in most towns and the word 'trash' in seventeenth-century Bristol. The word 'waste' is used throughout the book as an umbrella term encompassing all solid and liquid materials which inhabitants wanted to remove from their homes, businesses and neighbourhoods because they themselves had no further use for them. Some of this 'waste' was used subsequently by others, as in the case of urban manure having been used as a fertilizer by local farmers. Waste materials included: construction and demolition waste, butchery offal, stable manure, human excrement and urine, dirty water from cleaning, cooking and washing clothes, the corpses of animals such as horses and dogs and small amounts of manmade materials such as metal and glass.

This book is not an attempt to ascertain how clean or dirty early modern urban streets actually were. Rather, it delves beneath the 'chamber pot in the window' stereotype in order to explore and evaluate how local and national governors perceived sanitation, organized street cleaning, managed waste disposal and regulated the cleanliness of the macro-scale outdoor environment. It also analyses how typical urban inhabitants self-regulated the sanitary standard of their own neighbourhoods, making important efforts to shape environmental regulation themselves, from the bottom upwards. I do not argue that there was marked antagonism between inhabitants and urban governors in the management of waste disposal and environmental regulation, or indeed a gap between inhabitants' concern and governors' control. Clearly, pitting progressive, industrious and 'clean' urban governors against backward, generally unwilling and 'dirty' inhabitants would provide a misleading framework in which to reconstruct attitudes towards waste and insanitary nuisances in this period. It would be similarly misleading to approach the topic primarily as a socio-economic issue, pitting 'clean' and civilizing elites against the 'dirty' general populace. I argue, conversely, that there was actually significant symmetry and harmony between the efforts, perceptions and attitudes of governors and the governed in relation to outdoor cleanliness. Early modern waste disposal bylaws simply could not have functioned successfully had the majority of the urban population not wanted, welcomed and obeyed them. Far from waiting idly and passively for local and national governing institutions to take action to improve the sanitary condition of the outdoor urban landscape on their behalves, neighbours very often used their own initiative to pursue and then to maintain their own collective standard of cleanliness in the outdoor public spaces with which they were so familiar. Indeed, in relation to this area of urban management in the preceding late medieval period, Carole Rawcliffe firmly rejects the assumption that 'whatever initiatives were eventually adopted must have been imposed from above, by the crown, upon a resistant and ignorant populace'.[13] While the origins of such positive attitudes from the bottom-up are undoubtedly rooted in the medieval period, they underwent substantial further development in the sixteenth and seventeenth centuries, at least up to the dawn of the eighteenth century. Before 1700, inhabitants' concern over the cleanliness of outdoor public spaces was generally strong and their efforts to improve that aspect of urban life largely complemented and reflected those of their local and national governors to manage waste and to improve outdoor salubrity from above. The 'chamber pot in the window' myth should be thrown out of the window once and for all.

Contemporary literature

The 'chamber pot in the window' stereotype can be at least partly attributed to contemporary travel literature, diaries and poems, some of which have depicted sixteenth- and seventeenth-century urban streets, sewers and even houses as having overflowed with filth. Unsurprisingly, widely accessible, sensationalistic and dramatic examples of contemporary literature have attracted disproportionately higher levels of interest than manuscript legal court minute books and administrative and financial council records. Many unrepresentative samples of such legal, administrative and financial records have been printed while conversely most of these records' full extant versions are only available in their original manuscript format. The full manuscript collections, however, provide a much more balanced and realistic view of sanitation systems and daily urban life. It is, of course, much more entertaining to read contemporary literature. Ben Jonson's mock-heroic poem, 'On The Famous Voyage', for example, describes two imaginary travellers returning from the Mermaid Tavern on Bread Street to Holbourn, making their way up London's Fleet Ditch on a wherry as they face deeply unpleasant, successive scenes of a detestable cesspool decorated with rotting animal carcasses. The Fleet Ditch, which was covered in 1737, was a place where, according to Jonson, 'The sinks ran grease and the hair of meazled hogs/The heads, houghs, entrails, and the hides of dogs'.[14] Or, alternatively, one can step back in time and into Samuel Pepys' house in London, where in October 1660 he wrote in his diary, 'going down into my cellar … I put my foot into a great heap of turds, by which I find that Mr Turner's house of office [i.e. toilet] is full and comes into my cellar, which doth trouble me'.[15] Even a brief perusal of William Shakespeare's family background guarantees exposure to the heavily showcased and often completely uncontextualized anecdote of his father, John Shakespeare (1531–1601), having been fined 1s by the Stratford upon Avon Aldermen because he committed the apparently amusing crime of leaving a dunghill outside his family home in Henley Street.[16] Naturally, such entertaining examples, of which there are many more, have exerted a far greater influence on the historical imagination in relation to early modern sanitation than the heavy, dusty minute books of council meetings, treasurers' accounts and nuisance court cases.

Transcending the Anglo-Scottish border, one can listen to Rev. Thomas Morer, an English chaplain to an army regiment stationed near Edinburgh, who depicted a Scottish capital city in 1689 which was certainly not renowned for its cleanliness.

> Between … [Edinburgh's Cow Gate] and the High Street there are many little lanes of communication, but very steepy and troublesome, and withal so nasty (for want of boghouses, which they very rarely have), that Edinburgh is likened by some to an ivory comb, whose teeth on both sides are very foul.[17]

The ivory comb analogy can be appreciated by looking closely at the 'View of Edinburgh', by James Gordon of Rothiemay, drawn in 1647.[18] The closes were certainly very narrow and the numerous multi-storey tenements within them meant that they were very densely populated, but how foul they actually were is questionable. Morer's condemnation of Edinburgh was neither new nor unusual, but joined a long-established genre of purposely anti-Scottish literature.[19] Scotland's political, religious, administrative and legal centre hosted a myriad of prestigious visitors, who often observed, judged and wrote about their experiences in the city. Previously, in 1617, another Englishman, Sir Anthony Weldon, noted sardonically,

> The men of old did no more wonder that the great Messias [sic] should be born in so poor a town as Bethlehem in Judea, than I do wonder that so brave a prince as King James [VI and I] should be borne in so stinking a town as Edinburgh in lousy Scotland.[20]

Weldon's comments were shaped by his political stance against James VI and I. Subsequently, he was dismissed from King James's court and he eventually went on to support the Parliamentarians during the Civil Wars, holding and administering Kent.

Other sensationalistic accounts followed Weldon's lead. In 1635, the Englishman Sir William Brereton commented,

> [Edinburgh] is placed in a daintie health-full pure aire: and doubtless were a most health-full place to live in: were nott the inhabitants most sluttish, nastye and sloath-full people … Their houses of office [i.e. toilets] are tubs, or firkins, placed upon the end: which they never emptie, until they bee full, soe as the sent thereof annoyeth, and offendeth the whole house.[21]

Brereton's horror extended to the simple shutters which adorned Edinburgh's High Street too: 'this face of boardes … (wherein are round holes shaped to the proportion of mens heades) ... is a mightye disgrace'.[22] These commentaries, depicting Edinburgh's perceived low standards of sanitation and sophistication, are part of a wider literature on alleged Scottish incivility more generally.

Richard Franck also blamed the Scots for insanitary conditions, noting in 1656 that 'the natives in this northern latitude are naturally ... addicted to idleness and nastiness [i.e. uncleanness]'.[23] And John Ray included the following extract in his *Collection of English Proverbs*, published in 1684,

> A Scotch warming pan i.e. A Wench
> The story is well known of the Gentleman travelling in Scotland, who desiring to have his bed warmed, the servant-maid doffs her clothes, and lays her self down in it a while. In Scotland they have neither bellowes, warmingpans, nor houses of office [i.e. toilets].[24]

Clearly, poetic, dramatic and sensationalistic descriptions are not sufficiently reliable to underpin a realistic reconstruction of the sanitary, or indeed the insanitary, condition of the urban landscape. The English descriptions of Edinburgh in particular and of Scotland more generally are especially unreliable sources of information. They are purposely anti-Scottish and unhelpful to the objective historian, who must remain mindful that Englishmen were highly motivated to enhance England's relative civility and to offend and discredit their Scottish foreign rivals in no uncertain terms. In 1724, Daniel Defoe, who celebrated the recent Anglo-Scottish union in 1707, appreciated such accounts' intrinsic unreliability. He noted that Scotland's 'enemies' made her inadequate public hygiene 'a subject of scorn and reproach; as if the people were not as willing to live sweet and clean as other nations, but delighted in stench and nastiness'.[25] Indeed, the large extent to which early modern Scotland's insanitary urban streets appalled her foreign visitors has led Margaret Sanderson to ask 'may not at least some of ... [the] squalor have been in the eye of the beholders?'.[26]

Several contemporaries described York's sanitary conditions too, but dirty streets, filth and rubbish are curiously absent from such accounts. In 1586, for example, William Camden termed York 'the second city of England, the finest of this region and indeed of the whole North' and he elaborated that 'it is pleasant, large, and strongly fortified, adorned with private as well as public buildings, crammed with riches and with people'.[27] Clearly, Camden respected York and he notes that he found it a pleasant place. It is highly unlikely that Camden would describe a city as pleasant if he perceived it as intolerably filthy by his own standards, whatever they were. However it is also possible that such base subjects as human waste and filthy streets would never have been considered appropriate topics for inclusion in his *Britannia* regardless of the actual conditions. In 1639, the English poet John Taylor provided far less detail when he described York, but he, too, clearly admired it, deeming it 'a great, faire, and the second city in England'.[28] A few decades later, in 1673, Richard Blome agreed with Camden and Taylor that York 'next to London claimeth priority of all other cities in England' and he, too, described it positively, as 'a place of great antiquity and fame ... a fair, large and beautiful city, adorned with many splendid buildings, both publick and private', and he noted that it was 'very populous, much resorted unto and well inhabited by Gentry, and wealthy Trades-men'.[29] The marked contrast between the commentaries describing Edinburgh, penned by foreigners, and of York, penned by English natives, perhaps reveals more about the authors' attitudes towards Scotland and England than it does about the relative cleanliness of Edinburgh's and York's respective urban landscapes.

As a result of the daring adventures of the avid sole traveller, Celia Fiennes, one can also see York right at the end of the period under discussion, in 1698, through a woman's eyes. Fiennes was not quite as complimentary as her predecessors, Camden, Taylor and Blome, noting that York 'stands high but for one of the Metropolis and the See of the Archbishop it makes but a meane appearance'.[30] She elaborated, 'the streetes are narrow and not of any length, save one which you enter of from the bridge', by which she referred to Micklegate.[31] Fiennes also noted that 'the houses are very low and as indifferent as in any country town, and the narrowness of the streets makes it appear very mean'.[32] Despite her comparatively negative appraisal of the city, however, Fiennes does not highlight the presence of dirt or rubbish on the streets, which suggests that York was not excessively dirty, at least not below Fiennes' own standards of cleanliness. It is also possible, however, that Fiennes noticed dirty streets, but did not consider such matters an appropriate subject for a written description of a city. Indeed, David Palliser accounts for contemporaries' observations of the 'beauty and not the squalor' of York by suggesting that they took the squalor for granted and therefore did not consider it noteworthy.[33] It is also significant that Fiennes was not writing for publication, but rather for her own private recollections of her journey, within which descriptions of unsavoury matters might well have been personally unwelcome.

In the early eighteenth century, between 1724 and 1726, Daniel Defoe described York as 'a spacious city', which covered 'a great deal of ground, perhaps more than any city in England out of Middlesex, except Norwich'.[34] He also noted that York's buildings were 'not close and thronged as at Bristol, or as at Durham, nor is York so populous as either Bristol or Norwich'.[35] On a positive note, Defoe complimented York as 'very magnificent, and, as we say, makes a good figure every way in its appearance, even at a distance'.[36] Defoe's descriptions of York contrast significantly with his estimation of contemporary Darlington, a northern English post town on the Great Northern Road, which he concluded 'had nothing remarkable but dirt'.[37] Defoe's comments suggest that the perceived cleanliness or dirtiness of urban streets was something which observers and travellers might well have taken the time to include in their descriptions of places which they found shockingly, offensively or unusually insanitary. But it cannot be concluded on the basis of contemporary literature alone that places such as Edinburgh, London and Darlington were intolerably filthy and York boasted clean and salubrious streets. However widely read, easily accessible and admittedly entertaining contemporary descriptions of sanitary and insanitary urban scenes undoubtedly are, they form a very small part of the large body of extant documentary evidence in relation to urban sanitation. Such evidence, largely in manuscript format, contains much more positive, balanced and ultimately important information about attitudes towards sanitation and the processes, systems and technologies which were developed and improved over time to organize waste disposal and street cleaning more effectively, to suppress insanitary nuisances and to enhance urban salubrity.

Historiographical progress in the field

How townspeople and their local governors perceived and organized the disposal of waste was an important aspect of daily life which necessarily shaped the experiences of every person who lived in and visited early modern towns. Yet, by and large, historians of England and Scotland during this period have at best marginalized and at worst ignored the ways in which contemporaries perceived, experienced and regulated waste materials and insanitary nuisances which were present around homes and in streets and other public spaces. Historians' reluctance to engage with the topic leaves it vastly under-researched, and consequently misunderstood, perhaps a direct result of its explicitly unsavoury connotations and perceived repulsive details. In much the same way, today's public hygiene systems are maintained purposely hidden from the public eye, and nose, on the edge of settlements. As Bill Bryson highlights in his *Home: A Short History of Private Life*, 'that's what history mostly is: masses of people doing ordinary things', yet, he laments, 'we treat them as incidental and hardly worthy of serious consideration'.[38] This book is an attempt to shed light on the sixteenth- and seventeenth-century history of one such ordinary thing: the production, storage, processing, organization, reuse and disposal of waste in British towns.

The field of early modern British sanitation has been largely neglected by traditional social, political, cultural and economic historians of early modern Britain, yet several notable exceptions have contributed important cases studies, on the shoulders of which this book undoubtedly stands. Mark Jenner made several important contributions to the field following his pioneering 1991 doctoral thesis on cleanliness and dirt in London, 1530 to 1700, in relation to water supply, conceptions of plague, the removal of waste, street cleaning, insanitary nuisances, smoke pollution and smell.[39] And Walter King, John Harrison and I have completed highly detailed single case studies of seventeenth-century sanitation in the smaller towns of Prescot, Stirling and Carlisle, respectively.[40] Dolly Jorgensen has compared sanitation in Scandanavian and English towns, and focused in remarkable depth in one article on how the provision of sanitation services in two of England's regional centres, Norwich and Coventry, shaped civic governance between 1400 and 1600.[41] Recently, William Cavert contributed an in-depth study of Charles I's regulation of smoke pollution in London, between 1624 and 1640, in which he highlights, 'studies of pre-industrial cities do generally invoke – and sometimes revel in – dirtiness', arguing that the regulation of coal smoke was actually a purposeful attempt to improve air quality in the city.[42] Two literary scholars have contributed focused respective studies relating directly to the topic.

Douglas Biow analyses contemporary ideas pertaining to cleanliness as portrayed through an array of renaissance Italian literature in order to argue how integral cleanliness was to Italian culture in that period; and Sophie Gee uses a similar literary style to draw out eighteenth-century English contemporaries' attitudes and values in relation to food leftovers and the very idea of waste products, which was an important aspect of their daily lives.[43] All of these works agree that waste disposal and environmental regulation was much better organized and more progressive in their basic spirit than historians have previously tended to believe. More deep and narrow case studies of how this area of daily life was regulated in individual urban and rural settlements, together with some national and international comparative research projects, are needed urgently in order to shed light on important differences between processes and systems in settlements with markedly different characteristics and functions.

Historians of the medieval period are leading the way in relation to this important topic, having produced several important works which shed light on the positive attitudes of medieval urban governors towards sanitation and the highly sophisticated ways in which they processed and organized domestic and agricultural waste. This body of literature highlights that just as progressive attitudes towards outdoor sanitation and the environment did not originate in the Victorian era, nor did they originate in the sixteenth century.[44] Carole Rawcliffe's *Urban Bodies* articulates a passionate, persuasive and heavily researched argument that, between 1250 and 1530, regardless of the less than ideal conditions on the ground, often resulting from the lack of fiscal resources and rudimentary technology, English urban governors consistently aspired towards improving public health, in terms of the physical condition of the urban landscape, water supplies, food and drink and the provision of communal health services.[45] Pursuing a very similar argument to that articulated in this book, albeit in relation to the preceding period, Rawcliffe laments the 'belittling' of medieval health and hygiene as having resulted from 'the long shadow cast by a *cadre* of influential Victorian sanitary reformers and polemicists whose commitment to the ideal of scientific progress made them contemptuous of a society so different from their own'.[46] Rawcliffe is quite right to assert that 'the history of public health cannot be envisaged in terms of a slow but unwavering march towards the shining citadel of mains drainage'.[47]

It is important to understand the long-term historical development of the hard-won medals of modern civility which we all wear so proudly today, earned cumulatively by our forebears over millennia. As Robert MacFarlane explains, in his history of attitudes towards mountains, 'each of us is in fact heir to a complex and largely invisible dynasty of feelings: we see through the eyes of innumerable and anonymous predecessors'.[48] This can be applied to attitudes towards the environment, waste disposal, cleanliness and sanitation too. Sixteenth-century concerns were, of course, born out of medieval concerns which had developed in different contexts but broadly speaking in very similar veins. Indeed, Janet Loengard observes the 'outlines' of London's Assize of Nuisance, which regulated insanitary nuisances, 'in both form and subject' from the late eleventh century.[49]

Nuisance formally entered Common Law in 1166, when English King Henry II's Assize of Novel Disseisin's founding legislation referred to it specifically.[50] Henceforth, circuit justices held Assizes of Nuisance to which annoyed householders could complain in the localities.[51] Helena Chew and William Kellaway found that London's late medieval Assize of Nuisance upheld 'remarkably elaborate' regulations.[52] In 1996, Ronald Zupko and Robert Laures produced an important and revealing study of medieval urban environmental law in relation to northern Italy, arguing that insanitary nuisances were rigorously regulated and that waste disposal was well organized. As Zupko and Laures warn, it is misleading to perceive 'environmental awareness' as a completely modern movement, 'arising out of the tumult of a half-century of war and depression like some Venus given birth in the crashing surf of a Mediterranean shore'.[53]

Similarly productive progress has been made in relation to modern sanitation. A six-volume edited collection, *Sanitary Reform in Victorian Britain*, was published in 2012, providing a remarkably deep and lengthy analysis of several aspects of sanitary improvement over the course of the Victorian era.[54] Martin Melosi's *The Sanitary City* tracks the development of waste disposal and environmental regulation in America from colonial times to the present day.[55] Melosi highlights that there are some examples of limited regulation and attempts to improve conditions in colonial times, but he concludes, rather negatively, that 'erratic enforcement of sanitary laws undermined the effort to protect the public health throughout colonial America and continued to be the problem into the eighteenth and early nineteenth centuries'.[56] Dorothy Porter's ambitious study of public hygiene throughout history and across the world is inevitably uncomprehensive, but it does provide a high-level overview including some useful perspectives in terms of long-term continuity and change and in terms of geographical differences.[57]

Impressive progress has also been made in relation to sanitation in early modern Europe. Several authors have observed the fastidiousness of sanitation in the seventeenth-century Dutch Golden Age.[58] Moreover, Georges Vigarello's *Concepts of Cleanliness*, a primarily French study which was translated into English in 1988, marked the first historiographical attempt to understand what cleanliness meant in the context of seventeenth-century culture.[59] Although primarily concerned with the eighteenth century, Alain Corbin's pioneering work on smell and culture in France broke new ground in 1986 by emphasizing the huge importance of smell in early modern daily life and society.[60] More recently, in 2007, Jo Wheeler highlighted the strong links between malodorous nuisances and plague in sixteenth-century Venice and the consequently rigorous sanitation initiatives of the city governors.[61] And three years later, in 2010, John Henderson published some detailed research into sanitation in early modern Tuscany.[62] Comparatively, the field of early modern British sanitation has been left woefully behind and is unacceptably misunderstood. This book makes a purposeful effort to at least partially fill this lamentable gap.

The project

As well as analysing closely how and why the outdoor urban environment and key elements of sanitation infrastructure were regulated, cleaned, maintained and improved, from day to day, week to week and year to year, this book also tracks the ways in which such systems and processes changed in the longer term, over the course of fourteen decades. The study is purposely post-Reformation in both Scotland and England, in order to make meaningful comparisons in relation to religious beliefs and practices. From 1560, it continues up to 1700, which permits analysis of the post-Restoration period too. The period 1560 to 1700 was chosen because fourteen decades is a long enough period during which to track long-term continuities and discontinuities in waste disposal and street cleaning processes and systems and it is sufficiently short enough to allow deep analysis of all extant council minutes and court records without having to use sampling techniques. Council minutes, court records and financial accounts provide the main sources to explain the sanitation systems used in Edinburgh, York and many other towns and cities across Britain; though other documents, including national Parliamentary Acts, diaries, advice literature, property leases, travel literature, poetry and correspondence, have been used where relevant. Although research into extant council and court records has been exhaustive, without the use of any sampling techniques at all, the research was limited exclusively to matters directly relating to the disposal of waste, street cleaning and the regulation of insanitary nuisances. Other unrelated areas of urban management, such as gambling, prostitution, begging, slander and weights and measures, have been purposely excluded from the study. Whereas council minutes and financial accounts have survived fairly continuously in both Edinburgh and York and the minutes of Edinburgh's Dean of Guild Court have survived for most of the years throughout the period, detailed minutes of the presentments for insanitary nuisances exacted by the various courts which regulated York's environment have not. However, all sixty-one extant complete lists of court presentments which were recorded in York's Chamberlains' Accounts between 1560 and 1700 have been categorized and analysed alongside the consistent series of York Corporation House minute books.

The book blends a combination of statistical and anecdotal – quantitative and qualitative – evidence. Inevitably, almost all of the sources from which it draws its conclusions were written by scribes employed by governmental or legal institutions. However, a significant effort has been made to delve, as far as possible, beneath official records and to pay close attention to the many resourceful ways in which inhabitants used their own initiatives to self-regulate and improve the micro-scale environment of their neighbourhoods themselves. Townspeople throughout England and Scotland very often used their own initiative to pursue and maintain their own standard of outdoor cleanliness in the outdoor public spaces with which they were intimately familiar. A comparative, national methodology was chosen because while an in-depth case study of one city would have been useful and revealing in its own right, it would have provided merely one piece of a complex jigsaw to the overall topic of British public hygiene. Such a case study, however deep and comprehensive, would have failed to compare how this area of local government was managed in urban settlements of different sizes, geographical locations, populations, architectural styles, nationalities, administrative frameworks and political contexts. Focusing on the case studies of the large urban centres of Edinburgh and York, significant attention is also paid to sanitation systems in several other smaller urban settlements across the whole of England and Scotland, towns which Peter Borsay refers to collectively as 'the bedrock of urban system'.[63]

Whereas a large majority of England's and Scotland's population continued to live in rural settlements throughout the period, increasingly more settlements in both countries were becoming less 'rural' and and more 'urban', and although there are no precise definitions confirming exactly where the line lay between 'rural' and 'urban', a greater proportion of people in both countries were of the latter than the former in 1700 than had been the case in 1560. The largest urban settlement in England by far was London, in a league of its own housing a population of around 55,000 in 1520, 350,000 by 1650 and perhaps as many as 550,000 people by 1700. The largest English towns with populations of over 7,000 in 1500 and over 11,000 by 1700 were York, Bristol, Norwich, Exeter and Newcastle upon Tyne. The four 'premier' Welsh towns, defined by function rather than population because reliable population estimates are not available for Welsh towns during this period, were Brecon, Carmarthen, Denbugh and Caernarvon, which functioned as regional administrative and legal centres, or 'local metropoles'.[64] Scotland's larger burghs were Edinburgh, Glasgow, Aberdeen and Dundee, accounting for 64 per cent of total burghal taxation in 1705.[65] In each country, London and Edinburgh substantially dwarfed the main cities beneath them in their respective urban hierarchies in terms of both population and trade. Edinburgh's population of around 12,500 in 1560 rose to between 27,000 and 30,000 by 1700 whereas the population of Glasgow rose far less dramatically from around 4,500 in 1560 to 12,000 by 1700. Even in 1543, London paid a similar tax subsidy to that of all of England's main provincial centres and in 1705, Edinburgh paid 35 per cent of Scottish burghal tax.[66] A whole range of smaller market centres peppered England and lowland Scotland; many of these settlements, which would have been perceived in 1560 merely as large villages in today's terms, had become unambiguously and much more obviously urban by 1700. In 1520, English towns of more than 4,000 people represented 6 per cent of England's total population whereas by 1700 English towns of over 5,000 people represented 15 per cent of the English population.[67] The urban population was quite a small minority, but it was a growing minority.

Edinburgh and York were selected as the book's main case studies because of their differences, rather than their similarities. Melissa Hollander also used Edinburgh and York as comparative case studies in her study of early modern sexual relations.[68] As well as their obvious Anglo-Scottish differences in terms of government, law and culture, developed separately over several centuries, inner Edinburgh's population swelled while that of York remained relatively stagnant, fluctuating between 8,500 and 13,500 over the course of the whole period.[69] Using

Edinburgh and York for the project's main case studies, therefore, provided a useful framework within which the relationship between demographic change and sanitation provision could be analysed deeply. Moreover, York is relatively flat with more open space and featuring buildings of only two or three storeys, whereas Edinburgh's topographical gradients are severe, the housing was densely concentrated and some buildings were over ten storeys high. Edinburgh was a national capital city whereas York functioned as a regional centre. And Edinburgh lacked access to an immediately proximal river whereas York's inhabitants could access the River Ouse and the River Fosse.

The other urban settlements referred to (London, Southwark, Maidstone, Clare, Exeter, Bristol, Bideford, Southampton, Oxford, Norwich, Nottingham, Coventry, Warwick, Sheffield, Macclesfield, Salford, Liverpool, Scarborough, Newbottle, Barnard Castle, Durham, Darlington, Kendal, Whitehaven, Newcastle upon Tyne, Hexham, Carlisle, Berwick on Tweed, Hawick, Peebles, Dunfermline, Ayr, Glasgow, Lanark, Stirling, Perth, Aberdeen and Inverness) were chosen specifically because they feature a wide and diverse range of different characteristics. This plethora of settlements is referred to in order to emphasize the large range of different functions, needs and geographical situations of each unique urban settlement, and to explain why so many different sanitation systems were developed to meet the particular needs of unique towns and cities during this period. Each town's local governmental system had developed in a piecemeal manner, shaped much more by local than national conditions, and they were by no means uniform. Indeed, in 1908, Sidney Webb described the municipal corporations and manorial boroughs in 1835, by which point, he argued, they had developed into 'a collection of apparently heterogeneous individuals, showing signs of having been arrested in their development at different stages of their growth; some remaining in a rudimentary state; some even reverting to simpler types; and some again standing still at what seems full maturity'.[70] Within England, some towns were governed by corporations and others by manorial governments while urban Scots lived in burghs of barony or royal burghs. Some towns functioned as ports, major market centres or lived alongside major military garrisons; others did not. A town or city could be heavily agricultural, coastal, landlocked or a national or regional centre. Some urban populations specialized in fish trades, skinning or leather-making while others remained unspecialized and architectural traditions had a significant impact on the style and extent of drainage infrastructure. All of these factors, it is argued, shaped an urban settlement's necessarily unique sanitation systems and its environmental regulation to a large extent. The rich insights gained from the plethora of other towns and cities, in addition to Edinburgh and York, it is hoped, make an important comparative contribution to the main argument, even if they do not form its central focus.

The main issues under discussion are: the complex relationship between demographic change and efforts to improve the outdoor urban environment; how a city's architectural building tradition and geographical topography have shaped drainage, and the regulation of that drainage; the differences between environmental regulation in an English and Scottish administrative, governmental and legal framework; and how far the influence of Crown and Parliament shaped matters relating to sanitation in individual towns or cities. The decision to present Edinburgh and York as parallel case studies, albeit within thematic chapters, rather than meshing the case studies together more closely, was taken to ensure that the material from the respective cities could still be considered in its own right, in relation to the city within which it was produced and in its own particular local context, as well as in comparison to other towns and cities. The book consists of four chapters. The first chapter contextualizes sanitation in this particular period by explaining the character of the environmental challenges faced by early modern urban governors and populations. The second chapter explains the national, demographic, legal and governmental context of environmental regulation in Edinburgh, York and in many other urban settlements across Britain. The third chapter compares the management and provision of civic-funded sanitation services while the fourth compares how insanitary nuisances were regulated in Edinburgh, York and many other English towns. The conclusion situates the different systems and processes into a national framework, highlighting just how differently, and sometimes just how similarly, this area of daily life was managed in different urban settlements. Although, primarily, the book focuses on the detail of how environmental regulation and waste disposal functioned in English and Scottish towns and cities, it also engages with one larger question throughout: whether or not humans are necessarily motivated to live in clean surroundings devoid of excrement and malodorous waste material as a result of innate physiological senses or whether cultural influences, social status, governmental and legal control and wealth are the major driving forces behind such motivations.

Notes

1 R. Girling, *Rubbish! Dirt on our Hands and Crisis Ahead* (London: Eden Project Books, 2005), p. 3. Similar views can be found in S. Strasser, *Waste and Want: A Social History of Trash* (New York: Metropolitan Press, 1999).
2 Girling, *Rubbish!*, p. 4.
3 D. Snow, 'Filthy Cities' (BBC2 England, 05/04/2011, 9.00pm, 12/04/2011, 9.00pm, 19/04/2011, 9.00pm).
4 L. Stone, *The Family, Sex and Marriage in England 1500–1800* (Harmondsworth: Penguin, 1979), p. 62.
5 F. Emmison, *Elizabethan Life: Home, Work and Land* (Chelmsford: Essex County Council, 1976), p. 295.
6 T. C. Smout, *A History of the Scottish People, 1560–1830* (London: Fontana Press, 1969), p. 151.
7 P. Clark and P. Slack, *English Towns in Transition, 1500–1700* (London: Oxford University Press, 1976), p. 96.
8 J. Thomas, *Town Government in the Sixteenth Century* (London: George Allen and Unwin Ltd, 1933).
9 E. Cockayne, *Hubbub: Filth, Noise and Stench in England 1600–1770* (London: Yale University Press, 2007).
10 Cockayne, *Hubbub*, pp. 181, 192, 194.
11 B. Capp, Review of *Hubbub: Filth, Noise and Stench in England*, by E. Cockayne, *Renaissance Quarterly*, 61:1 (2008), pp. 277–278, on p. 278.

12 M. Jenner, 'Overground, underground: pollution and place in urban history', *Journal of Urban History*, 24 (1997), pp. 97–110, on 100–111.

13 Rawcliffe, *Urban Bodies*, p. 8.

14 B. Jonson, 'On The Famous Voyage', in B. Jonson, *The Works of Ben Jonson* (1573–1637), 8 vols, ed. William Gifford (London, 1875), vol. 8, pp. 232–239.

15 S. Pepys, *Diary of Samuel Pepys* (1660–1669), ed. R. Latham and W. Matthews, *The Diary of Samuel Pepys: A New and Complete Transcription*, 11 vols (London: G. Bell and Sons, 1970–1983), vol. 1, p. 269 (20/10/1660).

16 M. Hunt, *Shakespeare's As You Like It: Late Elizabethan Culture and Literary Representation* (Basingstoke: Palgrave MacMillan, 2008), p. 97.

17 Rev. T. Morer, *A Short Account of Scotland: Being a Description of the Nature of that Kingdom* (London, 1702), ed. P. Brown, *Early Travellers in Scotland* (Edinburgh: James Thin, 1978), pp. 266–290, on p. 290. Morer's description of Edinburgh, included in this wider 1702 publication, was based on notes taken during his trip to Scotland in 1689.

18 J. Gordon, *Edinodunensis Tabulam/Iacobus Gordinas P. Rothemayus* (Amsterdam, 1647).

19 These issues are discussed in L. J. Skelton, 'Pursuing improvement: public hygiene in Scottish burghs, 1500–1700', *History Scotland Magazine*, 9:6 (2009), pp. 22–27.

20 Sir A. Weldon, *A Perfect Description of the People and Country of Scotland* (London, 1617), ed. P. Brown, *Early Travellers in Scotland* (Edinburgh: James Thin, 1978), pp. 96–103, on p. 103.

21 Sir W. Brereton, *Journal of Sir William Brereton* (1635), ed. Hodgson, J. C., *North Country Diaries*, second series, 124 (Durham: Surtees Society, 1914), pp. 1–50, on pp. 30–31.

22 Brereton, *Journal*, pp. 29–30.

23 R. Franck, *Franck's Memoirs* (1656), ed. P. Hume, *Early Travellers in Scotland* (Edinburgh: James Thin, 1978), p. 190.

24 J. Ray, *A Collection of English Proverbs Digested into a Convenient Method for the Speedy Finding of Any One upon Occasions* (Cambridge, 1684), pp. 83–84.

25 D. Defoe, *A Tour through the Whole Island of Great Britain* (1724), ed. P. Rogers (London: Penguin, 1971), p. 577.

26 M. Sanderson, *A Kindly Place? Living in Sixteenth-century Scotland* (East Linton: Tuckwell Press, 2002), p. 69.

27 W. Camden, *Britannia* (London, 1586), quoted in E. Gibson (ed.), *Britannia* (London, 1695), p. 407.

28 J. Taylor, *Adventures* (London, 1639), quoted in J. Chandler (ed.), *Travels through Stuart Britain: The Adventures of John Taylor, Water Poet* (Stroud: Sutton, 1999), p. 167.

29 R. Blome, *Britannia* (London, 1673), p. 23.

30 C. Fiennes, *The Journeys of Celia Fiennes* (1702), ed. C. Morris (London: Cresset Press, 1947), p. 76.

31 Fiennes, *Journeys*, p. 76.

32 Fiennes, *Journeys*, p. 76.

33 D. Palliser, *Tudor York* (Oxford: Oxford University Press, 1979), p. 38.

34 Defoe, *A Tour*, p. 523.

35 Defoe, *A Tour*, p. 523.

36 Defoe, *A Tour*, p. 523.

37 Defoe, *A Tour*, p. 533.

38 B. Bryson, *Home: A Short History of Private Life* (London: Black Swan, 2010), pp. 20–21.

39 M. Jenner, 'Early modern English conceptions of "cleanliness and "dirt" as reflected in the environmental regulation of London c.1530–c.1700' (D.Phil. dissertation, University of Oxford, 1991). While Jenner's doctoral thesis remains unpublished in

monograph form, many insightful elements of it have been published as articles: Jenner, "'Another epocha"? Hartlib, John Lanyon and the improvement of London in the 1650s' in M. Greengrass et al. (eds), *Samuel Hartlib and Universal Reformation* (Cambridge: Cambridge University Press, 1994), pp. 343–356; Jenner, 'The Politics of London Air: John Evelyn's Fumifugium and the Restoration', *Historical Journal*, 38:3 (1995), pp. 535–551; Jenner, 'The great dog massacre' in W. Naphy and P. Roberts (eds), *Fear in Early Modern Society* (Manchester: Manchester University Press, 1997), pp. 44–61; Jenner, 'From conduit community to commercial network? Water in London, 1500–1725' in P. Griffiths and M. Jenner (eds), *Londinopolis: Essays in the Cultural and Social History of Early Modern London* (Manchester: Manchester University Press, 2000), pp. 250–272; Jenner, 'Civilization and deodorization? Smell in early modern English culture', in P. Burke et al. (eds), *Civil Histories: Essays Presented to Sir Keith Thomas* (Oxford: Oxford University Press, 2000), pp. 127–144; Jenner, 'The roasting of the rump: scatology and the body politic in Restoration England', *Past and Present*, 177 (2002), pp. 253–272; and Jenner, 'Follow your nose? Smell, smelling, and their histories', *American Historical Review*, 116:2 (2011), pp. 335–351.

40 W. King, 'How high is too high? Disposing of dung in seventeenth-century Prescot', *Sixteenth Century Journal*, 23:3 (1992), pp. 443–457; J. Harrison, 'public hygiene and drainage in Stirling and other early modern Scottish towns', *Review of Scottish Culture*, 11 (1998–99), pp. 67–77; L. Skelton, 'Beadles, dunghills and noisome excrements', *International Journal of Regional and Local History*, 9:1 (May, 2014), pp. 21–38.

41 D. Jorgensen, 'Co-operative sanitation: managing streets and gutters in late-medieval England and Scandanavia', *Technology and Culture*, 49:3 (2008), pp. 547–567; D. Jorgensen, '"All Good Rule of the Citee": sanitation and civic government in England, 1400–1600', *Journal of Urban History*, 36:3 (2010), pp. 301–315.

42 W. Cavert, 'The environmental policy of Charles I: coal smoke and the English monarchy, 1624–1640', *Journal of British Studies*, 53:2 (2014), pp. 310–333, on p. 315. For more information on the development of air pollution from the medieval period onwards, see P. Brimblecombe, 'Early urban climate and atmosphere', in A. Hall and H. Kenward (eds), *Environmental Archaeology in the Urban Context* (London: Council for British Archaeology, 1982); P. Brimblecombe, *The Big Smoke: A History of Air Pollution in London since Medieval Times* (London: Methuen, 1987); and W. Te Brake, 'Air pollution and fuel crises in pre-industrial London, 1250–1650', *Technology and Culture*, 16 (1975), pp. 337–359.

43 D. Biow, *The Culture of Cleanliness in Renaissance Italy* (London: Cornell University Press, 2006); S. Gee, *Making Waste: Leftovers and the Eighteenth-Century Imagination* (Oxford: Princeton University Press, 2010).

44 D. Keene, 'Rubbish in medieval towns' in A. Hall and H. Kenward (eds), *Environmental Archaeology in the Urban Context* (London: Council for British Archaeology, 1982), pp. 26–30; D. Evans, 'A good riddance of bad rubbish? Scatalogical musings on rubbish disposal and the handling of "filth" in medieval and early post-medieval towns', in K. De Groote et al. (eds), *Exchanging Medieval Material Culture: Studies on Archaeology and History presented to Frans Verhaeghe* (Brussels: Vlaams Instituut voor het Onroerend Erfgoed, 2010), pp. 267–278; E. Sabine, 'Latrines and cesspools of medieval London', *Speculum*, 9 (1934), pp. 303–321; E. Sabine, 'City cleaning in mediaeval London', *Speculum*, 12 (1937), pp. 19–43; L. Thorndike, 'Sanitation, baths, and street-cleaning in the Middle Ages and Renaissance', *Speculum*, 3 (1928), pp. 192–203; J. Greig, 'Garderobes, sewers, cesspits and latrines', *Current Archaeology*, 85 (1982), pp. 49–52; R. Jones, 'Manure and the medieval social order', in M. Allen et al. (eds), *Land and People: Papers Presented in Memory of John G. Evans* (Oxford: Oxbow Books, Prehistoric Society Research Paper 2, 2009), pp. 215–225; M. Beck and M. Hill, 'Rubbish, relatives, and residence: the family use of middens', *Journal of Archaeological Method and Theory*, 11:3 (2004), pp. 297–333; R. Zupko and

R. Laures, *Straws in the Wind: Medieval Urban Environmental Law: The Case of Northern Italy* (Oxford: Westview, 1996).

45 C. Rawcliffe, *Urban Bodies: Communal Health in Late Medieval English Towns and Cities* (Woodbridge: Boydell and Brewer, 2013).

46 Rawcliffe, *Urban Bodies*, p. 3.

47 Rawcliffe, *Urban Bodies*, p. 18.

48 R. MacFarlane, *Mountains of the Mind: A History of a Fascination* (London: Granta, 2003), p. 167.

49 J. Loengard, 'The Assize of Nuisance: origins of an action at common law', *California Law Journal*, 37:1 (1978)', p. 151.

50 J. Baker, *An Introduction to English Legal History*, 2nd ed. (London: Butterworths, 1979), p. 352; Loengard, 'Assize of Nuisance', p. 145.

51 W. Holdsworth, *A History of English Law*, 3rd edn (London: Methuen, 1903–1972), vol. 3, p. 154; Loengard, 'Assize of Nuisance', pp. 145–146, 158–159.

52 *London Assize of Nuisance, 1301–1431*, ed. H. Chew and W. Kellaway (London: London Record Society, 1973), p. x.

53 Zupko and Laures, *Straws in the Wind*, p. 1.

54 M. Allen-Emerson (ed.), *Sanitary Reform in Victorian Britain*, 6 vols (London: Pickering and Chatto, 2012).

55 M. Melosi, *The Sanitary City: Urban Infrastructure in America from Colonial Times to the Present* (Baltimore: John Hopkins University Press, 2000). For a more detailed analysis of American public hygiene in the modern period, see M. Melosi, *Garbage in the Cities: Refuse, Reform, and the Environment*, 2nd edn (Pittsburgh: University of Pittsburgh Press, 2005).

56 Melosi, *Sanitary City*, p. 21.

57 D. Porter, *Health, Civilization and the State: A History of Public Health from Ancient to Modern Times* (London: Routledge, 1999).

58 H. Deceulaer, 'Implications of the street', in M. van der Heijden et al. (eds), *Serving the Urban Community: The Rise of Public Facilities in the Low Countries, 1400–1800* (Amsterdam: Aksant Academic Publishers, 2009), pp. 194–216; B. Van Bavel and O. Gelderblom, 'The economic origins of cleanliness in the Dutch Golden Age', *Past and Present*, 205:1 (2009), pp. 41–69; M. van der Heijden, 'New perspectives on public services in early modern Europe', *Journal of Urban History*, 36 (2010), pp. 271–284; and S. Schama, *Embarrassment of Riches: An Interpretation of Dutch Culture in the Golden Age* (New York: Knopf, 1987).

59 G. Vigarello, *Concepts of Cleanliness: Changing Attitudes in France since the Middle Ages*, trans. J. Birrel, (Cambridge: Cambridge University Press, 1988), pp. 18, 58. For an in-depth and informative discussion of public hygiene improvements and attitudes towards waste in modern Paris, see D. Reid, *Paris Sewers and Sewermen: Realities and Representations* (London: Harvard University Press, 1991).

60 A. Corbin, *The Foul and the Fragrant: Odour and the Social Imagination* (Cambridge, MA: Harvard University Press, 1986).

61 J. Wheeler, 'Stench in sixteenth-century Venice' in A. Cowan and J. Steward (eds), *The City and the Senses: Urban Culture Since 1500* (Aldershot, 2007), pp. 25–38.

62 J. Henderson, 'Public health, pollution and the problem of waste disposal in early modern Tuscany', in S. Cavaciocchi (ed.), *Le Interazioni fra economia e ambiernte biologico nell'Europa preindustriale secc. XIII–XVIII. Economic and Biological Reactions in Pre-Industrial Europe from the 13th to the 18th Centuries* (Florence, Italy: Firenze University Press, 2010), pp. 373–382.

63 P. Borsay, *The English Urban Renaissance: Culture and Society in the Provincial Town, 1660–1770* (Oxford: Oxford University Press, 1989), p. 4.

64 H. Carter, *The Towns of Wales: A Study in Urban Geography* (Cardiff: University of Wales Press, 1965), pp. 35–37.

65 Clark and Slack, *English Towns in Transition*, p. 9; T. Devine, 'The merchant class of the larger Scottish towns in the later seventeenth and early eighteenth centuries', in G. Gordon and B. Dicks (eds), *Scottish Urban History* (Aberdeen: Aberdeen University Press, 1983), pp. 92–111, on p. 92.

66 Devine, 'The Merchant Class', p. 92.

67 Clark and Slack, *English Towns in Transition*, pp. 11–12.

68 M. Hollander, 'Sex in two cities: the formation and regulation of sexual relationships in Edinburgh and York, 1560–1625' (PhD dissertation, University of York, 2006).

69 H. Dingwall, *Late Seventeenth-Century Edinburgh: A Demographic Study* (Aldershot: Scolar Press, 1994), pp. 13, 16–21; W. Makey, 'Edinburgh in mid-seventeenth century' in M. Lynch (ed.), *The Early Modern Town in Scotland* (London: Croon Helm, 1987), pp. 192–218, on p. 205; C. Galley, *The Demography of Early Modern Towns: York in the Sixteenth and Seventeenth Centuries* (Liverpool: Liverpool University Press, 1998), pp. 43–45.

70 S. Webb, *English Local Government from the Revolution to the Municipal Corporations Act: The Manor and the Borough*, pt. 1 (London: Longmans, Green and Co., 1908), p. 5.

1 The character of the environmental challenge

Introduction

Throughout the period 1560 to 1700, early modern urban governors faced distinctly different, and arguably larger, sanitation and environmental challenges than those faced by town councils today. Malodours emanating from soap-boiling, slaughterhouses, candle-making, tanners' and dyers' vats, open sewers, dunghills, stables and pig sties characterized pre-modern, urban streets. Not a few contemporaries were engaged in a combination of domestic, industrial and agricultural activities in the same neighbourhoods, streets and even within the bounds of one property. Craftsmen's workshops were commonly situated above, below or behind their homes, to facilitate economic familial survival. Small agricultural outbuildings, such as pig sties, hen houses or stables, were common features of the areas of land behind houses (backlands).[1] Indeed, some Aberdonians even shared their homes with their livestock.[2] Urban dwellers relied on their landward counterparts for some foodstuffs, and, as important market centres, towns provided their rural hinterlands with a variable degree of urban services; but urban centres were not exclusively manufacturing settlements, which exchanged urban wares for rurally grown food, as some later became. It is important to remain mindful that early modern urban landscapes differed markedly from those of the industrial epoch. In the period 1560 to 1700, they were largely tripartite patchworks of residential, industrial and agricultural buildings. It is crucial to consider the sources of urban dirt within such aesthetically and practically chaotic scenes.

This chapter is split into five sections. The first explains the sources and disposal of domestic waste, how the drainage systems for liquid waste functioned and how such systems were shaped by the built infrastructure. The second section discusses privies and chamber pots and analyses the invention, in 1596, of Sir John Harrington's water closet. The third section explains perceptions of malodorous trades and the fourth contextualizes the meaning of smell in the early modern mind in relation to health and plague. The fifth and final section discusses urban agriculture and the urban-rural manure trade. The chapter draws from qualitative evidence in relation to a variety of British towns, providing a wider, national context for the much heavier focus on the major case study cities of Edinburgh and York in subsequent chapters.

Domestic waste, drainage systems and the built infrastructure

In the context of urban agriculture, which produced substantial volumes of manure, domestic waste actually constituted a proportionately small amount of a town's total waste. Of course, domestic waste included human excrement and urine, but it also included: dirty water from cooking, cleaning and washing; food waste and bones; hearth ashes; building waste, such as rubble and broken stones; and small amounts of non-organic material such as glass and metal. Most contemporaries recycled food waste, by feeding it to livestock, and they sold unwanted possessions, especially clothes, out of necessity, which limited how much waste was produced.[3] Unwanted materials which were intended to be removed from properties were supposed to be piled on forefronts, in backlands or on communal dunghills, also known as middens and in south-west England as mixons, until inhabitants or local governors transported, or paid a carrier to transport, such materials out of town. Rubbish and manure was usually hauled using pack horses or in horse-drawn carts or sledges, the former to be buried in the surrounding countryside and the latter to be sold to farmers to be used as fertilizer. In 1586, when Carlisle Castle was repaired at Queen Elizabeth I's expense, 7s 8d was paid each day to 'Martine Bone and James Tompson for leadinge the rubbishe and broken stones from the gait house for themselffes and their nages'.[4] Perhaps there was a proper location, officially set aside for waste disposal, to which these men travelled, but the document does not allude to one. Where there was sufficient space, rubbish pits could be dug on one's own land, obviating the transportation of rubbish out of town. When some building work was undertaken on Sheffield Parish Church, in 1622, the Church Burgesses paid a labourer 7d for 'making a pitt & removing of plankes & Rubbish'; whereas in 1691, they chose instead to pay 1s 2d 'for carriage of Rubbish'.[5] Perhaps, by this point, the Church Burgesses had run out of open space in which to dig rubbish pits.

Waste liquids, such as dirty water from domestic cooking and cleaning, butchery blood and urine, were supposed to be deposited carefully into proximal drainage channels. Where they existed, they were usually shared by at least two households or businesses, sometimes by many more. These channels were known as watergaits, gutters, ditches, watercourses, watergangs, cundiths, sinks, gouts, conduits and channels when they were open and they were known as syvers, syres or sewers when they were covered or they ran underneath buildings. Grooves were often carved into stone paving slabs in yards and in front of buildings, specifically to aid and direct the drainage paths of rainwater. As long as blockages did not impede their flow, which could and did occur, narrow secondary channels near to dwellings directed liquid waste and rainwater into wider, primary channels running down either the crown or both sides of main causeways. That Edinburgh's High Street drains were 'verye conveniently contrived on both sides of the street: soe as there is none in the middle' impressed Sir William Brereton in 1635.[6] Major drains then usually fed waste into rivers or the sea.[7] However, landlocked towns or those which lacked convenient access to rivers directed their waste into large cess pits such as Edinburgh's North Loch or Stirling's Meikle Dub.[8]

Whereas cooking pots and dishes tended to be scoured with sand, soap and water within the home, clothes tended to be washed outside. In England, clothes were usually washed by women in large tubs of water on riverbanks or in the streets; the resultant dirty water was supposed to be poured carefully into rivers or into open sewers leading to rivers. However, some householders washed clothes indoors, as an Elizabethan Chancery case confirmed that Godfrey Bradshaw and his family, who lived above a woollen goods shop in the London parish of St Augustine, near 'Powles Gate' in the ward of Bread Street, performed 'househoald works as washing clothes and other necessaries done and exercised in the said kitching'.[9] Notably, in Scottish towns, clothes were washed in tubs of soapy water under women's pounding feet, usually on riverbanks, but sometimes in the streets or other public areas. This characteristically Scottish method of washing clothes captured foreigners' attention. John Ray visited Dunbar in 1662 and noted Scottish women's 'way of washing their linen is to tuck up their coats, and tread them with their feet in a tub'.[10]

Dirty water from food preparation and cooking, washing dishes, domestic cleaning and washing clothes could threaten the purity of drinking water supplies. Although most women disposed of dirty water carefully into sewers or large rivers, some townswomen washed clothes and cleaned other items in or near to wells, which was expressly forbidden. In 1612, for example, Darlington's inhabitants were warned under the threat of a fine of 6s 8d that 'none shall wash cloathes fish or suchlike thinges at the tubbwell to putrifie the same'.[11] At Scarborough's Sheriffs' Tourn, in April 1631, Mr Francis Tomson was presented 'for his maide washinge clothes at the cundith [i.e. sewer]'.[12] And at Sheffield's Great Court Leet, in April 1609, inhabitants were warned under the threat of a fine of 3s 4d,

> That no person or persons shall at any time hereafter wash any clothes, calfe heads, calfe meates or … other things within three yarde of the Towne Head Well, New Hall Well, Burtland Well or any other common well in and about the same towne for corruptinge the said wells.[13]

Streams and burns from which inhabitants drew their drinking water could also be contaminated with dirty water. In 1638, Dunfermline's councillors forbade inhabitants from 'washing of barrells [of] cloathes … whairby the water may be trublit [i.e. troubled]'.[14] In this case, women were not banned from washing clothes in barrels, but rather from washing so close to the well that the water became contaminated. Similarly, in 1657, Lanark's councillors banned washing clothes at the 'Welgait Well' and 'at the burne that the filthe goe into the burne'.[15] Here, the councillors were concerned about the purity of the well's and the burn's water, which were both sources of drinking water. Moreover, Edinburgh's inhabitants were prohibited from washing clothes at the Nor' Loch in 1552.[16] And, in 1668, Inverness's councillors, 'considering the great abuse and prejudice the inhabitants ... [were] daylie susteaneing be the washers of cloath', banned washing clothes at the River Ness.[17] Stirling's council also banned washing 'ony maner of clais [clothes] at the toune bouirn' in 1522, and reiterated this ban in 1610 with the added threat of a fine of five pounds Scots and 'breking of thair [women's] tubes'.[18] A woman's washing tub was no mean possession. Urban governors regulated the practice of washing clothes because they were motivated to protect drinking water against pollution to ensure that it did not become dangerous. Berwick's Bailiffs permitted the disposal of waste water into the River Tweed, but only downstream from the town and thereby into the sea. As Christopher Smout argues, in relation to northern England and Scotland, when river water was commonly used as drinking water, before the construction of large-scale upland reservoirs provided preferable supplies, ensuring the cleanliness of river water, as far as technology and resources allowed, was a serious priority in local government.[19] Smout elaborates that it was only after towns stopped relying on rivers for their water supply, in the modern period, that industries and municipalities then 'felt free to pour greatly increased quantities of foul water into the rivers without giving the consequences much thought', by which time the 'convenience' of having 'a river in which to dump waste quickly outweighed complaints'.[20] Although significant efforts were made to protect the purity of water which was used for drinking and cooking, protecting water purity for the purposes of maintaining a clean water supply was not always the primary concern. Inverness's and Stirling's rivers were not sources of drinking water, but inhabitants were prohibited from corrupting them with perceived harmful liquid and solid waste. During plague epidemics, textiles and furniture were often cleaned in running water because contemporaries across Britain recognized running water's purifying effects. It is not obvious from the Stirling and Inverness regulations why contamination of their respective rivers was regulated, but generating income from fines and protecting the burghs' sources of running water for use in times of plague are potentially motivating factors.

Newcastle's River Tyne was protected from solid, but not from liquid waste. In 1613, Newcastle Corporation passed a bylaw ordering 'that strangers shall be appointed every week to cleanse the streets in Newcastle of their ashes and other rubbish, to prevent the rain from washing the same into the river through Loadbourn'.[21] That Newcastle was built on a steep gradient descending to the Tyne surely necessitated this bylaw. Another Newcastle bylaw, also passed in 1613, ensured that all gates in Newcastle's quayside town walls were locked up and watched every night, 'except one or two to stand open for the masters and seamen to go too and fro to their shipps, which will prevent servants casting ashes and other rubbish into the river'.[22] In Newcastle, liquid waste drained into the Tyne with rainwater through the drainage network of open sewers and tributary streams such as the Loadburn and the Ouseburn. The disposal of solid waste into the Tyne was forbidden to prevent the river from silting up and thereby reducing its efficiency as a navigable river and economic lifeline to the monopolistic Port of Newcastle, some eight miles inland. It was not until several decades after the passing of the 1613 bylaws that domestic water supplies were drawn directly from the Tyne, in 1680, when Cuthbert Dykes installed an engine to draw water directly from the river at Sandgate, Newcastle.[23] Before 1680, the town relied on spring water supplies drawn manually from public water pumps known as 'pants'.

Harbours were often protected from waste disposal too. Although inhabitants would certainly not have drawn their drinking water from harbours, they were busy places which were important for trade. Harbours had the potential to become malodorous and unpleasant, but the risk to maintaining sufficiently deep water capable of receiving large ships was surely the primary motivating factor for their protection from solid waste. In seventeenth-century Scarborough, a minority of contemporaries disposed of their waste onto the sand and directly into the harbour in explicit contravention of the town bylaws. In May 1622, for example, Scarborough's Sheriff's Tourn presented Mathew Woolf for 'throwing rubble on to the sand to the corruption of the port'.[24] In April 1623, moreover, the same court presented Elizabeth Rosdell, Thomas Hawkins, George Ruston, Christofer Duke and Christofer Thompson for 'casting moule [i.e. human waste] & ashes over Thomas Herd['s] staith upon the sand to the [an]noyance of the harbour'.[25] And, in October 1623, the court presented Robert Reynold for 'casting ballast in the harbour contrary to the order of the towne and noysome to the harbour' as well as Jeromy Thompson for 'casting his ballast in the harbour at the same time on the 27 October'.[26] That it was against the town bylaws to dispose of waste in this way indicates that the town governors respected the harbour and thought it was indecent and problematic to use it as a receptacle for waste. That only a minority of inhabitants contravened this bylaw, moreover, suggests that most of the town's population respected the bylaw, either because they, too, wanted to maintain the cleanliness of their harbour or because they didn't want to pay a fine. Fines ranged from 4d to 12d, depending on how many times one had committed the offence, which certainly acted as a deterrent, but it is not unreasonable to assume that inhabitants also wanted to preserve the cleanliness of their harbour and beaches themselves. Martin Melosi has discovered that similar harbour regulations were common in the American colonies by the late seventeenth century. In 1634, for example, Boston officials prohibited residents from throwing fish or rubbish near to the common landing, which was possibly the first sanitary ordinance passed in America before the 1650s. And, in 1647, additional regulations were passed to prevent the pollution of Boston Harbor.[27] Disposing of waste into a harbour, which is sheltered from the sea, was problematic because the waste would have lingered in the harbour before eventually entering the sea, thus creating malodours. That Scarborough functioned as a harbour shaped its environmental regulation.

A town or city's building tradition could have a significant impact on drainage, street cleaning and waste disposal. For example, Edinburgh featured multi-storey tenement buildings. In 1679, Thomas Kirke noticed some that were 'seven or eight stories high'.[28] By 1689, Morer had seen 'one row of buildings … with fourteen' storeys.[29] The human waste emanating from these chronically overcrowded residential mazes was substantial. It is significant that Edinburgh's multi-storey tenements had forestairs, which descended exterior walls in the street rather than within them.[30] Forestairs could fall into a poor state of repair and became unsafe. Indeed, as Morer confirmed, forestairs were 'so steepy, narrow and fenceless, that it requires care to go up and down for fear of falling'.[31] This may well explain why a minority of inhabitants residing on upper floors preferred, quite logically and rationally, to throw the heavy contents of chamber pots out of a window or upstairs door into the street below, a practice known as 'casting over', rather than to risk injury by carrying potentially cumbersome chamber pots down a hazardous, exterior staircase. Throughout the eighteenth century, 'casting over' became much more common in Edinburgh and the practice became known as 'gardy loo'. This derived from the French, *gardez l'eau*, meaning beware of the water, and was traditionally shouted down into the street before throwing one's chamber pot out of an upstairs window, in order to warn passers-by of the impending unsavoury shower. However, this practice was by no means widespread, permissible or normal before 1700; it contravened city statutes and both neighbours and local governors objected to the practice profusely. In 1674, for example, Lanark's council ordered inhabitants to 'keep the calsay frie of any watter comeing doun at everie one of ther heid roumes'.[32]

By the late seventeenth century, many main urban streets were paved. A substantial number of them had been paved since the medieval period and paving increased throughout the sixteenth century. They usually rose in the centre to a 'crown' to aid drainage. Regarding Carlisle, W. Hutchinson noted in 1794, 'about the beginning of the present [i.e. eighteenth] century ... the streets though spacious, were paved with large stones and the centre part or causeway rose to a considerable height'.[33] In the seventeenth century, Carlisle Corporation spent substantial sums of money repaving the city's three gates, two bridges, market place and around the Moothall, but individual householders were responsible for paving the area before their property to the middle of the street, known as the forefront.[34] Neighbours who neglected to pave their forefronts were often presented by civic officials through local courts as a result of civic street inspections. In 1594, Berwick Corporation found,

> The hiestrete in Castlegate which is yet unpaved is very noysome this winter time especiallie at the upper end of the new cawsey it is growen verye deepe and almoste not passable for horse nor catle. There woulde some good waye be taken for pavinge it up throughe the street.[35]

As Emily Cockayne rightly notes, regarding London, Oxford, Bath and Manchester, 'a hotch-potch of surfaces adorned each street' as respective neighbours used different sizes, colours and types of paving materials, such as pebbles, flint and rag stones.[36] Figure 1 shows an example of contemporary paving, completed in 1665, which survives intact today in Dartmouth in Devon, demonstrating stones which were typically incorporated into paving designs. Narrower lanes and vennels leading off the main streets were often left unpaved. According to Hutchinson, eighteenth-century Carlisle's 'lanes and avenues, even the church road, were not paved and in many places entirely covered with weeds and underwood. The streets, not often trode upon, were, in many parts of them,

Figure 1 Paving in Dartmouth, Devon (1665)
Photograph: Adrian Green

green with grass'.[37] Vennels and lanes of bare earth were harder to clean and could become muddy during heavy rainfall. This was not practical for main streets which supported heavy volumes of horse-drawn traffic. Unsurprisingly, councils and corporations tended to focus available investment for paving on the most strategically important thoroughfares, consequently often neglecting to pave smaller vennels and lanes.

Although sewers in this period were supposed to be limited to liquid waste and rainwater, a minority of inhabitants disposed of solid waste into them. Some properties in Edinburgh and in other Scottish towns had jaw holls in their floors or walls through which dirty water, but no human waste, could be poured from inside houses directly into watercourses.[38] Those without convenient access to open sewers or to jaw holls, however, had to make a large effort to deposit their liquid waste correctly. This method of liquid waste disposal was largely beholden to the compliance of householders, necessarily problematic and often became the source of contention between adjacent neighbours. In November 1671, Andrew Bands, of Perth, complained to the Burgh Council that his neighbour, Malcome Aissons, had allowed his sewer to fall into disrepair and had altered its course which was consequently harming Andrew's land. Perth's Dean of Guild, who normally judged such neighbourhood disputes, was out of town, so certain members of the Burgh Council, Baillie Robert Russell, Convener Robert Anderson, Treasurer Christopher Russell and a Merchant councillor, John Bands, inspected the drainage nuisance itself and decided,

> For the better saiftie of the said Andrew Bands land and the advantage of the miln dam [that] the said gutter on the bakside of Malcome Aissons hous run noe farder [i.e. further] down that way then to the corner dyke at the south

cheeke of the old port at the eist end of the said hous and that the hoill in the said dyke wherthrow the said gutter runs presentlie be built upe with stone & lime and a ... breastwark of stone be built therat for stopping the current of the said gutter and that a syver be made therat throw beneath the calsey to convoy the same to the Meikle Dub.[39]

The repair was paid for by the burgh, rather than by the offender. The Treasurer released sufficient funds to cover the repairs soon after this case was decided, probably because this nuisance posed a risk to the Miln Dam and the Dirt Raw Port, both of which were integral to the burgh's efficient functioning.

Early modern towns were, in Walter King's words, 'a maze of private ditches' which drained a range of urban buildings to the major open sewers which carried rainwater and liquid waste out of the town.[40] These complex networks of open and closed, private and public, main and secondary sewers were designed to drain liquid waste and rainwater only, but they were relatively rudimentary systems which relied largely on inhabitants' efforts and compliance to ensure that they flowed efficiently, and it is unsurprising that they often became blocked with solid waste. The complex webs of ubiquitous main and private sewers which drained early modern British streets were undoubtedly noxious, especially in hot weather, and they only functioned effectively so long as they were not blocked with solid waste, they were scoured frequently, they were not flooded by heavy rainfall and they did not dry up during droughts. Although sewerage networks were generally more comprehensive in larger, busier, more densely populated and more prosperous urban settlements, townspeople across Britain perceived at least the main street sewers into which their private ditches drained as a service provided and maintained for them at the expense of the civic purse. The majority of inhabitants were necessarily interested in maintaining private sewers and contributing to the maintenance of main sewers to minimize the malodours emanating from them. Excepting intermittent lapses and failures, these sophisticated constructions successfully drained liquid waste away from dwellings and businesses and without them early modern streets would certainly have been wetter, dirtier and more unpleasant.

Privies, chamber pots and Sir John Harrington's water closet

Human waste is perhaps domestic waste's most obvious component. Stationary toilets were called privies, but not everyone enjoyed access to one. Most were dry privies, which were deep pits below simple wooden seats, with holes cut out of them, built as separate outbuildings in backlands.[41] They had to be dug out at regular intervals between which lime and sand could be used to cover the waste and thereby suppress its malodour. A 1612 survey of some houses in the West Smithfield area of London, by Ralph Treswell, a mapmaker and surveyor who created many detailed surveys of London buildings, showed the exact location of privies, symbolized by grey holes within brown seats.[42] There were not enough privies in this particular location for each household to have had exclusive access to one. They might well have been shared by several neighbours who upheld strict informal rules governing which neighbours accessed and maintained particular privies. Access to wells within neighbourhoods was governed in a similar way. Unless one lived nearby the marketplace, the convenience of having a well close to one's dwelling was an amenity with a cost. A complex web of goodwill agreements, leases, rents and maintenance payments dictated who could use private and street wells. Regarding early modern London, for example, Mark Jenner argues 'access to water was mediated by the micropolitics of the neighbourhood' and 'clusters of relationships ... determined who could use particular sources'.[43] Town councils and corporations were not responsible for emptying householders' private privy pits, though they could enforce individuals to dig them out if they leaked into the streets or became offensively malodorous. A minority of inhabitants did create insanitary nuisances by digging their privy pits out infrequently. Nuisance courts, such as The City of London's Assize of Nuisance and Edinburgh's Dean of Guild Court, sent sworn viewers to assess such complaints of nuisance in the urban environment. Their reports contain insightful information about privies. In February 1547, the London viewers recorded

> there is a jakes [i.e. toilet] whiche is a noysaunce to the said tenement whiche is partable between the said partie defendaunt and one Maister Norres, Gentilman usher, and oweth of righte to be clensed and repaired at the costes and charges of bothe the said parties.[44]

This privy was shared between two neighbours, and they were expected to work together to keep it clean. In 1614, Alexander Bowie, of Steven Law's Close in Edinburgh, complained to the city's Dean of Guild Court that his neighbour, John Moffat, a stabler, had two privies in Steven Law's Close which 'daylie breks out and ryns [i.e. runs] in the laithe houses [i.e. basements] of his said tenement and rotts and consumes the walls thairof in the said close to his great hurt and skaith [i.e. damage]'; Moffat was ordered to clean the privies out immediately.[45] Privies could also be dangerous, as the Bristol Court Leet Jurors highlighted in October 1629, when they ordered the 'amendment of a house of office that is in the castle beinge very noisome & dangerous for children for falling in it as there hath bin one child already in it'.[46]

Noisome privies seem to have been much more problematic in the summer months. In April 1585, Edinburgh Council issued a proclamation ordering that 'nane suffer their privies to gorge, brek, and rin owt in the streits in dew times'.[47] And, in 1582, Edinburgh Council passed a statute, proclaiming,

> all persones that has scheildes [i.e. privies] clenye the same if they be full so they break furth nor run in the streets under the pain of 18s and if any open their closets in time of rain so that the filth thereof runs along the street the tenement sall be fined ... 18s and that none hold their closets open seeping or running furth but honestly covered ... as when any scheildes are clanyed [i.e.

cleaned] that the clenyer carie the same honestly and quietly away in the night not fouling the high streets therewith and that none presume to take on hand to empty the dry schields at close heads or cast the water over the stones upon the high streets under the pain of imprisonment ... at the will of the magistrates.[48]

Clearly, it was completely unacceptable to pour waste water 'over the stones upon the high streets', an offence which could lead to imprisonment. Here, privies are referred to as 'schieldes'; indeed, contemporaries used an array of names for privies during this period, from 'closets' to 'jakes' or 'jacques', to 'houses of office', 'houses of easement', 'close stools', 'easing chairs' or 'chairs of easement'. In most towns, the nuisance of noxious or leaking privies tended to be relatively rare, in comparison to other insanitary nuisances, such as throwing waste onto the streets, only accounting for 1 per cent of insanitary nuisances in seventeenth-century Carlisle, for example.[49] This suggests that the majority of households with dry privies had them dug out and cleaned sufficiently frequently, even if Samuel Pepys' neighbour did not. There is no firm evidence detailing how regularly dry privy pits should be dug out. However, the frequency would have depended on several variables, such as the size of the pit, the number of people using the privy and temperature.

Some documents refer to whether a privy was wet or dry. The ones which were described as having 'run out in the streets' may well have been wet privies, with cisterns of water to flush the waste into a relatively watertight, brick or clay-lined vault below or perhaps even through a pipe into a sewer or a river.[50] In the maze of Edinburgh's multi-storey tenements, neighbours' drainage systems were often interconnected. Indoor wet privies were certainly less common than outdoor dry privy pits, but they did exist. Some urban governments funded the maintenance of communal, public toilets, known as common houses of office or easement. The overwhelming majority of families, however, used simple chamber pots or portable indoor commodes known as close stools.[51] Chamber pots, made from pewter, wood, brass, earthenware or glass, were used at night for convenience, and by those without access to a stationary privy, as well as by the elderly and infirm. Buckets and pails were surely also used by those who could not afford chamber pots. The Carlisle City Chamberlains' accounts for the financial year 1634–1635 note a payment of 1s paid 'for a herring barrell and makeinge it new for a close stoole'.[52] This is a simple and inexpensive but remarkably effective invention which suggests that inhabitants might well have created their own similarly innovative facilities independently using inexpensive receptacles such as barrels. More elaborate chamber pots with cushioned seats, which were used upon normal chairs, were called plate jakes. Most elaborate of all was the mobile close stool, complete with a storage compartment underneath the seat and removable pans.[53] In 1605, George Denton, a Carlisle gentleman, died leaving an array of facilities including two pewter chamber pots, two 'plate jakes covered with cloth' and 'a joined easinge chaier with a quisshon' worth 2s 6d.[54] And John Pattinson, another Carlisle gentleman, died in 1667 leaving 'one close stool and pann' worth 16s.[55] For those of less prosperous social strata than these individuals, however, buckets, chamber pots and outdoor privies were the norm. Joined easing chairs, close stools and plate jakes were features of more wealthy households.

In many pre-industrial British towns, it was not uncommon for inhabitants, especially vagrants and young children, to urinate, and even to defecate, directly onto outdoor areas which offered seclusion, such as walled churchyards, derelict houses and poorly lit lanes and closes. It is highly probable that vagrants and some of the very poorest people inhabiting overcrowded and impoverished closes possessed no suitable receptacles at all.[56] In 1580, for example, Edinburgh Council prohibited inhabitants from 'doing thair ease at the said close heids as is maist uncomely to be sene'.[57] A similar statute was passed in April 1586,

> proclamatioun to be maid dischargeing all persouns of voiding of thair filth and doing thair eases at the close heids as thai haif done in times past, under the paine of wairding [i.e. imprisoning] thair persouns and punessing of thame that may be tryet or apprehendit at the will of the magestrats and payment of ane unlaw be the maisters of the hous[es] whose servands do the sam, so often as thai failyie.[58]

This issue was not exclusive to Edinburgh. In December 1573, moreover, a proclamation was passed in Berwick on Tweed to remind inhabitants,

> it is straightlie charged and commanded that no person childe or other shall by the filthe of his owne bodye anoye anye of the stretes lanes or walles of the same towne or the churchyardes or places of assemblies uppon paine aforesaid to be inflicted either [u]ppon the partie that dothe it, or elles if it be done by an infant uppon suche as have charge over them.[59]

Although such behaviour was more prevalent among vagrants and children, it was by no means exclusive to them. In June 1598, Robert Birrel, an Edinburgh Burgess, noted in his diary, 'Robert Cathcart [was] slaine pisching att the wall in Peibleis wynd heid be William Stewart, sone to Sir William Stewart'.[60] Although the more significant focus of this reference in Birrel's diary is that Cathcart had been killed, it does demonstrate, albeit coincidentally, that urination directly onto the street occurred in Edinburgh at this time. Notably, Cathcart was killed for political reasons and not in outrage *because* he was urinating onto the street, but it is highly likely that the fact that he was urinating enabled his killer to use the element of surprise. Edinburgh Dean of Guild Court sometimes intervened to clear derelict tenements and areas of waste land when they had been used by inhabitants effectively as open cess pits known as a 'common jacques'.[61]

Townspeople were capable of developing useful waste disposal facilities themselves because this was something which affected them every day. The common misconception that passive urban inhabitants waited idly until governing institutions implemented macro-scale improvements on their behalves in the nineteenth century is nonsensical. Householders used their own initiative to make their own arrangements in relation to this element of their daily routine. Contemporaries surely made many more ingenious and imaginative contraptions than those which were recorded in the documentary records. One can only learn about the converted herring barrel at Carlisle because the Corporation kept detailed Chamberlains' accounts, whereas the majority of householders did not. While much of the history of this aspect of everyday life has unfortunately been lost, there are clues which elucidate it in many documents, especially in nuisance court cases. From grand and elaborate contraptions, to simpler wet and dry privies, to close stools and easing chairs, right down to the pails, barrels and buckets used by the poor, contemporaries designed, built and maintained an impressive array of receptacles to facilitate the act of nature which they called 'taking their ease' or 'easie'. While such technology was arguably rudimentary, the 'chamber pot in the window' stereotype does not do justice to the array of ingenious mechanisms which contemporaries devised for use in what was an integral part of their daily lives.

In 1596, Sir John Harrington invented the water closet basically in its modern form. The Elizabethan courtier and writer was Queen Elizabeth's godson, being the son of Isabella Markham, who had served as one of Princess Elizabeth's maids of honour at the Royal Palace of Hatfield and who had remained a member of Queen Elizabeth's Privy Chamber until Isabella's death in 1579.[62] In 1596, Harrington published *A New Discourse of a Stale Subject called the Metamorphosis of Ajax* as a pamphlet in which he proposed his water closet invention as the solution to the domestic waste disposal problems of the day. The invention originated from a conversation in the early 1590s between Harrington and several other well-connected contemporaries, including Sir Mathew Arundell and the Earl of Southampton, Henry Wriothesley, at Wardour Castle in Wiltshire.[63] The pamphlet consists of three parts: firstly, the *Metamorphosis Proper* in which he justifies at length why such a high-born man is talking about such low matters. He asks the reader to 'let a publik benefit expell a private bashfulnes' and argues that discussion of such base matters is necessary for public benefit at large, the public benefit being sweeter smelling privies. The second section, the *Anatomie of the Metamorphosed Ajax*, is a detailed description, complete with diagrams, about how to construct the water closet, where to obtain various parts and at what price. Basically, it was a flushing mechanism with a cistern, which automatically stopped the running water after the waste had exited the bowl into an airtight storage vat below, which had to be emptied periodically. Thirdly, an *Apologie* offers further justification for his public discussion of such a foul subject in the form of a court case in which he is charged with writing about low-born matters.

Though Harrington published under the name Miscasmos, meaning 'hater of filth', allegedly as a series of letters between Miscasmos and his cousin and friend, Philostilpnos, meaning 'lover of cleanliness', Harrington's authorship is undoubted and he does actually sign off the last section in his own name. The word 'Ajax' refers to a common contemporary word for a toilet or chamber pot, jaques or jakes, and the title was designed to depict a metamorphosis, i.e. the cleaning out, of early modern privies themselves. In his pamphlet, Harrington personifies Ajax as an individual who must be improved:

> Sometimes with the heate of his breath he will be readie to overcome a strong man; another time he will take a weake man at the vauntage, and strike him behind with such a cold, that he shalbe the worse for it a moneth after [i.e. a reference to draughty garderobes]. Now many have wrastled with him, to seeke to stop his breath and never maime him but he makes them glad to stop their noses, and that indeed is some remedie, for such whose throats have a better swallow, then their heads have capacitie.[64]

Harrington then goes on to explain how integral good sanitation is to the commonweal, situating the need for such facilities in the long-term historical context.

> When companies of men began first to increase, and make of families townes, and of townes cities; they quickly found not onely offence, but infection, to grow out of great concourse of people, if speciall care were not had to avoid it. And because they could not remove houses, as they do tents, from place to place, they were driven to find the best meanes that their wits did then serve them, to cover, rather then to avoyd these annoyances: either by digging pits in the earth, or place the common houses [i.e. communal privies] over rivers … first they were provided for bare necessitie … then they came to be matters of some more cost … & I thinke I might also lay pride to their charge: for I have seene them in cases of fugerd sattin, and velvet …[65]

Close stools belonging to wealthy households were indeed sometimes covered in the rather impractical fabric of velvet to provide comfort and to display wealth, something at which Harrington clearly sneered.

Harrington's description of how to construct his proposed water closet is lengthy and detailed, but he wrote very easy-to-follow instructions, presumably for a craftsman to implement on behalf of the individual into whose house the privy was actually being installed. Admittedly, Harrington's invention was a court joke, which literary historian Jason Scott-Waren suggests might have even been designed to earn him notoriety.[66] It certainly was a shocking and indeed base subject for someone of his social standing to have published about at the time. Moreover, the pamphlet was never very widely disseminated and it was directed towards the people of his own social stratum; it was never intended as a panacea for the entire population's domestic waste disposal problems. While Queen Elizabeth had one of Harrington's water closets installed at Richmond, and Harrington installed one into his home at Kelston in Somerset, those at court and wider society were largely disgusted by the invention, which was generally ignored, because of its unsavoury connotations. The infrastructure of sixteenth-century towns, even in London, simply could not have coped with the much larger and more problematic volume of liquid waste which Harrington's design would have produced.[67] Dry privy pits were far more efficient in the context of pre-modern infrastructure and available technology. Indeed, the installation of so many flushing toilets in early nineteenth-century London drove increasingly more untreated liquid waste directly into the River Thames, causing the 'Great Stink' in the summer of 1858, and motivating the very urgent development of a large-scale underground sewerage network in the city. The Victorians have been admired immensely for their successful, tireless and monumental efforts to solve the urgent technological problem of how to dispose of the higher volume, increasingly liquid, human waste which had been both augmented and liquified by millions of gallons of flush water, and rightly so. But it is rarely mentioned that they had actually exacerbated the problem in the first place by installing thousands of water closets in the place of dry privy pits. Harrington's invention, albeit a relatively small technological step, was hugely sophisticated for its time and while sadly it did not solve the waste disposal problem of the day, this 'unsavory discourse' is significant as an insight into one Elizabethan man's proposed solution.

Malodorous trades

Urban dwellers contended with a myriad of malodorous trades and crafts in their environment – from butchers and fishmongers, to dyers and tanners, to candlemakers and soap-boilers, to skinners and cloth-bleachers. A rich variety of urban crafts produced a correspondingly rich assortment of malodours and waste materials. Tanners, skinners and dyers, who used urine and animal excrement in their production processes, created foul smells in their vats and caused a nuisance by drying noxious products over walls in public places, and urban inhabitants found the smell of candlemakers melting tallow (hard animal fat) very offensive. In April 1629, a Bristol weaver, Edward Kestell, was presented at the city's Court Leet because he 'useth brine otherwise pisse for skowringe of his stuffes which is an annoyance of his neighbours'.[68] The waste left behind at fishmongers' stalls and fleshers' deposition of offal in public areas continually annoyed contemporaries. In October 1628, Bristol Court Leet presented Thomas Bright and John Goare, butchers, for 'throwing the filth & inwards that cometh from the beasts bellies into the streete before their dores it being very noisome to all the inhabitants'.[69] They also presented Anne, the wife of Phillip Gillett, 'for that she doth throw out of hir shop … the stinking water of Newfoundland fishe and other saltfishe'.[70] The confluence of the various smells and waste materials emanating from urban workshops must, at times, have been overwhelming, especially in the heat of summer; but urban authorities devoted a great deal of time, effort and resources into suppressing malodorous nuisances. The regulation of so-called 'dirty' trades was motivated, first and foremost, by the noxious waste materials produced and the olfactory offence caused by their production processes. In relation to Charles I's regulation of London coal smoke, for example, William Cavert has argued convincingly, 'the harassment, fining, and arrest of large-scale brewers with the intention of improving air quality was … part of a much broader initiative to reform and improve the kingdom from the center outward'.[71] But however much inhabitants disliked the pollutants of such crafts, they all needed essential products such as leather, fish, beer, candles and meat, and both governors and inhabitants knew that these crafts could not be expelled from urban centres entirely, though they were regulated quite rigorously. Noxious crafts and trades tended to be tolerated to a larger extent than other nuisances, or they were confined to particular areas rather than banned outright, out of economic interest and the widely appreciated necessity of producing vital products.

In 1592, for example, Edinburgh's councillors recorded 'divers nichtbours hes havilie complenit upoun the candilmakers who, throw rinding and melting of thair tallow ... raises such vile, filthie and contagious savoures that nane may remaine in thair awin houssis'.[72] That these neighbours actually felt that they could not remain in their houses suggests that they perceived candle-making's malodour less as an annoying inconvenience and more as a dangerous health risk which they felt obliged to avoid. Edinburgh Council responded to this complaint by passing a statute prohibiting candlemakers from melting tallow in 'common vinells or other places where the savour thairof may cum to the Hie Gait ... or common streits'.[73] As a direct response to the petition from Edinburgh's inhabitants, this was a purposeful attempt to improve the air quality in the most populous and most strategically important neighbourhoods, near to important civic buildings where prestigious visitors were entertained, by moving a noxious trade to more sparsely populated areas on the urban periphery. Dolly Jorgensen found similar examples of 'harmony' in Norwich and Coventry, between 1400 and 1600, noting that when the city councils responded to inhabitants' petitions requesting improvements in sanitation provision or regulation, 'officials then acted as the representatives of the community'.[74]

Many other noxious trades required significant regulation. In October 1663, Kendal's Court Leet Jurors presented and fined John Swale 3s 4d 'for setting the water which he dyes with into the streate, & it standes in a poole in the street'.[75] In Bristol, in October 1628, the city's Court Leet jurors presented Edward Belsure, a sopemaker, for 'throwing sopers lime in the streete in Duke Lane'.[76] Elsewhere, in Berwick, those who processed and packed salmon for export and for local consumption were regulated. In 1568, the corporation declared that nobody involved in the trade 'shoulde presome to washe them within the towne & neither in their houses nor in their backsides', but they were to do so 'onelye withoute the Brig Gate or Shoregate for avoidinge of corrupte aire and other noisome deseases'.[77] Again, in October 1594, Berwick's washers of salmon were reminded not to wash their products in the public streets because

> there is suche corruption and stinche all the sommertime in the streets by washinge of salmon in sondrye places in the towne especiallye in the Westerlane and other places ... that is verye like to poison & infect all the towne.[78]

Their proaction in relation to preventing foul-smelling miasmas, which were perceived as possessing the potential to transmit infectious diseases such as plague, could not be clearer. The bleaching of cloth was also a nuisance in Berwick, and in 1592 the bleachers were presented at the Bailiffs' Court because the

> streame issuinge frome the well on the Grenes is turned frome the customed course by the bleachinge of clothe in somer time whiche hathe ... brede mires and bogges on the Grenes to the grete hurte and annoyance of the dwellers there and of the whole towne.[79]

In this case it was not the bleaching of the cloth itself which was regarded as the nuisance, but rather the consequent diversion of the watercourse by those who were conducting the bleaching. By moving the channel, the bleachers caused parts of the bleach greens to become waterlogged, which caused wider inconvenience to the town.

In 1568, Carlisle Corporation 'orderid that no tanner shall drye anye barke within houses but onlye in the common kilnes withoute the citie upon paine of 6s 8d'.[80] It is impossible to say for certain whether this bylaw was passed to reduce the risk of fire or to regulate the malodour of the bark while it dried. That in 1596, John Haithway, a tanner of Carlisle, died leaving a 'lime croke', 'bark', 'working and chipping knives' and a 'tanning vat' in the 'barkhouse' behind his dwelling house, however, suggests that this bylaw might not have been enforced rigorously, if indeed he was actively using the equipment.[81] At Carlisle City Court Leet, in April 1597, four glovers, Warwicke Rogersonne, Richard Warwicke, Ingrame Teasdall and Robert Bradfurthe, were each fined 6d for 'hinging of sheip skines in [the] streat'.[82] Very similarly, in October 1628, Thomas James and Henry Northall of Bristol were presented to the Court Leet for 'hanginge of skinnes at their dores below Newgate where the streete is very narrow which is very noisome to passers by'.[83] Producers of leather needed to dry their animal skins, which had been soaked in noxious substances such as urine and dog or bird excrement, in the open air, usually draped over walls or fences for long periods of time. It is highly likely, therefore, that the malodours emanating from these skins concerned inhabitants more so than their unsightly appearance. Later, in 1665, Carlisle Court Leet regulated the glovers again, emphasizing the skins' foul smell:

> (Whereas complainte is made unto us that the glovers of this Citty do frequently hang up there sheepe skins in the shambles to the greate anoyance of the neighbours ther adjacent, by ther loathsome smell and savor they have) wee order that from hence forth noe glovers hand [i.e. handle/work on] any ther but carry them to dry without the walls of this citty.[84]

Skinners who contravened of this bylaw were threatened with a fine of 12d. However, the complaints continued and the glovers received a further leet order in 1668, stipulating that 'noe glovers or others shall hang up any sheepe skines in the shambles to the greate anoyance of their neighbours and others by ther loathsome smell but that they carry the same out of the citty to dry'.[85] The word 'loathsome' suggests that inhabitants were not merely annoyed by these malodours, as people might be today, but that they literally feared them in a much more serious manner. In Bristol, in April 1635, John Arthur was presented at the Court Leet 'for beating his lymed skines or such as are dressed with meale before his dore in Redcliffe Streete to the greate annoyance of the neighbours'.[86] While there was an element of considered planning efforts in urban settlements during this period, in the absence of strictly enforced zoning and town planning, industrial processes were often carried out in and around inhabitants' dwellings. While everyone needed meat, leather and candles, the waste materials and particularly the malodours emanating from noxious crafts and trades' production processes often reduced the quality of people's daily lives. Urban governors worked hard throughout the period to curtail the impact of such noxious trades and crafts, often by removing them to peripheral areas of town, but complaints about industrial nuisances continued in earnest throughout the period.

Natural or divine causes? Plague and the meaning of smell

Foul-smelling insanitary nuisances caused contemporaries so much concern because they perceived them as dangerous, potentially fatal, health risks rather than merely as annoying inconveniences. An understanding of contemporary perceptions of and reactions to insanitary nuisances in this period is ultimately flawed if the way in which townspeople perceived smell is not fully appreciated. In many respects, an insanitary nuisance was defined by its smell; and its smell, above any other of its characteristics, was what alerted people to the nuisance's presence in the first place and also what motivated them to suppress the nuisance. Reconstructing olfactory perception from written sources is a difficult, but by no means impossible, task. Historians' attempts to historicize and contextualize early modern sensory experiences have transcended the traditional boundaries of historical enquiry. Innovative work has been published, which will surely inspire and encourage other historians to follow, such as: Christopher Woolgar's *The Senses in Late Medieval England*, published in 2006; Jo Wheeler's 2007 study of smell and plague epidemics in sixteenth-century Venice; and Elizabeth Foyster's 2010 essay on smell, sound and touch in early modern Scotland.[87] Clearly, historians are coming to realize that the senses must be taken into account if they are to understand and reconstruct contemporaries' daily life experiences in a significant way. Borough Court and council records are full of clues as to which features of the outdoor olfactory environment annoyed, and which features pleased, urban inhabitants. Bio-physicists have researched how the brain's insula constantly monitors and controls physical reactions to bacteria-filled air, as perceived by scent receptors, by creating a perceived 'bad' smell in order to motivate an individual's withdrawal from the area in which the malodorous air is being inhaled.[88] Both rich and poor early modern contemporaries, too, had brains complete with insulas and were therefore necessarily repelled by bacteria-filled air, which they perceived negatively. Contemporaries sought to remove insanitary or dirty features of their urban landscape, which in the anthropologist Mary

Douglas's seminal *Purity and Danger* would be deemed 'matter out of place', because of the malodours which emanated from such nuisances, first and foremost, and only because of their unsavoury, 'dirty' or 'out of place' appearance, secondarily, though physical obstruction of thoroughfares was also an important motivating factor.[89] While non-noxious rubbish which physically blocked streets was regulated, contemporaries responded to malodorous nuisances with a special sense of urgency. Indeed, they feared intensely that malodours emanating from insanitary nuisances could permeate their bodies and consequently disrupt the necessary balance of the four internal bodily liquids – blood, yellow bile, black bile and phlegm – known as humours, according to Greco-Roman medicine propounded by classical scholars such as Hippocrates and Galen. This fuelled motivation to improve air quality by regulating the practice of dirty crafts and trades.

Why were urban dwellers in this period so seriously concerned about the quality, or in their words the 'wholesomeness' or the 'sweetness', of the air which they inhaled? That contemporaries judged a place's cleanliness by its air quality, and described the air in terms of wholesomeness, reveals that they judged air and food in a similar light. They believed that the air which they inhaled possessed a similar capability with which to nourish or damage their bodies as did the food which they ingested. Indeed, Mark Jenner also found that Londoners 'perceived themselves as ingesting, almost eating' their environment, and he notes that 'smells that we might consider simply unpleasant could be as fatal as mustard gas' in contemporaries' minds.[90] Early modern people inherited such understandings from their late medieval ancestors, among whom Christopher Woolgar found 'there was an enduring belief in the regenerative or debilitating effects of odours'.[91] To late medieval people, Woolgar highlights, 'unpleasant smells indicated danger, corruption and even death', though he emphasizes that contemporaries believed that the effects of bad smells on the body 'varied with the humoural composition of both the odour and the person perceiving it'.[92] In the early modern mind, smell held a symbolic significance above and beyond mere unpleasantness. Indeed, contemporaries deemed it potentially threatening to their physical wellbeing and, understandably, sought to avoid its dangerous properties.[93]

There is much documentary evidence to suggest that contemporaries' fears of malodours were reinforced by, and very much heightened during, plague epidemics as a result of their perception of how miasmatic plague contagion functioned. Modern research has now revealed that the black rats, which carried plague-infested fleas, must have flourished among the ubiquitous dirt and refuse in early modern towns. Although Sir Theodore de Mayerne, a physician, submitted a report to King Charles I in 1631 recommending the killing of rats and mice during plague epidemics, contemporaries were largely unaware of the role which rats played in spreading plague.[94] Indeed, rats rarely featured in the archival material.[95] The earliest extant Scottish anti-plague legislation was passed in 1456 to enforce quarantine, the regulation of inhabitants' movements and the burning of infected buildings. Subsequent legislation to combat plague epidemics tended to be passed by local burgh, non-parliamentary governing institutions due to a relatively weak Scottish central government.[96] Comparatively, the first English anti-plague legislation dates from 1518 and subsequent plague orders included clauses regarding the removal of middings and increased cleansing of streets. Some contemporaries attributed plague contraction to God's wrath, and perceived it as a form of divine punishment from which condemned inhabitants had little, if any, means of escape. Carlisle Corporation, for example, was in no doubt that the epidemic of 1597–1598 was God's doing, describing those spared from death as 'anye person to whom god has granted life ether by not contracting the sicknes though beinge in the visiteds company daily, or otherwise that have had it & yet it has pleased god to spare them life'.[97] Most contemporaries understood that plague was contagious and consequently endeavoured to curtail contraction after God had initiated a plague epidemic, but sanitation improvements were deemed useless by many as deterrents in the first place because, ultimately, in the early modern mentality, God's vengeance was insuperable.

Mark Jenner appreciates the logic of sixteenth- and seventeenth-century Londoners' dog culls from a contemporary perspective.[98] Keith Thomas interpreted such culls as a 'sanitary measure', and both Frank Wilson and Brian Pullan merely pointed to the irony that, by killing rats' natural predators, such culls increased contagion.[99] Furthermore, Ronald Hutton mistakenly assumed that dog culls reveal that contemporaries linked fleas, which inhabited dogs' fur, to plague contraction.[100] But, by making a commendable effort to appreciate what such culls meant to contemporaries, Mark Jenner explains why contemporaries believed that having fewer dogs in London would reduce contagion. Using an anthropological approach, Jenner cleverly highlights that dogs, and to a lesser extent cats, had significant contact with humans; indeed, dogs even had human names.[101] Moreover, because dogs and cats, unlike other animals such as pigs, lived a 'liminal lifestyle' between people's homes and public areas, where their owners often expected them to find their own food, contemporaries believed that dogs could infect humans with plague directly.[102] This is a revealing example of contemporary Londoners' belief in a natural explanation of plague.

It is undeniable that some urban dwellers perceived malodorous nuisances as sources of potentially fatal plague miasmas. Consequently, during plague epidemics, some contemporaries cleared the streets of dunghills and refuse and swept streets and scoured sewers more frequently – in addition to lighting bonfires in the streets, wearing pomanders and burning incense in plague victims' houses to overpower miasmas. In 1568, the Aberdonian Dr Gilbert Skeyne wrote a treatise entitled *An Brave Description of the Pest* in which he asserted 'the cause of pest in our private citie [i.e. Edinburgh] is stink and corruption and filth, which occupies the common stretis and gaittis', emphasizing that plague 'always … has the cause frome … corruptioun of the air'.[103] However, Archibald Skeldie's book of preventatives, *The Only Sure Preservative against the Plague of Pestilence*, written almost a century later in 1645, diverges from Skeyne's tracts. Skeldie admitted that hygienic, or in his words 'humane', preventative measures, such as reducing 'immediat and mediat touching', could curtail plague's spread after a town had contracted it.[104] But he believed, ultimately, if God decided one's sins warranted a plague contraction, one 'cannot be secure from the avenging hand of God in any place where they can live'.[105] He also believed that there was no better preservative than 'true and unfeined repentance'.[106] Improving public hygiene to prevent future plague epidemics would have seemed nonsensical to someone of Skeldie's mentality. But both Skeyne and Skeldie, like most contemporaries, agreed that once a town had contracted plague, it subsequently spread through airborne, foul-smelling miasma clouds. Skeyne believed plague 'alwais … hes the cause frome the heavins or corruptioun of the air'.[107] Similarly, Skeldie called plague, 'that infection which commeth of the aire, which is polluted and corrupted … by the huge number of unburied carkases of men and beasts, which polluting the aire, breedeth a pestilence to such as live in those places…'.[108]

This is why people wore sweet-smelling pomanders on clothing and lit bonfires in the streets to overpower plague-infested air. Indeed, Constance Classen, David Howes and Anthony Synnott go as far as to call efforts to overpower malodours during early modern plague epidemics an 'olfactory war'.[109] It is important, however, to bear in mind Richard Oram's observation that Skeyne's work potentially overshadowed and consequently impeded the circulation of other more 'modern' medical texts regarding plague contagion during the early seventeenth century.[110] For example, the eradication of mice and rats as possible vehicles for the transmission of plague was ordered as early as 1647 in Aberdeen, possibly originating from De Mayerne's report to King Charles I in 1631. Richard Oram highlights this as 'evidence for the circulation of ideas relating to epidemics, plague prevention and cures within academic and other intellectual circles that is otherwise invisible in the literary record'.[111]

Local governors clearly linked the phenomena of malodour and infection, or plague, in their minds. In October 1585, for example, Edinburgh's councillors declared,

> Finding that the middings, muck, and filth in the common closes, venells, old walls, and other places out of houses and suchlike … lying in the said places, is dangerous and an occasion of infection, therefore ordain the baillies or quarter masters to pay such persons as will clenye and remove the said rubbish.[112]

Similarly, in Bristol in April 1635, the Court Leet Jurors presented John Arthur for 'drying of skinnes in the High Way at Batt Haven which is both a great annoyance and also infection by passers by'.[113] These examples reveal that an unambiguous link existed in contemporaries' minds between malodorous nuisances and plague contagion. This explains why contemporaries perceived such noxious nuisances as dangerous rather than as merely annoying. Regarding sixteenth-century Aberdeen, moreover, Patricia Dennison notes that there was a 'long established' and 'widely-held notion' that plague was spread through a 'miasma of noxious air that adhered to infected people and the things and spaces around them' and she highlights the 'association of stinking dung-heaps and middens with infection'.[114] Similarly, regarding sixteenth-century Venice, Jo

Wheeler emphasizes 'an analysis of contemporary perceptions of stench is essential to understanding the increasing regulation of the urban experience in the sixteenth century' because in contemporary medical theory 'stench was equated with disease'.[115] Wheeler even goes as far as to suggest that to sixteenth-century Venetians, the air 'literally reeked of death' during plague visitations.[116] At such times, malodours were neither merely unpleasant nor unwholesome, but they actually threatened death. It is difficult to comprehend just how terrifying this was, but it explains the logic of removing malodorous nuisances, lighting bonfires in the streets, wearing pomanders and burning incense in plague victims' houses. Mark Jenner concludes that in the sixteenth and early seventeenth centuries, 'the idea of cleanliness was bound up with that of sweetness' when people were principally concerned about the malodours of noxious trades, refuse and human waste. After the 1660s, however, by which time the threat of plague had passed, he argues that London's authorities became more concerned about keeping thoroughfares physically passable and less concerned about air quality. He calls this 'the shift in concern from corruption to obstruction'.[117] Edward Wrigley suggests that thought did indeed become increasingly rational between 1650 and 1750, and that people living in pre-modern society, in the period before 1650, displayed non-rational modes of thought.[118] While there was an increasing trend towards more rational modes of thought towards the end of the seventeenth century, driven forward by the Englightenment, mistaken ideas that foul-smelling miasma clouds emanating from malodorous material could permeate the skin, thus causing disease, were present until at least 1700. Such irrational theories were certainly more prevalent in the sixteenth and early seventeenth centuries, than after 1650, though intense fears of malodours did continue after 1650, certainly in northern English and Scottish towns. Improving public hygiene to improve air quality was the right action for the wrong reasons, but contemporaries' conception of plague contagion explains why they were so afraid of malodours.

The meanings which contemporaries attached to certain features of their urban landscape are complex and somewhat ambiguous, but it is clear that contemporaries' perception of the dirt and waste which peppered their urban landscapes was integral to the way in which the built, urban environment was experienced on a daily basis. Indeed, as Jill Steward and Alexander Cowan highlighted in their innovative study of early modern urban sensory history,

> In ... early modern ... cities ... the history of the senses was bound up with their material and cultural development, contributing to the way that the urban environment was experienced, understood and represented by those who inhabited it.[119]

Dirt and dung was perceived in a deeply symbolic way, and sometimes people used it specifically as a way of disrespecting or shaming others by signifying their immorality metaphorically. Martin Ingram found that the victims of rough ridings, who were paraded through communities sitting backwards on a horse, were 'pelted with filth' *en route*.[120] Urban dwellers demonstrated that they found dirt offensive by throwing dung at opponents during arguments. In 1574, Glasgow Burgh Court found Jonet Dunlop guilty of 'casting of dirt at hir [Agnes Martene's] windo and filing hir stuff sett thair'; Agnes must have retaliated because she was also 'fund in the wrang for casting furth of weshe [i.e. urine] at ... Jonet'.[121] In 1667, Sir Hugh Middleton hired some 'ruffians' to wreak his revenge on Rebecca Marshall, an actress at The King's Company in London, for denouncing him 'roundly' at the Theatre Royal's backstage retiring room in response to his insults towards the entire King's Company; they interrupted Rebecca's journey home by rubbing filth all over her body.[122] These cases prove that contemporaries were deeply offended when dirt encroached upon their person; they understood throwing dung as an explicit symbol of disrespect.

The aspects of the environment which were regulated most rigorously, we can assume, are the ones which contemporaries were most concerned about. While they lacked an in-depth understanding of the link between dirt and disease, they protected water purity and air quality in a simple, but progressive way. The way in which sixteenth- and seventeenth-century urban dwellers perceived malodours' impact on their health was neither irrational nor illogical from their point of view. They might have sought to suppress malodours for what we can see with the benefit of hindsight were the wrong reasons, but it was, albeit coincidentally, the correct action. Ridding the streets of refuse, and especially of edible food waste, would have impeded rats' survival. Sixteenth- and seventeenth-century urban dwellers' intense fear of malodours, inherited from their medieval ancestors, fuelled efforts to enhance urban air quality by cleaning streets, regulating noxious trades and managing waste disposal more efficiently. In sixteenth- and seventeenth-century towns, breathing sweet-smelling air was hugely important to contemporaries because they believed it enhanced their health and wellbeing whereas they believed that evil-smelling air, conversely, would adversely affect their health at best and potentially endanger their lives at worst. It is important to remain mindful that it was contemporaries' perceived need to breathe 'sweet and clean' air in order to preserve their health, wellbeing, and sometimes even their lives, rather than aesthetic considerations, which fuelled their efforts to improve public hygiene first and foremost; and for this reason, sixteenth- and seventeenth-century urban dwellers might well have been more concerned about outdoor sanitation than are their twenty-first-century descendants today.

Urban agriculture and the urban-rural manure trade

Writing in 1665, Robert Seymore noted that Dorset farmers 'use all sorts of dung indifferently for all sorts of arable land. Shovellings of streets, and highways, with straw or weeds rotted amongst it'.[123] For this reason, manure was a valuable resource. Large volumes of it were produced in many backlands of pre-modern towns. Townhouses often stood in front of long narrow backlands, also known as rigs or crofts in Scotland and burgage plots in England, upon which livestock could be raised, horses stabled and crops grown. They were demarcated when many medieval towns and burghs were originally planned.[124] It was not uncommon for townsmen to own or manage small-holdings of arable land within the urban landscape. For example, in 1670, Carlisle Dean and Chapter filed a suit in the Court of Chancery against Erasmus Towerson, a gentleman, over the details of a lease of 'tenements, stables, barnes, gardens, orchards and other houses ... scituate in Castle Gate'.[125] Castle Gate was a busy and major thoroughfare in the heart of Carlisle. Similarly, within the City of Bristol, in 1636, on Grotelane there was a 'tenement then or late used as a sope house or workehouse to make blacksope' with an 'iron furnace sett up ... for the making of sope', and 'belonging thereunto' were 'one stable and one little garden or backside ... and also one hayloft being over the porch of the same sope house' and a 'pigstye adjoininge' the tenement.[126] Hens', pigs' and horses' presence behind both residential quarters and industrial workshops were common features in all early modern towns and cities. In addition to human, domestic and industrial waste, therefore, urban inhabitants had also to deal with substantial volumes of agricultural waste, which formed a large proportion of urban dirt. Though cows were primarily kept on common pastures beyond the town, townspeople also typically kept milk cows, hens for eggs, and both pigs and geese for meat, on their backlands. Moreover, burgesses usually stabled a horse for their own transportation. Therefore heaps of dung, known as middings, dunghills, muck heaps or mixons, were accumulated amongst buildings as a matter of course. That urban dwellers engaged in agriculture not only increased urban dirt's physical volume, but it also created the potential for free-ranging animals to spoil inhabitants' efforts to contain such dirt:

> in the churchyard they [i.e. the pigs] have cassin up ... graves and uncoverit dead corpses ... and they ... doe converse in all the filthie dunghillis, middings, gutters and sinkes of all sorts of excrements and by their working ... spoill the streets ...[127]

And, in 1574, Berwick's inhabitants were warned not to let geese or swine wander freely in the streets or on the ramparts.

> No person or persons shall kepe any swine or geese to rune abroade in the strete or upon the rampers or walles of this towne. But shalbe forfited to any that shall take them. And that it shalbe lawfull for any mane to kill all such curr doges as are found ... either barkinge or bawlinge which is contrarye [to] the Statute of this towne.[128]

Allowing livestock to roam freely was such a serious offence because free roaming swine or geese could deposit their own waste on the streets, eat and trample crops, rummage in sewers or even graves and charge into market stalls and dunghills, damaging goods and spreading carefully piled animal manure across the streets. In 1661, John Bushbie of Carlisle was fined 3s for 'his swine goeing unringed in the streets ... & other places'.[129] And in 1672, Thomas Lowson, also of Carlisle in Finkle Street, was fined 6s 8d 'for suffereing his Barne end to ly downe soe that the swine goes through to Thomas Hewells Gardon'.[130] Such offences must have frustrated Carlisle Corporation because inhabitants had been given the facility of Kingmoor complete with a herdsman, albeit at the cost of 1d per month, specifically to avert this nuisance. Many inhabitants could not or would not take advantage of Kingmoor and stubbornly kept their swine in insecure pig pens in their backlands. Clearly, Broadwood, a gentleman, could afford to keep his swine on Kingmoor, but stubbornly chose not to, presumably for convenience. Wandering livestock could cause much more serious problems than disturbing dunghills. Maureen Meikle notes that in 1551, in Dundee, a mad cow charged into a brewhouse and in 1615, in Lanark, pig ownership had to be restricted after a sow attacked a baby in a cradle.[131] In Bristol, in October 1635, the Court Leet Jurors presented Mary Dobson 'for not keeping a gate at the lower ende of the greene goinge to the waterhouse for the keeping out of cattell'.[132] Agricultural activity, however necessary for urban inhabitants' survival, was clearly impractical in densely populated urban settings. All towns regulated the presence of livestock to some extent.

Dunghills inevitably ensued from raising livestock and stabling horses on the backlands which, for many, provided essential components of familial diet and income. Manure could be sold to local farmers who were keen to apply it to their arable holdings as fertilizer. In 1612, Dunfermline Burgh Council ordered some stable owners to remove 'all impure matters' down the back road because loading manure onto carts in front of James Kinghorne's tenement offended him.[133] In this case, it is highly probable that these stable owners sold the manure from their stables to a local farmer and this is why it was periodically loaded onto carts in front of the tenement. Indeed, men even fought over this valuable commodity. In 1564, after having borrowed eight muck loads from James Duff, of Inverness, James Kar subsequently claimed he 'misknew [i.e. forgot] how monye [i.e. many]' he had borrowed.[134] Sometimes, dung trading was regulated by legal contracts, which resulted in a few court cases if and when dung was short measured and contracts were contravened. To ensure that he did not lose any of this valuable resource, Duff approached Inverness Burgh Court to ensure he received his muck's full value.[135] Indeed, dunghills were so integral to pre-industrial life that even royal palaces featured them. John Damien, an alchemist and King James IV's friend, attempted ambitiously to fly from Stirling Castle to France in September 1507 wearing artificial wings. After having taken flight from the castle, he fell into a dunghill. Heaps of manure even decorated the entrance to the Sheldonian Theatre in Oxford before 1700.[136] Dunghills were an immoveable fact of life for pre-industrial urban dwellers, but they were noxious if they were not properly maintained and cleared away sufficiently frequently, and their deposition had to be regulated to protect inhabitants' property and to keep streets physically passable for the purposes of trade and facilitating access to businesses and dwellings. For example, in April 1699, the Clare Baron Court in Suffolk threatened Thomas Weavell and Daniell Hearenton with a fine of 1s each, not for storing a dunghill outside of their dwelling, but rather for storing it there for too long; they were given 'a month thime for the careing [i.e. carrying] it away'.[137]

Manure was highly valuable in the early modern period and while dunghills were seen in a negative light when they became excessively noxious, damaged or leaked through the walls they leaned against or blocked thoroughfares, it is important to remain mindful of their economic value and how important they were in the context of the integrated household economy which was not yet fully specialized, and which had largely retained its medieval pattern. Throughout the sixteenth and seventeenth centuries, many urban inhabitants across Britain took responsibility for their own manure and removed it out of town themselves to apply to their own arable land, sold it directly to a local farmer or arranged for it to be removed and sold by a middle man. Inhabitants were careful to heap solid rubbish and manure separately because the latter was a valuable fertilizer. Manure mixed up with lots of domestic and industrial rubbish would have been less desirable to local farmers, who bought urban dunghills to fertilize their arable land; though some fragments of rubbish were inevitably taken away with the manure, as revealed by modern archaeologists who recover ubiquitous fragments of early modern urban rubbish in rural fields.[138] Dung trading between townsmen and farmers was probably negotiated verbally, perhaps when farmers came to urban markets, which would explain why they have left few traces in the written records. As Richard Jones warns in relation to dung in the medieval period, however, 'the silence of the sources should not be equated with any ignorance or rejection of their utility'.[139] Townsmen who owned arable land in local manors surely used urban dunghills to improve their own arable land's fertility; others might have sold them to middle men, who transported them to nearby farms. In any case, arable farmers used animal and human waste which had been produced in towns as fertilizer. When in March 1698, Thomas Child, an innkeeper of Bristol, signed a fourteen-year lease to rent a tenement, garden and close of meadow and pasture known as Riglings, some thirteen acres of arable land within the suburbs of the city in the parish of St James, part of his contract with the landowners was that he would 'every yeare during the terme hereby granted carry into and upon the said demised premises threescore loades of dung and shall and will throw abroade the same in good husband like manner on the premises' in order to fertilize the land.[140]

An East Lothian agricultural improver, Baron John Hamilton Belhaven, published a pamphlet in 1699, entitled *Advice to the Farmers in East Lothian*, in which he advised 'If your Grounds ly within three Miles of a Burgh or Village, it is worth your pains to lead Dung all the Summer time, and lay it upon your Wheat Fauch, especially having a Cart way thereto'.[141] Sir John Archer noted the application of dung on his arable land in his diary: on 5 January 1663, he noted 'dung spread'.[142] As early as 1967, leading agricultural historian Joan Thirsk unveiled several important discoveries in relation to the use of urban dung as a rural fertilizer in *The Agrarian History of England and Wales, 1500–1640* and many others have subsequently contributed to her findings.[143] Thirsk discovered, for example, that Newcastle upon Tyne's local farmers 'used to cart dung from the town to their fields' and 'boats which carried corn and malt down River Colne and River Lea to London brought back manure on the return journey'.[144] Substantial volumes of seventeenth-century London's manure was loaded onto barges at Dung Wharf on the Thames and sold to market gardeners upriver.[145] According to Liam Brunt, manure trading occurred 'mainly in towns', after which farmers 'shipped the fertilizer back to their farms by horse and cart'; notably, he found 'all available waste products were traded', including human excrement.[146] Similarly, Richard Oram notes that the 'modern Western cultural aversion' to the use of human waste as manure in the production of crops to be used as food, arising from nineteenth-century medical developments which linked such practices to the spread of disease, has 'perhaps limited past discussion of pre-modern urban waste disposal in Britain, and has helped to embed deep in the public consciousness a vision of our ancestors wallowing in their own filth'.[147]

Significantly, in May 1651, a few months before Oliver Cromwell captured Perth in August that year, the landowners around Perth sent a supplication to King Charles II, who had been crowned at nearby Scone on New Year's Day that year, complaining that the Provost of Perth, Andrew Grant, had,

> infix certain stakes or posts of great timber in the midst of his majesty's ... highway within the Castle Gavel Port of the said burgh and by an act has discharged the whole inhabitants thereof to sell refuse or muck to the supplicants, through which neither cart nor sled can have access to the said burgh ... for transporting ... muck and refuse for bettering the supplicants' lands adjacent to the said burgh according to use and custom ... and that the buying and transporting of the said muck not only occasions the streets of the said burgh to be cleaned but also renders commodity to the inhabitants thereof, owners of the same muck.[148]

Evidently, there was a healthy trade in manure and refuse between Perth's inhabitants and local arable farmers. Although the blocked highway meant that Perth's inhabitants were unable to remove their muck from the streets, it was the landowners who drove the complaint, and clearly they needed the muck with which to fertilize their arable holdings more urgently than the townspeople needed to clear their streets of the commodity. This suggests that the rural buyers were the real driving force behind the urban-rural manure trade.

In Stirling, too, inhabitants sold their muck to landward farmers. In October 1675, Stirling Council passed a proclamation, entitled 'Act anent the Carying of fulyie [i.e. refuse] out of the Town', forbidding,

> the haill nighbours and others to tack any muck out of the Towne unles they ingadge themselves to bring ther haill grindable cornes growing upon the ground of lands that they carie ther fuilyie to to the townes milnes ... under the paine of five pounds scottis money.[149]

Thereby, Stirling Council maximized its income by ensuring that farmers whose corn grew with the aid of the burgh's muck used the burgh mill, for which Stirling received a fee, to grind their corn. Muck was also transported out of Inverness to the surrounding countryside. In December 1677, Inverness Council promulgated the following act:

> considdering & finding the harme & prejudice that the bridge susteanes throw transporting & carieing of dung & muck alongest the samen, therfor the Magistrats & Counsell prohibit & discharge all the inhabitants to carie or transport any muck or dung alonges the said bridge in time comeing be any maner of way nather be cairts, slaids [i.e. sledges], wheel barows or be creills [i.e. baskets] on horseback under the paine of ten punds scots.[150]

Over a period of years, substantial volumes of muck were being transported out of town across the bridge, probably to local arable farmers. Unfortunately, regulatory documents, references to contracts of supply, complaints of breaches of contract and the court cases arising from such instances are the only archival vestiges of the oral early modern urban-rural manure trade, but selling manure to be used as fertilizer was clearly common in this period, and it is a hugely important aspect of urban sanitation in that it provided an easy means of removing manure from urban centres.[151] As Brunt concludes, 'there was an active and sophisticated market for manure by 1770 ... despite the lack of formal scientific knowledge, farmers in 1665 ... used manure rationally and in a similar fashion to the farmers of 1840'.[152] Donald Woodward laments the severe lack of farmers' and urban sellers' records, but concludes that the use of off-farm fertilizers, which often included urban waste, 'undoubtedly did rise' between 1500 and 1800.[153] Clearly, the presence, smell, sale and transportation of manure were integral to urban life in this period.

Conclusion

This chapter has characterized and contextualized the environmental challenges faced by pre-industrial urban governors and communities in the period 1560 to 1700, emphasizing the large extent to which inhabitants were directly engaged in the day-to-day functioning of the systems and processes which managed waste disposal and drainage in urban settlements. Waste consisted of domestic, industrial and agricultural material and pre-industrial urban streets hosted a chaotic array of domestic, industrial and agricultural activities. Solving the sanitation problems of early modern English towns and Scottish burghs was a complex task, retarded by rudimentary and somewhat unreliable technology, limited fiscal and material resources, sluggish communication systems and the presence of urban agriculture in the heart of urban centres. Establishing the cultural attitudes and values of early modern people towards the cleanliness of outdoor, public spaces is an urgent historiographical task, and understanding contemporary perceptions of malodours is a prerequisite to developing such an understanding accurately and meaningfully. How sixteenth- and seventeenth-century urban dwellers perceived malodorous nuisances impacting on their health was logical in their own minds. They might have sought to suppress malodours for what we can see with the benefit of hindsight were the wrong reasons, but it was, albeit coincidentally, the correct action. Ridding the streets of refuse, and especially of edible food waste, would have impeded rats' survival. Contemporaries' intense fear of malodours, inherited from their medieval ancestors, fuelled efforts to enhance urban air quality by cleaning streets, regulating noxious trades and managing waste disposal more efficiently. In sixteenth- and seventeenth-century towns, breathing sweet-smelling air was hugely important to contemporaries because they believed it enhanced their health and wellbeing whereas they believed that evil-smelling air, conversely, would adversely affect their health at best and potentially endanger their lives at worst. It is important to remain mindful that it was contemporaries' perceived need to breathe 'sweet and clean', 'wholesome' air in order to preserve their health, wellbeing and sometimes even their lives, rather than aesthetic considerations, which fuelled their efforts to improve urban sanitation first and foremost.

Each town had its own unique dividing line between householders' and civic authorities' sanitation responsibilities. Contemporaries surely understood exactly where this line lay, and the majority of inhabitants fulfilled their obligations without complaint. That most urban governments in this period did not fund regular municipal refuse and night soil collections perhaps did not seem unreasonable to inhabitants because they produced relatively little unusable rubbish, manure was sold easily to local farmers and contemporaries were unfamiliar with the idea of having a right to publicly funded rubbish collections. It is important to bear in mind that not every urban inhabitant wanted their urban governors to get rid of their manure as soon as possible. Many of the middling sorts whose livestock produced large volumes of manure had a vested interest in storing it on their property until they could either sell it to local farmers as fertilizer or apply it to their own arable holdings. It is possible that those urban inhabitants who were more directly involved in the production of primary foodstuffs, largely of the middling sorts, viewed manure as personal property and retained it on their properties for longer periods of time and either sold it or used it themselves. Conversely, those who were less directly involved in food production, largely the very rich and the very poor, may well have begun at an earlier stage than their middling-sort counterparts to view manure as an unwelcome and unsavoury waste material to be expelled from the burgh as soon as possible, preferably at the expense of the public purse.

The character of the early modern environmental challenges, faced by sixteenth- and seventeenth-century urban governors, differed from those faced by urban councillors today in many important ways. Fiscal and material resources were limited, technology was rudimentary and the combination of industrial, residential and agricultural activities in streets and other public areas tested the inventiveness and tenacity of local governors and urban inhabitants alike. Now that that historically specific scene has been set, and some of the issues have been considered in detail, we can consider the demographic, legal and governmental parameters within which such environmental challenges were embraced, managed and driven hopefully and enthusiastically towards the heartfelt hope of resolution.

Only within this context can a true understanding be gained of the motivations for and the impact of the sanitation services, infrastructure and process and systems which were developed and provided across the urban landscape.

Notes

1 M. Palmer, 'The workshop: type of building or method of work?' in P. Barnwell et al. (eds), *The Vernacular Workshop from Craft to Industry, 1400–1900* (York: Council for British Archaeology, 2004), pp. 1–16, on pp. 2–3; P. Barnwell, 'Workshops, Industrial Production and the Landscape' in Barnwell et al. (eds), *The Vernacular Workshop*, pp. 179–82, on p. 181.

2 G. Still, 'Housing in the two towns', in E. Dennison, D. Ditchburn and M. Lynch (eds), *Aberdeen Before 1800. A New History* (East Linton: Tuckwell Press, 2002), pp. 97–108, on p. 107.

3 B. Lemire, 'Consumerism in pre-industrial and early industrial England: the trade in second-hand clothes', *Journal of British Studies*, 27 (1988), pp. 1–24.

4 The National Archives [hereafter TNA], E101/545/16: Scottish Marches: Accounts of repairs at Carlisle, 1577–1602.

5 Sheffield Archives, CB/161: Sheffield Church Burgesses' Account Book, 1574–1727.

6 Brereton, *Journal*, p. 29.

7 Harrison, 'Public Hygiene', p. 68.

8 Makey, 'Edinburgh', p. 201.

9 TNA, C 2/Eliz/N2/36: Court of Chancery: Edmund Nicholson and Thomas Yates v Godfrey Bradshawe (1558–1603, exact date unknown).

10 J. Ray, *Select Remains of the Learned John Ray* (1662), p. 231. Also depicted by John Slezer's 'Prospect of Dundee' in 1678, see J. Slezer, *Theatrum Scotiae: Containing the Prospects of his Majesties Castles and Palaces* (London, 1874), plate 33.

11 Durham County Record Office [hereafter DCRO], Da/DM/5/2: Darlington Borough Book, 1612–1633.

12 North Yorkshire County Record Office [hereafter NYCRO], DC/SCB/II/1: Scarborough Corporation Minute and Order Book, 1621–1649.

13 *Records of the Burgery of Sheffield, commonly called the Town Trust*, ed. J. Leader (London: Elliot Stock, 1897), p. 312.

14 *Extracts from the Burgh Records of Dunfermline in the Sixteenth and Seventeenth Centuries*, ed. A. Shearer (Dunfermline: Carnegie Dunfermline Trust, 1951), p. 186 (20/12/1638).

15 *Extracts from the Records of the Royal Burgh of Lanark: with Charters and Documents relating to the Burgh, AD 1150–1722*, ed. R. Renwick (Edinburgh: Scottish Burgh Record Society, 1893), p. 160 (28/04/1657).

16 *Extracts from the Records of the Burgh of Edinburgh, 1403–1589*, 4 vols, ed. J. Marwick (Edinburgh: Scottish Burgh Record Society, 1869–82), vol. 2, p. 165 (06/07/1552).

17 *Records of Inverness, 1556–1637*, 2 vols, ed. W. Mackay, H. Cameron and G. Laing (Aberdeen: New Spalding Club, 1911–24), vol. 2, p. 234 (26/05/1668).

18 *Extracts from the Records of the Royal Burgh of Stirling, 1518–1666*, 2 vols, ed. R. Renwick (Edinburgh: Scottish Burgh Record Society, 1887–9), vol. 1, pp. 17, 124 (27/10/1522 and 30/04/1610).

19 T. C. Smout, *Nature Contested: Environmental History in Scotland and Northern England Since 1600* (Edinburgh: Edinburgh University Press, 2000), p. 109.

20 Smout, *Nature Contested*, p. 109.

21 Anon., *Reprints of Rare Tracts and Imprints of Ancient Manuscripts Chiefly Illustrative of the History of the Northern Counties*, 3 vols (1847), vol. 3, pp. 14–15.

22 *Rare Tracts and Imprints of the Northern Counties*, vol. 3, pp. 14–15.
23 D. Archer, 'Kielder Water: White Elephant or White Knight?', in D. Archer (ed.), *Tyne and Tide: A Celebration of the River Tyne* (Ovingham: Daryan Press, 2000), pp.138–156, on p. 139; R. Rennison, *Water to Tyneside: A History of the Newcastle & Gateshead Water Company* (Newcastle upon Tyne: Newcastle and Gateshead Water Company, 1979), p. xvii.
24 NYCRO, DC/SCB/II/1: Corporation Minute and Order Book, 1621–1649 (08/05/1622).
25 NYCRO, DC/SCB/II/1: Corporation Minute and Order Book, 1621–1649 (21/04/1623).
26 NYCRO, DC/SCB/II/1: Corporation Minute and Order Book, 1621–1649 (14/10/1623).
27 Melosi, *The Sanitary City*, p. 21
28 T. Kirke, *A Modern Account of Scotland by an English Gentleman* (1679), ed. P. Brown, *Early Travellers in Scotland* (Edinburgh: James Thin, 1978), pp. 251–265, on p. 256.
29 Morer, *Short Account*, p. 279.
30 For an explanation of the development of Edinburgh's and other Scottish burghs' building tradition, see D. MacGibbon and T. Ross, *The Castellated and Domestic Architecture of Scotland from the Twelfth to the Eighteenth Century*, 5 vols (Edinburgh: Douglas, 1887–92).
31 Morer, *Short Account*, p. 279.
32 *Records of Lanark*, p. 195 (15/01/1674).
33 W. Hutchinson, *The History of the County of Cumberland*, 2 vols (Carlisle, 1794), vol. 2, p. 659.
34 Carlisle Record Office [hereafter CRO], Ca4/1–3: Carlisle Chamberlains' Accounts. See also Skelton, 'Beadles, dunghills and noisome excrements'.
35 Berwick on Tweed Record Office [hereafter BRO], C1/1–3: Berwick Bailiffs' Court Book, 1568–1601 (23/10/1594).
36 Cockayne, *Hubbub*, p. 182.
37 Hutchinson, *History of Cumberland*, p. 659.
38 Harrison, 'Public hygiene', p. 69.
39 Perth and Kinross Archives [hereafter P&KA], B66/20/5: Council Record, 1659–1680.
40 King, 'How high is too high?', p. 448.
41 M. Adams, 'Darlington Market Place: Archaeological Excavations', (unpublished archaeological report, Durham Sites and Monuments Record, nos., 4000, 4812, 1994), p. 24.
42 *The London Surveys of Ralph Treswell*, ed. J. Schofield (London: London Topgraphical Society, no. 135, 1987), p. 141.
43 Jenner, 'Water in London', p. 251; Skelton, 'Beadles, dunghills and noisome excrements', pp. 50–51. See also D. Hartley, *Water In England* (London: MacDonald and Jane's, 1964); and C. van Lieshout, 'London's changing waterscapes: the management of water in eighteenth-century London' (PhD dissertation, King's College London, 2013).
44 *London Viewers and their Certificates, 1508–1558: Certificates of the Sworn Viewers of the City of London*, ed. J. Loengard (London: London Record Society, 1989), p. 206.
45 Edinburgh City Archives [hereafter ECA], SL144/1/4: Edinburgh Dean of Guild Court Minutes, 1613–1623.
46 Bristol Record Office, JQS/Pr/1: Presentments to the Grand Jury to the Bristol Leet, 1628–1666 (27/10/1629).
47 ECA, SL1/1/7: Edinburgh Town Council Minutes, 1583–1585.
48 ECA, SL1/1/6: Edinburgh Town Council Minutes, 1579–1583.
49 Skelton, 'Beadles, dunghills and noisome excrements', p. 55.
50 For a very detailed archaeological report of one of Worcester's fifteenth-century barrel latrines, see J. Greig, 'The investigation of a medieval barrel-latrine', *Journal of Archaeological Science*, 8 (1981), pp. 265–282.
51 Sanderson, *A Kindly Place?* p. 97.

52   CRO, Ca4/2: Carlisle Chamberlains' Accounts.
53   L. Wright, *Clean and Decent: The Fascinating History of the Bathroom and the Water Closet* (London: Routledge and Kegan Paul, 1960), pp. 65–79; V. Smith, *Clean: A History of Personal Hygiene and Purity* (Oxford: Oxford University Press, 2007).
54   CRO, Carlisle City Probate, Wills and Inventories, 1605.
55   CRO, Carlisle City Probate, Wills and Inventories, 1667.
56   A. Green, 'Heartless and unhomely? Dwellings of the poor in East Anglia and North-East England', in J. McEwan and P. Sharpe (eds), *Accommodating Poverty: the Housing and Living Arrangements of the English Poor, c. 1600–1850* (Basingstoke: Palgrave MacMillan, 2010), pp. 69–101.
57   *Records of Edinburgh, 1403–1589,* vol. 4, p. 187 (11/11/1580).
58   ECA, SL1/1/8: Edinburgh Town Council Minutes, 1585–1589.
59   BRO, C1/1–3: Berwick Bailiffs' Court Book, 1568–1601.
60   R. Birrel, 'The Diary of Robert Birrel, Burgess of Edinburgh, 1552–1605', quoted in J. Dalyell (ed.), *Fragments of Scottish History*, 2 vols (Edinburgh: Printed for Archibald Constable at the Cross, 1798), vol. 2, p. 46.
61   ECA, SL144/1/6–9: Edinburgh Dean of Guild Court Minute Books, (05/10/1664, 22/07/1691, 19/08/1691, 20/07/1692, 28/08/1695, 17/03/1697, 04/05/1698, 14/12/1698, 26/04/1699, 10/05/1699).
62   J. Scott-Warren, 'The privy politics of Sir John Harrington's *New Discourse of a Stale Subject, Called the Metamorphosis of Ajax*', *Studies in Philology*, 93:4 (1996), pp. 412–442, on pp. 412–413.
63   Scott-Warren, 'Privy politics', pp. 414–415.
64   Sir J. Harrington, *A New Discourse of a Stale Subject, called the Metamorphosis of Ajax: Written by Misacmos, to his Friend and Cosin Philostilpnos* (London, 1596), ed. E. Story Donno (London: Routledge and Kegan Paul, 1962), pp. 78–79.
65   Harrington, *Metamorphosis of Ajax*, pp. 112–113.
66   Scott-Warren, 'Privy politics', p. 437.
67   T. McLaughlin, *Dirt: A Social History as Seen Through the Uses and Abuses of Dirt* (Dorchester: Dorset Press, 1988), pp. 50–52.
68   Bristol Record Office, JQS/Pr/1: Presentments to the Grand Jury to the Bristol Leet, 1628–1666 (28/04/1629).
69   Bristol Record Office, JQS/Pr/1: Presentments to the Grand Jury to the Bristol Leet, 1628–1666 (21/10/1628).
70   Bristol Record Office, JQS/Pr/1: Presentments to the Grand Jury to the Bristol Leet, 1628–1666 (21/10/1628).
71   Cavert, 'Coal smoke', p. 331.
72   ECA, SL1/1/9: Edinburgh Town Council Minutes, 1589–1594.
73   ECA, SL1/1/9: Edinburgh Town Council Minutes, 1589–1594.
74   Jorgensen, 'Sanitation and civic government', p. 303.
75   Kendal Record Office, [uncatalogued]: Sundry Court Leet Papers, sixteenth and seventeenth centuries.
76   Bristol Record Office, JQS/Pr/1: Presentments to the Grand Jury to the Bristol Leet, 1628–1666 (21/10/1628).
77   BRO, C1/1–3: Berwick Bailiffs' Court Book, 1568–1601.
78   BRO, C1/1–3: Berwick Bailiffs' Court Book, 1568–1601.
79   BRO, C1/1–3: Berwick Bailiffs' Court Book, 1568–1601, Michaelmas, 1592.
80   CRO, Ca2/2/1: Corporation of Carlisle Order Book, 1639–1654 [including an earlier insert of bylaws dated 1568].
81   CRO, Carlisle City Probate Wills and Inventories, 1596. For more detailed information on leather production in this period, see L. Clarkson, 'The organization of the english leather industry in the late sixteenth and seventeenth centuries', *Economic History Review*, new series, 13:2 (1960), pp. 245–256.
82   CRO, Ca/3/2/18, Ca/3/2/20: Carlisle Court Leet Rolls.

83 Bristol Record Office, JQS/Pr/1: Presentments to the Grand Jury to the Bristol Leet, 1628–1666 (21/10/1628).
84 CRO, Ca3/2/18: Carlisle Court Leet Rolls.
85 CRO, Ca3/2/20: Carlisle Court Leet Rolls.
86 Bristol Record Office, JQS/Pr/1: Presentments to the Grand Jury to the Bristol Leet, 1628–1666 (21/04/1635).
87 C. Woolgar, *The Senses in Late Medieval England* (London: Yale University Press, 2006); Wheeler, 'Stench in Venice', pp. 25–38; and E. Foyster, 'Sensory experiences: smells, sounds and touch in early modern Scotland' in E. Foyster, and C. Whatley (eds), *A History of Everyday Life in Scotland, 1600–1800* (Edinburgh: Edinburgh University Press, 2010), pp. 217–33. See also Jenner, 'Civilization and deodorization'; Jenner, 'Follow your nose?'; and M. Smith, *Sensory History* (Oxford: Berg, 2007).
88 S. Greenfield, *The Private Life of the Brain* (London: Allen Lane, 2000); W. Miller, *The Anatomy of Disgust* (London: Harvard University Press, 1997). See also R. Jutte, *A History of the Senses from Antiquity to Cyberspace* (Cambridge: Polity, 2005).
89 M. Douglas, *Purity and Danger: An Analysis of Concept of Pollution and Taboo* (London, Routledge, 2002), pp. 46–50, 208.
90 Jenner, '"Cleanliness and "dirt"', p. 155.
91 Woolgar, *The Senses*, p. 126.
92 Woolgar, *The Senses*, p. 126.
93 M. Dorey, 'Controlling corruption: regulating meat consumption as a preventative to plague in seventeenth-century London', *Urban History*, 36:1 (2009), pp. 24–41; M. Dobson, *Contours of Death and Disease in Early Modern England* (Cambridge, 1997); K. Jillings, 'Preventing plague in Post-Reformation Aberdeen', *International Review of Scottish Studies*, 30 (2005), pp. 108–134; Jenner, 'Dog massacre'; C. Mullett, 'Plague policy in 16th and 17th century Scotland', *Osiris*, 9 (1950), pp. 435–456. For a medieval perspective, see E. Sabine, 'Butchering in mediaeval London', *Speculum*, 8 (1933), pp. 335–353.
94 R. Oram, '"It cannot be decernit quha are clean and quha are foulle." Responses to epidemic disease in sixteenth- and seventeenth-century Scotland', *Renaissance and Reformation*, vol. 30, no. 4 (2006–2007), pp. 13–39, on p. 16; J. Shrewsbury, *A History of Bubonic Plague in the British Isles* (London: Cambridge University Press, 1971); P. Slack, 'The response to plague in early modern England: public policies and their consequences', in J. Walter and R. Schofield (eds), *Famine, Disease and the Social Order in Early Modern Society* (Cambridge: Cambridge University Press, 1989), pp. 167–187.
95 There is also a distinct lack of references to flies, as one might expect in relation to insanitary nuisances, dung and waste food material. Perhaps flies were so commonplace, that writers did not perceive them as noteworthy.
96 Oram, 'Responses to epidemic disease', p. 22.
97 CRO, D/MH/10/7/1: Carlisle Chamberlains' Accounts, 1597–1598, f. 68.
98 Jenner, 'Dog massacre', pp. 41–61.
99 K. Thomas, *Man and the Natural World: Changing Attitudes in England, 1500–1800* (London: Penguin, 1983), p. 105; F. Wilson, *The Plague in Shakespeare's London* (London: Oxford University Press, 1963), pp. 36–40; B. Pullan, 'Plague and perceptions of the poor in early modern Italy', in T. Ranger and P. Slack (eds), *Epidemics and Ideas: Essays on the Historical Perception of Pestilence* (Cambridge: Cambridge University Press, 1992), pp. 101–123, on p. 120.
100 R. Hutton, *The Restoration: A Political and Religious History of England and Wales, 1658–1667* (Oxford: Oxford University Press, 1987), p. 228.
101 Jenner, 'Dog massacre', p. 53.
102 Jenner, 'Dog massacre', pp. 52, 55.
103 Dr G. Skeyne, *Ane Breve Description of the Pest Quhair in the cavsis, signis and sum speciall preseruation and cure thairof ar contenit* (1568) in W. Skene (ed.), *Tracts by Dr. Gilbert Skeyne, medicinar to his majesty* (Edinburgh: Bann. Club, 6.111, 1860), p. 6.

104 A. Skeldie, *The Only Sure Preservative against the Plague of Pestilence* (Edinburgh, 1645), p. 5.
105 Skeldie, *Preservative against Plague*, p. 3. For a wider discussion of providentialism in early modern England, see A. Walsham, *Providence in Early Modern England* (Oxford: Oxford University Press, 2000).
106 Skeldie, *Preservative against Plague*, p. 29.
107 Skeyne, *Breve Description*, p. 5.
108 Skeldie, *Preservative against Plague*, p. 10
109 C. Classen et al., *Aroma: The Cultural History of Smell* (London: Routledge, 1994), p. 62.
110 Oram, 'Responses to epidemic disease', p. 16.
111 Oram, 'Responses to epidemic disease', p. 16.
112 ECA, SL1/1/7: Edinburgh Town Council Minutes, 1583–1585.
113 Bristol Record Office, JQS/Pr/1: Presentments to the Grand Jury to the Bristol Leet, 1628–1666 (21/04/1635).
114 E. P. Dennison, G. Desbrisay and H. Lesley Diack, 'Health in the two towns', in E. P. Dennison, D. Ditchburn and M. Lynch (eds), *Aberdeen Before 1800. A New History* (East Linton: Tuckwell Press, 2002), pp. 70–96, on p. 73. For an overview of the history of Scottish medical theories, see J. Comrie, *History of Scottish Medicine to 1860* (London: Balliere, Tindall and Cox, 1927).
115 Wheeler, 'Stench in Venice', p. 25.
116 Wheeler, 'Stench in Venice', p. 27.
117 Jenner, '"Cleanliness" and "dirt"', p. 155.
118 E. Wrigley, 'A simple model of London's importance in changing English society and economy, 1650–1750', *Past and Present*, 37:1 (1967), pp. 44–70. See also E. Wrigley and R. Schofield, *The Population History of England, 1541–1871: A Reconstruction* (London: Edward Arnold, 1981).
119 J. Steward and A. Cowan, 'Introduction' in J. Steward and A. Cowan (eds), *The City and the Senses. Urban Culture since 1500* (Aldershot: Ashgate, 2007), pp. 1–24, on p. 11.
120 M. Ingram, 'Ridings, rough music and the reform of popular culture', *Past and Present*, 105 (1984), pp. 79–113, on p. 93. See also McLaughlin, *Dirt: A Social History*; and P. Withington, '"Tumbled into the dirt": wit and incivility in early modern England', *Journal of Historical Pragmatics*, 12 (2011), pp. 156–177.
121 *Extracts from the Records of the Burgh of Glasgow*, 6 vols, ed. J. Marwick (Edinburgh: Scottish Burgh Record Society, 1876–1916), vol. 1, p. 11 (18/05/1574).
122 A. Fraser, *The Weaker Vessel: Woman's Lot in Seventeenth-Century England* (London: Orion Books, 2002), pp. 525–526.
123 R. Seymore, *An Account of the Husbandry used in some parts of Dorsetshire*, Royal Agricultural Society of England, *Classified Papers*, X (Agriculture, 3), paper no. 10 (1665), quoted in L. Brunt, 'Where there's muck, there's brass: the market for manure in the industrial revolution', *Economic History Review*, 60, no. 2 (2007), pp. 333–378, on p. 338.
124 D. Palliser, 'The origins of British towns', in D. Palliser (ed.), *The Cambridge Urban History of Britain, vol. 1, 600–1540*, pp. 17–24; D. Palliser, T. Slater and E. Dennison, 'The topography of towns, 600–1300', in Palliser (ed.), *The Cambridge Urban History of Britain 600–1540*, pp. 153–186. See St Andrews' demarcated crofts in J. Geddy's *The Bird's Eye View* (1580), originally entitled: *S. Andre sive Andreapolis Scotiae Universitas Metropolitina*, held at The National Library of Scotland, Edinburgh.
125 TNA, C 6/192/35: Court of Chancery, Carlisle Dean and Chapter v Erasmus Towerson, gent.
126 Bristol Record Office, 28048/D1: Lease of a Sope Workhouse, Grotelane, Bristol, between James Birkin and Abraham Barnes (21/05/1636).

127 *Extracts from the Council Register of the Burgh of Aberdeen, 1625–1747*, 2 vols, ed. J. Stuart (Edinburgh: Scottish Burgh Record Society, 1871–2), vol. 2, p. 143 (09/08/1654).

128 BRO, C1/1–3: Berwick Bailiffs' Court Book, 1568–1601.

129 CRO, Ca3/2/16: Carlisle Court Leet Rolls.

130 CRO, Ca3/2/22: Carlisle Court Leet Rolls.

131 M. Meikle, *The Scottish People, 1490–1625* (Raleigh, NC: Lulu, 2013), p. 44.

132 Bristol Record Office, JQS/Pr/1: Presentments to the Grand Jury to the Bristol Leet, 1628–1666 (27/10/1635).

133 *Records of Dunfermline*, p. 96 (12/03/1612).

134 *Records of Inverness*, p. 117 (25/10/1564); R. Oram, 'Waste management and peri-urban agriculture in the early modern Scottish burgh', *Agricultural History Review*, 59:1 (2011), pp. 1–17, on pp. 11–16.

135 N. Macdougall, *James IV* (East Linton: Tuckwell Press, 1997), p. 288.

136 M. Reed, 'The urban landscape, 1540–1700', in P. Clark (ed.), *The Cambridge Urban History of Britain, volume II, 1540–1840* (Cambridge: Cambridge University Press, 2000), pp. 289–313 on p. 307.

137 TNA, DL 30/883, Bundle 2: Clare, Suffolk, Court Leet, Court Baron and General Court Rolls, 1698–1761 (18/04/1699).

138 R. Jones, 'Signatures in the soil: the use of pottery in manure scatters in the identification of medieval arable farming regimes', *Archaeological Journal*, 161 (2004), pp. 159–188.

139 R. Jones, 'Understanding medieval manure', in R. Jones (ed.), *Manure Matters: Historical, Archaeological and Ethnographic Perspectives* (Farnham: Ashgate, 2012), pp. 145–158, on p. 146.

140 Bristol Record Office, 37941/1: Lease of the Ridlings between John Bubb, esq., and Thomas Child (25/03/1698).

141 J. Hamilton Belhaven, Baron, *An Advice to the Farmers in East Lothian how to Labour and Improve their Ground or The Countrey-man's Rudiments* (1699), p. 35.

142 Huntingdon Library, San Marino, HM MS 70160: Diary of Sir John Archer, 1663.

143 J. Thirsk, 'The farming regions of England' in J. Thirsk (ed.), *The Agrarian History of England and Wales, volume IV, 1500–1640* (Cambridge, 1967), pp. 1–112, on pp. 27, 52; D. Woodward, '"An essay on manures": changing attitudes towards fertilization in England, 1500–1800', in J. Chartres and D. Hey (eds), *English Rural Society, 1500–1800: Essays in Honour of Joan Thirsk* (Cambridge, 1990), pp. 251–278; Brunt, 'Where there's muck, pp. 333–378; Jones (ed.), *Manure Matters*.

144 Thirsk, 'The farming regions of England', pp. 27, 52.

145 Jenner, '"Cleanliness" and "dirt"', p. 92.

146 Brunt, 'Where there's muck', p. 363; Oram, 'Waste management', pp. 11–16.

147 Oram, 'Waste management', p. 4.

148 National Archives of Scotland, PA3/2/3: 'Supplicatioune of the heretours of the landwart parrosche of Perth', Charles II Scottish Parliament held at Stirling on 23/05/1651, (Additional Sources, 28/05/1651) [filed in error with May 1650], f. 42.

149 Stirling Archives, B66/20/5: Council Record, 1659–1680 (02/010/1675).

150 Highland Council Archives, BI/1/1/5: Inverness Town Council Minutes, 1662–1680 (17/12/1677).

151 D. Davidson, et al., 'The legacy of past urban waste disposal on local soils', *Journal of Archaeological Science*, 33:6 (2006), pp. 778–783; Oram, 'Waste management', pp. 1–17.

152 Brunt, 'Where there's muck', p. 367.

153 Woodward, '"An essay on manures"', p. 276.

2 York's and Edinburgh's sanitation in national, demographic, legal and governmental context

Introduction

Managing and regulating the drainage and disposal of the large amount of domestic, industrial and agricultural waste which was produced within the urban landscape occupied a significant proportion of urban governors' time and effort. Today, public hygiene matters are managed exclusively by separate and dedicated administrative departments within large-scale and complex urban councils, but in the sixteenth and seventeenth centuries, waste disposal, street cleaning and the regulation of insanitary nuisances were truly integral parts of the whole, overarching system of government by which a city's 'commonweal' was maintained. In a typical weekly council meeting, drainage and waste disposal problems, such as a blocked sewer or the disposal of offal, tended to be discussed between or even alongside other urban problems, such as card-playing, begging or forestalling. This seamless system of urban government had been established and handed down by the civic leaders' medieval predecessors. Dolly Jorgensen studied sanitation in two English regional centres, Norwich and Coventry, with populations broadly between 8,000 and 12,000 from 1400 to 1600, and found that although sanitation services were 'neither the most costly nor the highest profile activity', that by 1500 both city councils perceived sanitation services as 'necessary for the commonwealth' and 'one of the components of good and godly rule in the late medieval/early modern English city'.[1] In relation to the late medieval period, Carole Rawcliffe found that although 'ordinances for the removal of the intimidating quantities of garbage, dung and other detritus' which accumulated in urban centres were common by the mid-fourteenth century, they 'increased exponentially after the Black Death' and 'the financial and logistical challenges faced by magistrates remained daunting'.[2] Thus, urban governors' tenacious efforts to combat inadequate sanitation in the early modern period were not unprecedented, but rather medieval initiatives dovetailed quite seamlessly into the early modern epoch, with some modification, as part and parcel of the medieval inheritance of civic governance.

The monumental and pioneering multi-volume work contributed by Sidney and Beatrice Webb in the early twentieth century provides historians of the early modern English town with a very detailed mine of information on the micro-scale development of local government and urban infrastructure up to the Municipal Reform Act of 1835. The Webbs' very obvious conclusion, embedded into every page of their epic step-to-step guide through the development of local government in a plethora of different regions, counties, cities, towns, villages, wards and parishes across England, is that each respective settlement pursued a markedly different, indeed unique, course of piecemeal development which can only be understood properly when each settlement is considered in its own particular local context. It is therefore impossible to generalize about the style of local government, organization of local governors, courts, bylaws and management of urban issues in any two towns or cities with a very wide brush.[3] Indeed, Allan Kennedy asserts that although the systems of burgh government 'conformed to the basic patterns of other Scottish towns in the early modern period', such conformity was 'albeit with some local twists'.[4] He also highlights how the burgh's 'local colour' reminds us that 'while accepting the fundamental commonality of the burgh experience in seventeenth-century Scotland, historians should be wary of underestimating the importance of local distinctiveness'.[5] As Peter Clark and Paul Slack observed, such respective towns' and cities' different characteristics are complex, 'defying and vexing the historian who tries to generalize about their character'.[6]

The chapter begins by explaining the national legal context of urban environmental regulation in the national kingdoms of England and Scotland respectively. England's national environmental regulation and its relevance to the suppression of insanitary nuisances in individual English urban communities is subsequently discussed in some depth, followed by an analysis of how the Scottish Convention of Burghs, the Scottish Privy Council and the Scottish Parliament impacted on urban sanitation in Scotland. The chapter then introduces the major case studies of York and Edinburgh. The respective cities' demography, geographical situation and functions are explained, as are the systems which Edinburgh's and York's governors inherited from their medieval predecessors in 1560, how and why they were modified from decade to decade and finally which systems the cities' respective governors passed onto their eighteenth-century descendants in 1700. In Edinburgh, the original sanitation systems continued from 1560 well into the seventeenth century, until they eventually began to give way in the second half of the seventeenth century, under the pressure of population increase, to more specialized and centralized processes featuring committees and sub-councils which were appointed specifically to deal with particular urban problems, including waste disposal and street cleaning, in a much more focused manner. In York, however, where the population remained relatively stagnant, the medieval systems were preserved largely intact right up until the end of the seventeenth century, albeit with a few modifications. The chapter emphasizes the large extent to which each early modern urban settlement's geographic, demographic, administrative, governmental and legal context, which developed differently over centuries, necessarily shaped its sanitation needs and the unique style, scope and ultimately the efficacy of its environmental regulation.

Part 1: York's sanitation in context

England's national environmental regulation

By 1500, English Common Law judges defined nuisances as activities undertaken on one's property, which disturbed another's enjoyment of theirs. Easements which were vital to the enjoyment of real property, but which did not generate profit, developed from this definition. For example, whereas Common Law protected free passage, ancient light, wholesome air and unpolluted water it did not protect access to fisheries.[7] When householders' neighbours deprived them of easements, they could submit a writ to either King's Bench or Common Pleas requesting an action on the case for private nuisance. Such an action would order one's neighbours to abate their offensive activity.[8] How far inhabitants' right to obtain an action deterred their neighbours from committing nuisances depends on how explicitly people understood nuisance at English Common Law. Though at least one book articulated 'what manner of speciall nusance … a man may have his remedy by assise or other action', it is unlikely that this London publication reached most of England's literate population.[9] Those lacking such legal knowledge, however, could obtain advice from readily available attorneys.[10] Admittedly, one's economic wealth shaped the likelihood that they could or would pursue an action for nuisance. Submitting a writ cost approximately 5s, but numerous additional costs ensued for summoning the defendant, entering pleas on court rolls and the attorney's time.[11] Nevertheless, such modest inhabitants as tailors and artisans utilized the central courts and litigation could be obtained on credit.[12] Moreover, lawsuits pursued in King's Bench and Common Pleas were cheaper than were those pursued in Chancery and Star Chamber.[13] Though debt suits cost between six and eight pounds in the late 1620s, actions on the case were less costly. Also, increasingly ubiquitous attorneys could be hired easily in urban centres. Central court litigation increased between 1560 and 1640, which, as Chris Brooks suggests, contemporaries may have seen 'in a positive light, as the spread of valuable remedies to greater numbers of people'.[14]

Thomas Barnes highlights the proactive and noteworthy attempt in the first half of the seventeenth century to address the root problems of London's over-population, including insanitary conditions, by the passing and enforcing of building regulations rather than simply dealing with the consequences. Indeed, Barnes called it 'the most considerable, continuous, and best documented experiment in environmental control in the Common Law tradition', describing it as a 'remarkable example of governmental perspicacity'.[15] While it ultimately failed, derailed by the British Civil Wars, he asserts, nevertheless, 'from this early experiment, had it survived, we might have derived a solid procedural foundation, some lines of doctrinal development, and even a modicum of substantive rules upon which to build today's environmental law'.[16]

Chris Brooks and Chris Harrison highlight the large extent to which social relationships were reflected in litigation, emphasizing the importance of analysing the wider context of legal cases in terms of complainants' motivations to file a case.[17] It is possible that other unrelated social or economic grievances might well have been at the heart of a complainant's real motivation to pursue a defendant in a case which was ostensibly focused on an alleged insanitary nuisance. It is also important to consider the potentially large number of quite serious insanitary nuisances which might well have been resolved privately and informally with a few words exchanged verbally between one neighbour and another, which are now irretrievable. Janet Loengard emphasized the potentially large extent to which the official nuisance cases submitted to law courts could well represent the tip of a much larger iceberg of inhabitants' concern over the environment.[18]

To obtain an action on the case for a private nuisance, complainants had to convince the jury that they had suffered from it to a greater extent than their neighbours. In 1617, Fowler, of Coggeshall, in Essex, submitted a writ to King's Bench after having fallen from his horse as it tripped over 'divers loads of logs' in the highway before Sander's house. King's Bench awarded Fowler an action for private nuisance 'because he [had] ... special damage ... although the nuisance be a public nuisance'.[19] Although the logs in the highway were defined as a public nuisance, that Fowler had fallen over the logs and suffered a physical injury as a result of the public nuisance enabled it to be defined as a private nuisance. Insanitary nuisances were defined in the same manner as other private and public nuisances. William Aldred, of Harleston, Norfolk, submitted a writ to King's Bench in 1610 because his neighbour, Thomas Benton, had erected a noxious pig sty next to the hall and parlour of Aldred's home. Aldred resorted to King's Bench after Norfolk's Assize Judges had concluded 'the building of the house for hogs was necessary for the sustenance of man: and one ought not to have so delicate a nose, that he cannot bear the smell of hogs'.[20] Thus, judgements made at a county level were by no means final and could be pursued to England's central courts at Westminster. Eventually, Benton was found guilty of polluting Aldred's environment, and he had to remove the pig sty and pay damages to Aldred.[21] King's Bench resolved this nuisance for Aldred after his highest county court had failed to protect him against this insanitary nuisance.

In 1628, John Jones, of Gloucester, submitted a writ to Common Pleas accusing his neighbour, John Powell, of having created a nuisance by building a brewing house and privy, in which Powell burned much coal, next to Jones's house. The 'smoke, stench, and unwholesome vapours coming from the ... coles and privy' prevented Jones and his family from enjoying the environment of their home, which was also Jones's office, where he completed his duties of 'register' to the Bishop of Gloucester.[22] The judgement was that although 'brew-houses are necessary', they should be used in such a way 'that they be not prejudicial to their neighbours'.[23] The judges agreed that Powell's 'brew-house and privy was maliciously erected to deprive the plaintiff of the benefit of his habitation and office', and they ordered Powell to demolish them.[24] This is a revealing example of England's central courts having provided a middling-sort ecclesiastical clerk with a satisfactory, and seemingly affordable, solution to a nuisance. In 1638, moreover, an innkeeper, named Morley, of Eastgestock, complained to King's Bench that a nuisance threatened his livelihood. Innkeepers needed a salubrious environment effectively to sell to their guests; thus nuisances were especially problematic. It was alleged that Morley's neighbour, Pragnel, had 'maliciously erected a tallow furnace, and boiled therein much stinking tallow, to the great annoyance of him and his guests'.[25] King's Bench ordered Pragnel to remove the furnace. Despite Eastgestock's need for candles, these common law judges recognized that a salubrious environment was integral to Morley's livelihood. Furthermore, in 1663, Lightfoot complained to King's Bench that his neighbour, named 'Salt', had erected a pig sty, privy and dunghill against his house. He complained that 'the walls ... were putrid, and became ruinous', and Lightfoot had consequently abandoned his home.[26] King's Bench ordered Salt to remove the offending structures, thus protecting Lightfoot from the nuisance.[27] These functional central courts could and did offer real solutions to real insanitary nuisances suffered by real people. Actions on the case for nuisance were pursued in England's central courts throughout the early modern period. Travelling circuit Assize Courts also dealt with insanitary nuisances at the county level. In 1601, Surrey's Assize Judges presented several inhabitants of St George, Southwark, for obstructing the highway with dunghills.[28] In 1633, the Somerset Assize Judges forbade Francis Russell, 4th Earl of Bedford, to continue building some houses in Covent Garden because they predicted that inadequate sewers would make the houses a 'public nuisance'.[29] Even at the expense of economic development, seventeenth-century common law judges protected urban inhabitants' life quality against nuisances. Their progressive attitude towards urban salubriousness was remarkably similar to that of their counterparts who served on local courts.

English Parliamentary Statutes were also passed to provide nationwide protection against insanitary nuisances. While town courts primarily upheld their own local bylaws, they sometimes enforced Parliamentary Statutes in order to combat public nuisances. In 1616, for example, Durham's Court of Quarter Session fined six butchers for slaughtering livestock within Durham in contravention of a 1489 statute forbidding 'any butcher ... [to] kill any beast within the walls ... of any ... town'.[30] Well over a century after the statute was initially passed, it was still being used to abate and prevent insanitary nuisances which would reduce the life quality of Durham's inhabitants and the city's salubriousness more generally. Similarly, in 1603, Southampton Court Leet fined nine butchers for erecting slaughter houses in Southampton, which was deemed 'most unfitt and unlawfull ... beinge a matter expresly against the lawes of the Realm'.[31] These examples reveal not only that the English Parliament passed legislation to enhance urban inhabitants' life quality but also that local courts subsequently supported that legislation by enforcing it in the localities. Even monarchs acted to enhance urban salubriousness. Having realized that residential overcrowding caused London's numerous public nuisances – industrial smoke, impaired light and filthy, noxious streets – Elizabeth I, James VI and I and Charles I issued successive building regulations, between 1580 and 1640, to curtail London's rapid growth. Royal proclamations banned both building on new foundations and subdividing existing buildings into tenements. Parliament did not actually enact the initial proclamation of 1580 to that effect until 1592, and it was repealed on expiry in 1601, but between 1602 and 1640, fifteen further proclamations were issued largely reiterating its initial stipulations.[32] These proclamations' 'weighty sanctions', which Star Chamber judges meted out to contraveners, maximized their efficacy, but after 1592, as Thomas Barnes laments, Parliament refused to make these royal proclamations statutory, and by 1640 'building control was dead'.[33]

William Cavert interprets the regulation of London coal smoke pollution between 1624 and 1640, as an 'attempt to turn a messy metropolis into an image of virtue'.[34] Cavert highlights the importance of this period of environmental regulation, during which 'the English Crown found that the reform of urban air was an important aspect of its governmental program, a part of attempts to create a beautiful, orderly court and capital as showpieces of a well-governed kingdom', but he emphasizes that 'the push for clean air' was not motivated by wider environmental concerns for their own sake or for the public health of the inhabitants.[35] Rather, Cavert claims, it 'was explicitly political, part of a broader project to strengthen and glorify the Crown'.[36] Notwithstanding the premature death of these environmental initiatives, that only Londoners benefited from their enforcement and that they may well have had alterior political motives, these building and coal smoke regulations demonstrate long-term, sustained attempts to curtail insanitary nuisances in England's capital city. Although Parliamentary Statutes, royal proclamations, the circuit Assize of Nuisance and the Westminister central courts which permitted people to obtain actions on the case for nuisance functioned throughout the early modern period and were theoretically available to all subjects, the overwhelming majority of insanitary nuisances were dealt with by local legal facilities in the towns in which such nuisances occurred.

Introduction to York

Widely accepted as England's second city, York provides a revealing case study for the close analysis of changing attitudes towards environmental regulation, waste disposal and sanitation systems and processes in the late sixteenth and seventeenth centuries. As the seat of an archbishop, York had long been considered the capital of the northern province of the Church of England, and the city hosted the Council of the North from 1485 until its dissolution by the Long Parliament in 1641. As the ecclesiastical, legal, administrative and to some extent social centre of northern England, York played host to many prestigious visitors from far and wide, travelling up and down the Great North Road between Edinburgh and London. Moreover, its role as a strategic regional trading centre meant that it was an imperative that its main thoroughfares were kept clear and passable at all times. Environmental regulation was an important part of York's local government during this period. York Corporation also administered an area some twelve miles beyond the city itself, known as the Ainsty, thus functioning as the central government of a significant geographical area. York boasted substantial walls, sandwiched between concentric inner and outer dry moats, which ran almost continuously for more than two miles, interrupted only by the River Ouse, the

River Fosse and the marsh next to the Fosse, encompassing some 263 acres of the city.[37] Five gates known as bars defended the access points from the main radial roads into the city (Monk Bar, Fishergate Bar, Bootham Bar, Micklegate Bar and Walmgate Bar) and seven smaller gates known as 'posterns' guarded the points where the rivers crossed the walls.[38] York was originally divided into six secular, administrative wards, which were simplified into four wards during the 1520s (Bootham Ward, Monk Ward, Walmgate Ward and Micklegate Ward), of which the latter two had significantly more open space. The city was also split ecclesiastically into twenty-six parishes.[39] York had several bridges, the most important being Fosse Bridge and Ouse Bridge – the latter collapsed in 1565 but had been rebuilt by 1567 with impressive speed.[40] The city also boasted twenty-eight occupational guilds.

The population estimates for the city, detailed in Figure 2, indicate that while York may well have experienced a brief increase in population of as much as 71 per cent between 1548 and the turn of the seventeenth century, that it actually fell into gradual, but steady decline henceforth until well into the eighteenth century due to the decline in the cloth market and the downturn in the economy more generally. Therefore, it is fair to say that while York's sanitation and waste disposal systems and processes might have been placed under some strain during the latter half of the sixteenth century, this pressure diminished considerably throughout the seventeenth century, and it is highly likely that the city did not

Source	Year	Households	Population	Minimum (4.25)	+25%	% change since last count
Domesday Book	1066	–	9,000a	–	–	–
Poll Tax	1377	–	10,872b	–	–	+20.8
Chantry Commissioners' Survey	1548	–	6,431c	–	8,038	–26.1
Parish Registers	1601–1610	–	11,000d	–	13,750	+71.0
Corporation House Count	1639	2,156	–	9,163	11,454	–16.7
Hearth Tax	1671	1,869	–	7,943	9,929	–13.3
Parish Registers	1760	–	12,400e	–	–	+12.0

Figure 2 The estimated population of York, 1066–1760

Source:
a) D. Palliser, 'Domesday York', *Borthwick Papers*, 78 (1990), pp. 1–31.
b) J. Russell, *British Medieval Population* (Albuquerque: University of New Mexico Press, 1948), p. 142.
c) Communicants, including relative adjustments for parishes which lack extant records.
d) Including relative adjustments for parishes which lack extant records.
e) G. Forster, 'York in the 17th century', in P. Tillot (ed.), *A History of the County of York, The City of York* (London: Victoria County History, 1961), pp. 160–206.

suffer from significantly augmented urban waste over the course of the whole period. The city's demography must be considered in the context of the relatively large geographical area within its walls, especially when it is compared directly to Edinburgh. Not only did York have a relatively low and gradually declining population, but it was also a very sparsely populated city, albeit with a relatively more densely populated area east of the River Ouse and a substantially less populous area west of the river.[41]

York's legal, governmental and administrative context

In sixteenth and seventeenth century York, a range of legal and administrative authorities and institutions regulated and managed waste disposal and environmental regulation. This was a complex edifice of simultaneous and competing bodies with overlapping functions and jurisdictions, yet each and every one of these institutions was integral to the functioning of environmental regulation in the city. Figure 3 splits the fines received by the Chamberlain for insanitary nuisance and street cleaning offences according to the type of court which imposed the penalty, based on the sixty-one extant annual lists of fines paid to the Chamberlain which are available between 1560 and 1700. Figure 3 demonstrates very clearly the higher relative importance of York's Wardmote Court, compared to that of the Searchers of Occupations, Sessions of the Peace and Sheriff's Tourn. York had been a 'county corporate' since 1396, which meant that it was legally and administratively separate from the county of York. The county's Sheriff and Justices of the Peace had no jurisdiction in the city, which was governed instead by two of York's own Sheriffs and its twelve aldermen, who acted as Justices of the Peace.[42] Citizens of York, therefore, were restricted to using city courts only, except for England's central courts at Westminster and the Council of the North.

Court	Number of Fines for Insanitary Nuisances
Wardmote	549
Sessions of the Peace	68
Sheriff's Tourn	66
Searchers of Occupations	44
Sessions of the Peace and Wardmote [mixed in the same list]	282
Sessions of the Peace, Wardmote and Exchequer [mixed in the same list]	143
Total	**1,152**

Figure 3 Insanitary nuisance fines exacted from various courts in the city of York, 1559–1689

York Corporation was tripartite: a senior council consisting of an annually elected mayor and twelve aldermen; a junior or 'Privy' council, known as the 'Twenty-Four', two Sheriffs, a recorder and a town clerk; and there also existed a common, but more representative, council of forty-eight men, drawn from the searchers of the city's guilds.[43] The senior and junior councils, the main body of around thirty-five men, met in the Council Chamber on Ouse Bridge or the Common Hall on Coney Street between once and a few times weekly to discuss urgent city matters whereas the common council met only occasionally. However, when the senior and junior councils met effectively as a court to pass an official bylaw, they usually made a point of stating in the preamble to a bylaw, 'it is ordered by this Court with the consent of the Common Counsell'.[44] As well as discussing citywide, macro-scale waste disposal problems and designing appropriate solutions to keep the streets passable and the city functioning, the Court of Mayor and Aldermen also sometimes decided legal disputes between neighbours in issues such as boundaries and drainage, which often involved insanitary nuisances. Sessions of this court were conducted on an *ad hoc* basis within council meetings and hearings were simply slotted between discussions of other city issues. Although the mayor, aldermen and councillors were elected annually, many served on more than one council for successive years. As Paul Halliday observes, the hundreds of corporations spread across England were 'by no means democratic institutions', but they 'touched directly the daily lives of a large part of the English population'.[45] Although Halliday notes that corporations provided 'an environment where partisan groups could spawn and grow', he also emphasizes that 'partisan politics was not the politics of instability'.[46] Despite the strong forces which punctuated the period 1560 to 1700: the Reformation, the British Civil Wars, non-monarchical national government, the Restoration and the Glorious Revolution, York Corporation remained relatively united and relatively strong. Philip Withington draws attention to the importance of York's status as a county, which allowed its citizens to hold their own Assizes and to muster their own militia, observing that the city 'through the complex and overlapping structures of corporation, ward, parish and guild, possessed many of the responsibilities of the modern state'.[47] He asserts that although such power was ultimately checked by sovereign authority, the corporation nevertheless enjoyed 'high degrees of discretion and autonomy' and that such powers 'induced a powerful civic territorialism' leading to the development of 'a political culture which can at best be described as civic republicanism'.[48] York Corporation was a strong and confident body which acted as an autonomous government within the Ainsty boundaries, albeit within limits set by the Crown.

The Sessions of the Peace, both petty sessions and quarter sessions, were conducted by a quorum of any three of the mayor and aldermen in their role as Justices of the Peace.[49] This court presented and fined inhabitants for a large array of offences, from eavesdropping to card-playing, to slander, to petty violence, to insanitary nuisances, to failure to carry out neighbourhood duties such as cleaning one's forefront. Each parish had its own constable, who was responsible for disbursing poor payments, but constables also sometimes paid one-off sums to inhabitants for conducting urgent waste disposal duties within the parish. The corporation also delegated responsibility to the constables to ensure that the bylaws they passed were promulgated, implemented and adhered to in their own bounds. They had particular responsibility to ensure that all householders cleaned their forefronts thrice weekly, and especially after markets had ended, for example. Two wardens were appointed to each ward annually and were sometimes referred to as the officers of the wards. Wardens were senior to the constables of as many as six respective parishes which fell within their jurisdiction and the corporation often charged the wardens of the wards with implementing bylaws and changes to street cleaning systems made by York Corporation.

Building disputes had been viewed and surveyed throughout the medieval period by the searchers of the carpenters and tilers, who possessed significant expertise and knowledge in these areas. Many building disputes involved insanitary and drainage nuisances and thereby the searchers of the occupations of carpenters and tilers came to have an influence over environmental regulation. This court of the searchers of occupations was responsible for extracting many of the fines in the Chamberlains' accounts pertaining to insanitary nuisance, street cleanliness and waste disposal and it continued to exert a strong influence over the regulation of insanitary nuisances throughout the seventeenth century. Sheriff's Tourn and the Wardmote Courts were York's court leets, which were held twice yearly, and which functioned to fine inhabitants who had been presented as a result of the wardens' street inspections for having contravened city bylaws. This court had traditionally dealt with insanitary nuisances and minor infringements on properties throughout the medieval period, but it became increasingly less important into the early modern period, as the sessions of the peace became more active in the city.

Increasingly, over the course of the period 1560–1700, York's Sessions of the Peace court gradually took over the traditional jurisdiction of York's Court Leet, known as the Wardmote Court, leaving it to regulate more prosaic contraventions, including street cleaning offences and insanitary nuisance. In this respect, York's Wardmote courts reflected the national pattern of the decline in importance of Court Leets over the course of the early modern period.[50] Figure three shows the relative importance of the various courts which were responsible for regulating the environment throughout the period. However, the change in the respective courts' functions was more the result of a nationwide pattern than of definitive action taken by York Corporation to reorganize the regulation of the environment. In Bristol, whereas the medieval City Court Leet had previously regulated serious offences, the rise in the power of the Justices of the Peace over the fifteenth and sixteenth centuries, together with a statute passed by Edward IV which transferred matters of indictment exclusively to the circuit Assizes, led to a substantial reduction in the importance of the city's Court Leet. By the seventeenth century, Bristol Court Leet was only presenting minor neighbourhood disputes and nuisance cases and, as in York, the seventeenth-century Bristol Courts of Sessions encroached to a certain extent even on this remaining area of the Leet's jurisdiction too. Indeed, as Sidney Webb observed in relation to English local government in the seventeenth century, 'the suppression of nuisances ... was practically monopolized by the Leets of private Lords and enfranchised Boroughs'.[51] As we shall see, whereas Edinburgh Council was forced, under the pressure of the escalating problems ensuing from an increasingly densely populated and dirtier city, to rationalize and simplify their regulatory system, making a purposeful effort to improve environmental regulation, by delegating neighbourhood nuisances to the Dean of Guild Court, York Corporation saw no apparent need to simplify the complex and overlapping system which had been passed down to it by their medieval predecessors and it took no action to reorganize the courts which regulated insanitary nuisances in the city. This can be explained by the immense population increase in Edinburgh compared to the relatively stagnant population in York. Seemingly, early modern urban councils were reluctant to make significant changes to the systems which they had inherited from their predecessors unless they were forced to do so by significant demographic changes which rendered such systems inadequate.

Despite the lack of demographic pressure in York, the corporation did make some efforts to devote more focused attention to waste disposal problems in isolation from the array of other urban problems which required attention. The corporation rationalized and developed their administrative mechanisms for managing this area of city government. As is discussed much more fully and on a more practical level in the next chapter, the corporation appointed four Scavengers, one for each ward, to clean and remove waste from the streets on three days each week and they charged inhabitants for this non-negotiable, citywide service.[52] This heavily centralized and markedly different street cleaning and solid waste disposal system was designed to reduce the city's reliance on individual householders' compliance. The 'constables of everie parishe' collected 'the money assessed upon the inhabitants within ther severall parishes for the skavengers', and this money was collected twice yearly at the Annunciation and Michaelmas, from 1581 henceforth. In addition to the scavengers receiving 'all the donge and filth for their paines' the constables paid wages to them.[53] This change in the organization of the city's waste disposal was promulgated and explained to inhabitants through the medium of their parish churches.

In September 1654, moreover, in response to inhabitants' continual waste disposal in a prohibited area, a small party of three council officials were sent to survey 'the waiste peece of ground at staith'.[54] To all intents and purposes, York Corporation effectively delegated this specific task to a committee with a specific objective. Whether or not they viewed environmental regulation as a separate part of urban government, worthy of special, focused attention, they certainly perceived this as an issue which required the exclusive attention of a team consisting of three men. Just as in Edinburgh, where a committee was appointed to oversee street cleaning across the whole city, this delegation seems to have resulted from the pressure of augmented waste, albeit in one particular location rather than across the whole city, as was the case in Edinburgh. It is remarkable that both cities took the similar steps of appointing a committee to deal with sanitation problems, ableit on very different scales. This distinctly more modern, focused treatment of problems marks an important discontinutity in the respective cities' administration, management and government. Between 1560 and 1700, the systems and processes designed to prevent insanitary nuisances and problematic accumulations of waste underwent acute change in Edinburgh and relatively minimal modification in York. Yet both Edinburgh Council and York Corporation responded, in line with their very different levels of respective sanitation challenges, quickly, efficiently and in a similar manner using increasingly proactive approaches. While York's householders' sanitation responsibilities decreased somewhat, after the introduction of the scavenger system in 1580 – the most significant change in this area of city government over the course of fourteen decades – inhabitants still retained many of their traditional responsibilities due to the survival of the medieval forefront system alongside the scavenger system. While the scavengers were paid by means of what was essentially a tax on householders to remove as much waste as a man put out at his door and to clean the main thoroughfares thrice weekly, in reality householders were still responsible for cleaning their forefronts, scouring their gutters and transporting a large proportion of their own waste. They still had to move it to a designated disposal point in their ward or parish or transport it to boats on the Fosse so that it could be transported down the river to Tang Hall pastures near Heworth.

Environmental regulation in York functioned in a primarily top-down manner, with orders originating from the corporation to the officers of the wards, then to the constables and then down to the inhabitants through the medium of their parish churches. Householders seemingly had no choice but to obey such orders. However, inhabitants could petition the corporation to complain about nuisances which were reducing their daily life quality or to request liberty to implement solutions to insanitary nuisances themselves, such as the erection of a locked door to prevent inhabitants from dumping rubbish on one's land. They could also organize their own informal waste disposal methods and facilities within their own neighbourhoods, such as communal dunghills, and they could report their neighbours to the array of local courts which regulated the environment. Inhabitants could flout bylaws and dump their rubbish where they saw fit, taking care to remove it beyond the city walls, or they could take it down to the Staith even though such behaviour was officially forbidden. On the surface, the official records give a misleading impression that York Corporation tried to control the city's inhabitants by limiting their dirty, unthoughtful and chaotic waste disposal arrangements and techniques. But in reality they came up against a lot of resistance from inhabitants who made significant efforts to shape waste disposal themselves, even by flouting bylaws and dumping rubbish where they saw fit, which forced the corporation, eventually, to make such informal waste disposal locations official, by building walls around what were already functioning as established waste disposal locations.

While there was a distinctly and unmistakably more serious tone as well as a numerical increase in the council discussions and bylaws pertaining to this area of city government in the first half of the seventeenth century, and the corporation clearly made a significant effort to improve street cleanliness to combat plague during that period, for the most part of the period 1560 to 1700, the corporation reacted to problems on an *ad hoc* basis. Apart from establishing the scavenger system in 1580, and several minor innovations throughout the seventeenth century in terms of allocating specific locations at which to bury offal, managing the movement of livestock and regulating the sale of urban muck to local rural farmers to be used as fertilizer, waste disposal processes and systems remained relatively stagnant. Indeed, the medieval forefront system, which was dependent on householders' accountability, survived intact right up to the turn of the eighteenth century and despite the need to remind inhabitants several times to perform their duty to keep their forefronts clean, it seems to have functioned quite well. Such continuity in environmental regulation undoubtedly resulted from the city's stagnant, perhaps even declining, demography, which meant that the corporation was never forced to adapt this area of city government to meet the increasing needs of an accelerating population and its augmented waste. The fact that bylaws and reminders of previously passed bylaws were repeated several times throughout the period does not infer that the system was failing. In terms of the lengthy period of fourteen decades, it is an achievement that such bylaws only needed to be promulgated every few years, sometimes only once a decade.

Part 2: Edinburgh's sanitation in context

Scotland's national environmental regulation

Scottish urban sanitation did not fall exclusively under the jurisdiction of each burgh's local governmental and legal institutions. Burgh councils were subservient to Scotland's national governing institutions. They often had to obey direct orders in relation to sanitation which were issued by the Scottish Parliament, the Privy Council of Scotland and the representative urban body of the Convention of Burghs. Scotland's national institutions were particularly concerned about Edinburgh's sanitation due to the city's important function as the capital, its increasing population and the publication of several internationally embarrassing travellers' accounts which depicted the city as having been overwhelmed by filth, which were discussed at length in the introduction.

Scotland's Privy Council sometimes interfered in Edinburgh's sanitation when it believed it was in the national interest to do so. On 14 April 1590, for example, in reaction to a complaint from the Privy Council, Edinburgh Council passed an ordinance stipulating 'during the remaining of the strangers' that will be staying in Edinburgh, 'in cumpany with his Majestie', that 'all middings and staines be removet and the streitts and venellis kepit clene' within forty-eight hours of the order's promulgation.[55] Clearly, the Privy Councillors would have been embarrassed if King James VI's important visitors noticed muck, stones and rubbish on the streets of Edinburgh. In 1618, moreover, the Privy Council intervened to ban Edinburgh's fleshers from depositing 'the blood and filth of slaughtered goodis upoun the streits', and it ordered them to transplant their slaughter houses to 'remote pairts of the burgh ... whair thair is no houses'.[56] The city needed meat, but the malodours and unsavoury waste materials produced in a flesher's booth were incongruous in a well-organized urban landscape. Again, in March 1619, the Scottish Privy Councillors recorded their reaction to the typically condemnatory nature of travel literature written about Edinburgh by foreign visitors:

> [Edinburgh] is now become so filthie and uncleine, and the streits, vennalls, wyndis, and cloisis thairof so overlaide and coverit with middings, and with the filthe and excrements of man and beast, as the nobilmen, counsallors, senators, and uthers his Majesteis subjects who ar ludgeit [i.e. lodged] within the said burgh can not have ane clene and frie passage and entrie to thair ludgings ... And forder [i.e. further] this schamefull and beistlie filthienes is most detaistabill and odious in the sicht [i.e. sight] of strangers, who, beholding the same, ar constrained with reassoun to gif oute mony disgracefull speichs aganis this burgh, calling it a most filthie pudle of filth and uncleanness, the lik whairof is not to be seine in no [i.e. any] pairt of the world.[57]

The words 'with reassoun' speak volumes, suggesting that while the Privy Councillors thought that the travellers' descriptions were 'disgracefull', they admitted that they were not completely unjustified. Evidently, civic pride in relation to Scotland's capital city was strong, Scotland's Privy Councillors cared about travellers' perception of it, and the cleanliness of Edinburgh's streets was a nationally significant, arguably political, issue.

Scotland's national, representative, exclusively urban assembly, The Convention of Burghs, which had jurisdiction over Scottish incorporated royal burghs and which assembled commissioners from burghs across Scotland to debate and resolve specifically urban issues, was a remarkably effective facility of which there was no equivalent institution in England. Scottish burgh officials had been meeting formally to discuss urban issues, such as the enforcement of burgh laws, weights and measures and trade regulations, since at least the thirteenth century, but the Convention of Burghs started to meet as a truly representative assembly as early as 1487. The Convention of Burghs emerged as what Alan MacDonald calls a 'virtually autonomous national institution' after 1500 and began to meet more regularly from the 1550s onwards.[58] As well as discussing legislation and regulations which affected all Scottish burghs, it also controlled the admission of burghs to parliamentary status and was even able to veto the monarch's decisions in relation to urban affairs.[59] From the 1580s, incorporated burghs were regularly sending their commissioners to attend the 'general' convention of burghs, held every July in a different burgh each year.[60] Disposing of waste and keeping streets and other public places relatively clean was not an exclusively urban problem, but it was more challenging in an urban than in a rural context. Rural waste disposal problems never equalled those in the burghs because the countryside was less densely populated, and landward Scots were able to dispose of their waste directly onto their cottage gardens and fields. Consequently, urban, far more so than rural, squalor became the object of foreign visitors' condemnation. Indeed, Peter Clark and Paul Slack list 'public hygiene' as one of the 'problems which rural society experienced only to a far lesser degree' than their urban counterparts.[61] The increasingly serious problem of inadequate outdoor sanitation in Scottish burghs in general, but particularly in Edinburgh, attracted the attention of the Convention of Burghs several times throughout the period. Edinburgh's sanitation provision, waste disposal and street cleanliness had a far wider importance and a far larger impact on national politics than its smaller counterparts.

On 6 July 1608, the Convention of the Royal Burghs met at Selkirk and passed a statute which revolutionized urban waste disposal. It declared that in each burgh 'particular acts and statutes' are 'sett doun for removeing of all ... filth', and it ordered that each burgh 'sall put the samyn to dew executioun mair cairfulle and delegentle' than had been done previously, within the time period of twenty days and the filth was to be removed in each burgh in the future within forty-eight hours under the pain of forty pounds Scots.[62] Though this order stipulated that accumulations of muck had to be cleared away within twenty days, it also ordered burgh officials to regulate waste disposal 'mair cairfulle and delegentle' henceforth to improve long-term sanitation. Indeed, it imposed its own time limit of forty-eight hours on future waste deposits to ensure that urban streets would contain cyclically replaced, limited amounts of muck. Though simple, this had the potential to protect burghs from previous chaotic situations whereby muck had accumulated to unlimited levels. The commissioners returned to their respective burghs and relayed the statute to their councils, some of whose responses were recorded. The Glaswegian councillors took the statute very seriously after James Inglis, Baillie, returned from that particular Convention of Burghs and delivered a copy of King James VI and I's letter to the convention. Glasgow Burgh Council recorded that henceforth no muck could be 'had, laid, or keippit upone the streits' anywhere in the burgh because it is 'uncumlie and incivill' because 'the commissioners of burrows hes sett doun act and ordinance inhibiting and forbidding the same in all time cumming, and for taking away of the present fuilye hes appointit the space of xv days' under the pain of forty pounds Scots to be taken from the burgh which fails to put the said act into execution.[63] Therefore, 'for obedience of his Majesteis will and pleasour and act of burrowis sett doun', Glasgow Council ordered that 'na maner of fuilye be laid upone the foirgait nor pairt of this bruche in time cuming' under the pain of five pounds Scots and the confiscation of the muck.[64] Any muck which was 'lying presentlie' on the streets and closes was ordered to be removed within fifteen days under the threat of the same penalty.[65] By 16 July, therefore, only ten days after the statute's promulgation at the Convention of Burghs, 'fuilyie' had been banned from all Glaswegian streets 'in time cuming'.[66]

Edinburgh Council also responded to the convention's statute, but they did not make a record quite as swiftly. On 21 October 1608, they recorded that 'the Kings

Majestie be his letter directed unto the burrowes' has ordered that the burghs should take a 'substantiall ordour for purgeing of thair townes' from 'filth and middings' after 'the commissioners of burrowes in thair last conventioun haldin at Selkirk in July last' commanded to all of the burghs to have 'ane speciall cair for … honor of the haill [i.e. whole] realme to see that thair streitts and vinells may be kept cleyne'.[67] Though Edinburgh Council did not record their response until three months after the convention, the city councillors clearly understood that they had to change their attitude towards sanitation by addressing long-term waste disposal. Stirling's councillors did not record a specific response; a statute was passed only nineteen days after the convention, on 25 July 1608, adopting the convention's time limt of forty-eight hours and clearly aspiring towards improving street cleanliness in the long term. It ordered that no neighbours were to suffer any 'muk or fuilyie' to lie at their gates or doors on the high streets for longer than forty-eight hours 'unremovit or takin away' under the pain of 'five punds'.[68] It is highly likely that this burgh statute was a direct response to the Selkirk convention. The Convention of Burghs provided an invaluable means of rolling out to the burghs very quickly, efficiently and uniformly considered responses to specifically urban problems.

The Scottish Parliament could also interfere in the management of a particular burgh's sanitation if the burgh council was failing to cope and conditions were impacting negatively on wider national politics. In a Scottish Parliamentary Act of 8 June 1686, entitled the 'Act for Cleansing the Streets of Edinburgh', the magistrates of Edinburgh were ordered 'to lay down effectual ways for preserving' Edinburgh, the Cannongate and suburbs from the 'nastiness of the streets, wynds [and] closes'.[69] Clearly, the unwanted waste material which polluted the Scottish capital's streets, to the annoyance of 'his majesty's lieges', was given attention as an important, urgent and national problem. Edinburgh's insanitary streets became such a nationally significant issue because it impeded the functions of the nation's capital city.

Introduction to Edinburgh

Scotland's capital city was, and still is, situated on a prominent basalt crag, which descended steeply from Edinburgh Castle down the densely populated High Street (Royal Mile) – with all of its numerous, cramped closes running down steeply from its north and south sides – down to the lower part of the High Street, descending to the separate burgh of Canongate. Situated below the Netherbow, the burgh of Canongate boasted its own council, tolbooth, and market and at its base was the Palace of Holyrood House at the bottom of the Royal Mile. Although Canongate was made a dependency of Edinburgh in 1639, it was not legally incorporated within Edinburgh until 1856. The Nor' Loch was a natural boundary to the north of the High Street, submerging the area now covered by Princes Street Gardens, and Edinburgh's port at Leith was a short distance away to the north-east of the landlocked city. Around 70 per cent of Scotland's staple exports left the country through the port of Leith.[70]

Estimates suggest that Edinburgh's population swelled from around 12,500 in 1560 to perhaps between 27,000 and 30,000 by 1700, which meant that it was slightly larger than Dublin, around twice as large as Dundee and Aberdeen, but nowhere near as populous as its English counterpart, London, which housed around 550,000 people by 1700.[71] Indeed, David Buchanan, a Scot writing between 1647 and 1652, observed of Edinburgh that 'I am not sure that you will find anywhere so many dwellings and such a multitude of people in so small space as in this city of ours'.[72] Consequently, between the 1590s and the 1630s, the area bounded by Edinburgh's Old Flodden Wall and its High Street hosted a twofold housing-density increase.[73] Edinburgh was quartered for ease of administration, and these four areas functioned effectively as parishes until 1655, when inner Edinburgh was divided into smaller sections. After 1655, greater Edinburgh consisted of eleven parishes in total, of which the following seven were situated in inner Edinburgh: College Kirk, Greyfriars' Kirk, Lady Yester Kirk, New Kirk, Old Kirk, Tolbooth Kirk and Tron Kirk.[74] Edinburgh was an important centre for trade, with a tax assessment in the early seventeenth century of over two and half times that of Dundee, the second largest economic centre in Scotland, and over twenty markets were held within the city walls.[75] Edinburgh was a bustling, highly populated, densely built and increasingly densely inhabited city, employing a range of prosperous craft guilds and hosting an array of important foreign and native visitors.[76]

Edinburgh's legal, governmental and administrative context

Although, as we have seen, Edinburgh Council had to submit to nationwide orders from the Scottish Parliament, the Privy Council of Scotland and the Convention of Burghs, for the most part burgh councils enjoyed significant autonomy over the management of their own sanitation services, infrastructure and environmental regulation, certainly exerting the most influence over those elements of urban life throughout the period. In all Scottish burghs, including Edinburgh, urban affairs were debated, managed and regulated by burgh councils of men based in their respective tolbooths, each council consisting of a Provost, two, three or four Baillies and a body of elected councillor burgesses who assembled regularly, usually once weekly, to discuss various local issues which required deliberation, as well as to renew old burgh statutes and to design and promulgate new ones. While all burgesses were eligible to serve as councillors, and inhabitants could write petitions to the councils in order to shape sanitation services from the bottom upwards, burgh councils could become oligarchic. For example, Allan Kennedy found that in Inverness, where the outgoing council elected the successor, the burgh government was 'tightly controlled by an oligarchy of around ten office-holding dynasties'.[77] Between 1660 and 1688, the annually elected Inverness Council consisted of only sixty-one different men representing only thirty-two families.[78] However, Kennedy emphasizes that 'the entrenchment of oligarchic government' was a feature of most post-Reformation Scottish burghs.[79] However oligarchic a burgh council was, however, inhabitants could still approach the council in order to complain about and bring about real changes to inadequate sanitation systems or particular insanitary nuisances. Whatever its inherent weaknesses in terms of failing to meaningfully represent the burgh's inhabitants at large, oligarchy was not a major limiting factor in the management of a burgh's sanitation.

The Dean of Guild Courts, consisting of the Dean of the Merchant Guild and his council of various craftsmen and merchants of the Guildry, presided over mercantile issues, such as indentures and trade disputes, as the court's title suggests. However, these courts also decided questions of neighbourhood, such as boundary disputes, the obstruction of neighbours' window light, the safety of new or modified buildings, access rights and, of most importance here, drainage and insanitary nuisances. Burgh Courts held no supervisory jurisdiction over Dean of Guild Courts, which were established in around two-thirds of royal burghs in this period.[80] Complaints of neighbourhood were submitted by a Pursuer (complainant), usually the heritor (landlord) of the property being offended on behalf of their tenant, against the heritor of the property housing the tenant who had failed to 'keep neighbourhood', known as the Offender (defendant). The Dean of Guild and his council always undertook a physical inspection of the property or properties in question before passing judgement in the form of a court Decreet, and a Court Officer travelled around a burgh on the Dean of Guild's behalf, issuing warnings, executing warrants and summoning individuals to appear at court.[81] Richard Rodger goes as far as to conclude that 'the backbone to municipal involvement in the fabric of urban life was provided by the continuing and extended concern of the Dean of Guild Courts in the field of building regulations', elaborating that the name of the court minute books, 'The Neighbourhood Book', 'may in itself be an indication of the Dean of Guild Courts' own assessment of their community function'.[82] Thirty-seven men who served as Edinburgh's Dean of Guild between 1551 and 1650 had also served on Edinburgh Council; twenty-four of those men were hereditary burgesses and one had earned his burgess status through an apprecticeship.[83] Some of these men also served on several of Edinburgh's councils. George Suttie, James Rucheid and James Stewart were listed as councillors on six or more occasions and Suttie served as Dean of Guild successively between 1643 and 1650.[84] Indeed, Helen Dingwall concluded that 'the political affairs of Edinburgh were firmly in the hands of those who had the sort of background deemed necessary for the maintenance of the merchants' aims and ideals' and that 'election to civic duty was subject to similar controls in 1650 as had applied in 1550'.[85]

In 1560, both Edinburgh Town Council and Edinburgh Dean of Guild Court had joint jurisdiction over deciding complaints of neighbourhood in the city. However, a Decree Arbitral, passed by Edinburgh Council on 3 March 1584, which clearly stated 'the said dene of gild and his counsall' were to 'beir the haill burding in deciding all questiouns of nichtbourheid' and that no neighbour's construction work could be suspended by anyone but the Dean of Guild, changed this situation, effectively giving sole jurisdiction over neighbourhood disputes to Edinburgh's Dean of Guild and his council.[86] The decision to delegate all cases of neighbourhood to the Dean of Guild was perhaps designed to alleviate the council's increasing workload or even simply to rationalize, organize and simplify its workload by allowing the Dean of Guild to take over that particular area of city government. This is an example of a clear move from an overarching, overlapping and wider system of environmental regulation to one which was more specialized and better organized, under the pressure of increasing population density. Indeed, as Margaret Wood observed in 1940,

> It was undoubtedly the increase in building which produced the Neighbourhood Court ... with the increasing number of houses many other problems were bound to arise, and, as such problems recurred and became complicated, it is a natural step to the appointment of a court to deal with them and to relieve the Council of the work.[87]

Had Edinburgh Council continued to decide questions of neighbourhood itself in addition to its other responsibilities and jurisdictions, they would have started to spend necessarily less time on each case, perhaps even having been forced out of necessity to stop visiting the properties to inspect the nuisances before making a decision. Consequently, the quality and justice of this important area of environmental regulation would have suffered and sanitary conditions could have worsened. As Margaret Wood observes, the delegation of this jurisdiction to the Dean of Guild and his Council was timely and well considered. One can see with the benefit of hindsight that this decision was beneficial to Edinburgh's inhabitants in the long term. However, Richard Rodger observes that the Dean of Guild Court 'exerted absolute power both before and after the Decreet in matters relating to building control'.[88] It is true that even after the Decree, Edinburgh Council decided a few cases of neighbourhood, but the Dean of Guild and his council decided the overwhelming majority of such disputes.[89] Although Richard Rodger plays down the court's important adjudication of drainage and insanitary nuisances as 'minutiae', he does appreciate the wider function of Dean of Guild Courts, as they 'were increasingly disposed to protect a more broadly defined public interest and to shape and control town development generally'.[90]

There is no evidence to suggest that the two institutions were in fierce competition to decide cases of neighbourhood or that Edinburgh Town Council decided a few cases after the Decree explicitly against the Dean of Guild's will or without his knowledge. The two institutions may well have been communicating frequently, working together towards common goals in relative harmony. The 1584 Decree was subsequently ratified on 12 September 1600, when the Dean of Guild gained further powers to reverse and modify Decreets, providing that he informed Edinburgh Council of any such modifications:

> That when the deine of gild or gild counsall hes past or passis to visit ony nichtbourheid and hes producet and produces thair decreitt obsolvitour or condamnitour thairupoun, the partie, whether he be persewer or defender, if he finds himself hurt be the said decreit, shall instantlie before thay pas from

the grund to the deine of gild and his brether [i.e. council] that he estems and thinks that decreit wranguslie gevin and reclame to the greit counsall and thairupoun consigne in the hands of the deine of gild ane unlaw of fourtie schillings and offer to give in his bill to the greitt counsall the nixt counsall day conteining the points and heids.[91]

That Edinburgh Council confirmed and extended the Dean of Guild Court's jurisdiction over cases of neighbourhood sixteen years after the original Decree Arbitral suggests that the system was working well and that it was in the council's interests to extend the Dean of Guild's power.

As is explained more fully in the next chapter, in October 1682, Edinburgh Council delegated the whole area of street cleaning and waste disposal in the city to a 'constant comittie', which was appointed to oversee a street cleaning team of thirty muckmen, and which met each Friday immediately after Edinburgh Council's weekly meeting.[92] By 1684, this committee, headed by a General Scavenger with two overseers working under him, supervised a highly centralized team of thirty muckmen. This delegation of one area of urban management to a separate, albeit subservient, body of men marked a significant transition in urban administration. Edinburgh's councillors were under immense pressure, as a result of an expanding population and consequently augmented waste, to create a system capable of maintaining a basic standard of street cleanliness in such a frequently visited and nationally significant city. It is clear that they appointed a street cleaning committee, not because they wanted to change the administrative systems of the council, but because they could see that the increasing problem of dirty, insanitary streets needed more focused attention than they were able to devote to it. This administrative discontinuity was born out of practical necessity first and foremost. Practical necessity, therefore, inspired the beginning of a gradual shift towards more bureaucratic modes of administration. What is the difference, one might ask, between this centralized street-cleaning system and 'modern Western public servants who perform jobs according to formal rules, who receive fixed salaries and budgets for their services and whose operations are monitored by supervisors', which Manon van der Heijden claims are 'hardly comparable' to those who 'worked in the service of the early modern town'?[93]

By the late seventeenth century, Edinburgh Council had successfully created a highly centralized and well-organized street cleaning system which managed this area of urban government underneath, but separately from, Edinburgh Council. This is a shining example of what could be done towards solving early modern urban waste disposal problems, but it has to be said that it was born out of necessity rather than proaction or foresight; forced adaptation rather than an explicitly progressive movement of reform. It was unfortunate that increasing horse-drawn traffic and population growth absorbed much of the improvement which should have ensued from the development of this street cleaning committee. Foreigners continued to complain about Edinburgh's insanitary conditions into the eighteenth century, and even Edinburgh's proud burgh councillors admitted, in February 1681, that despite their best endeavours Edinburgh was 'still mor dirtie then formerlie'.[94] That the councillors rose to the challenge and confronted Edinburgh's street cleaning problem, however, is far more important than their ultimate failure to combat it once and for all. Edinburgh's centralized and very well-organized street cleaning and waste removal system goes a long way towards discounting the unfounded conclusions of contemporary English writers, such as Sir William Brereton and Sir Anthony Weldon, who denegrated Scotland as uncivilized. It also undermines Michael Reed's conclusion that change in Scottish towns was 'often lagging as much as a century behind that in English ones'.[95]

Since 1584, the Dean of Guild Court had held almost exclusive jurisdiction over neighbourhood disputes, including insanitary nuisances, which enabled it to devote specialized, focused and adequate attention to resolving such nuisances to satisfactory conclusions for the benefit of Edinburgh's inhabitants and the citywide standard of sanitation and air quality. Having only one court to deal with the bulk of such disputes was beneficial because the Dean of Guild and his council accumulated more specialized expertise as a result of hearing such cases. They understood the details and complexities of such disputes and were consequently better equipped to make fair and consistent judgements. The systems which were designed to manage waste disposal and environmental regulation in Edinburgh, which were passed down to Edinburgh's eighteenth-century governors, were very different from those which had been handed down from the medieval governors in 1560. The systems were certainly better organized and more efficient from an administrative perspective. However, they were not necessarily better equipped to deal with the waste produced by the much larger population which resided in Edinburgh in 1700 than the systems present at the start of the period had been equipped to deal with the waste produced by the much smaller population living in the Edinburgh of 1560. While the systems undoubtedly improved in actual terms, they might well not have improved in relative terms.

Conclusion

The governmental, legal and administrative systems which dealt with sanitation, street cleaning and waste disposal were handed down intact in 1560 still very much in their long-established, medieval form. As Dolly Jorgensen observes, the Reformation and the political changes which came as a result of Elizabeth I's accession 'did not radically alter the way cities dealt with the physical problems of urban life'.[96] The systems underwent far more significant changes subsequently, in the seventeenth century, but in a much more dramatic manner in Edinburgh than they did in York. This historically important and revealing difference can be explained largely by Edinburgh's population increase and York's demographic stagnation. However, Edinburgh should not be viewed as having boasted the more progressive, modern and proactive council complete with better and more effective local and national systems for improving sanitation. If anything, Edinburgh Council was far more reactive than proactive, and they overhauled the way in which waste was managed in the city because they had no other choice in the face of population expansion and consequent augmented waste in a relatively small area. While Edinburgh Council arguably handed over a far more rational, more efficient and reformed organized system for managing urban waste in 1700 than that handed over by York Corporation in the same year, Edinburgh's inhabitants produced more waste in a smaller area and therefore that city needed an improved system whereas York did not. Similarly, London needed a more efficient system for handling its waste than Edinburgh. The systems which were handed down respectively to eighteenth-century Edinburgh and York cannot be compared in the same context because the cities were so different in character, function and demography. They should be compared only in the particular context of the problems which they were designed to manage and regulate. Had York experienced a similar demographic increase, then its corporation, too, might well have designed a much more robust, centralized and efficient system for managing the city's waste. Similarly, had Edinburgh's population stagnated between 1560 and 1700, its councillors might not have felt the urgent need to alter, and thereby modernize, their system. It can be argued, therefore, that in the light of York's demographic stagnation, its corporation perhaps went to greater lengths to improve this area of urban government, certainly above and beyond what was required in relation to the size of their waste disposal problems, than did Edinburgh Council.

Notes

1 Jorgensen, 'Sanitation and civic government', pp. 301, 303.
2 Rawcliffe, *Urban Bodies*, pp. 8–9.
3 S. Webb and B. Webb, *English Local Government from the Revolution to the Municipal Corporations Act: The Parish and the County* (London, Longmans, Green and Co, 1906); S. Webb, *English Local Government from the Revolution to the Municipal Corporations Act: The Manor and the Borough*, pt. 1 (London: Longmans, Green and Co., 1908); B. Webb, *English Local Government from the Revolution to the Municipal Corporations Act: The Manor and the Borough*, pt. 2 (London: Longmans, Green and Co., 1908); S. Webb and B. Webb, *English Local Government from the Revolution to the Municipal Corporations Act: The Story of the King's Highway* (London, Longmans, Green and Co, 1913); and S. Webb and B. Webb, *English Local Government from the Revolution to the Municipal Corporations Act: Statutory Authorities for Special Purposes* (London, Longmans, Green and Co, 1922).
4 A. Kennedy, 'The urban community in Restoration Scotland: government, society and economy in Inverness, 1660–c.1688', *Northern Scotland*, 5 (2014), pp. 26–49, on p. 34.
5 Kennedy, 'Inverness', p. 45.
6 Clark and Slack, *English Towns in Transition*, p. 2.
7 Baker, *English Legal History*, pp. 354–355.
8 Sir W.S. Holdsworth, *A History of English Law* (London: Methuen, 1923–1925), vol. 3, p. 154.
9 R. Monson, E. Plowden, Sir C. Wray and J. Manwood, *A Briefe Declaration for What manner of special Nusance concerning private dwelling Houses, a man may have his remedy by Assise, or other Action as the Case requires* (London, 1636).
10 C. Brooks, *Lawyers, Litigation and English Society since 1450* (London: The Hambledon Press, 1998), p. 19.
11 C. Brooks, *Pettyfoggers and Vipers of the Commonwealth: The Lower Branch of the Legal Profession in Early Modern England* (Cambridge: Cambridge University Press, 1986), pp. 102–105.

12 Brooks, *Pettyfoggers and Vipers*, pp. 61, 106.

13 Brooks, *Litigation and Society*, p. 20.

14 Brooks, *Litigation and Society*, p. 22.

15 T. Barnes, 'The prerogative and environmental control of London building in the early seventeenth century: the lost opportunity', *California Law Review*, vol. 58 (1970), pp. 1332–1363, on pp. 1332, 1334.

16 Barnes, 'Environmental control', p. 1335.

17 Brooks, *Litigation and Society*; C. Harrison, 'Manor courts and the governance of Tudor England', in C. Brooks and M. Lobban (eds), *Communities and Courts in Britain, 1150–1900* (London: Hambledon Press, 1997), pp. 43–60.

18 J. Loengard, 'The Assize of Nuisance', p. 144. For a sociological and anthropological interpretation of wider conflict resolution and the law in early modern society, see S. Roberts, 'The study of dispute: anthropological perspectives', in J. Bossy (ed.), *Disputes and Settlements: Law and Human Relations in the West* (Cambridge: Cambridge University Press, 1983), pp. 1–24. For further important insights on the complex historical development of Nuisance Tort Law, see J. Brenner, 'Nuisance law and the Industrial Revolution', *Journal of Legal Studies*, 3 (1973), pp. 403–433; D. Cooper, 'Far beyond "the early morning crowing of a cock": revisiting the place of nuisance within legal and political discourse', *Social and Legal Studies*, 11:1 (2002), pp. 5–35; and J. McLaren, 'Nuisance law and the Industrial Revolution – some lessons from social history', *Oxford Journal of Legal Studies*, 3:2 (1983), pp. 155–221. See also QC. J. Gaunt and QC. P. Morgan (eds) *Gale on the Law of Easements*, 17th ed. (London: Sweet & Maxwell, 2002); and J. Getzler, *A History of Water Rights at Common Law* (Oxford: Oxford University Press, 2004).

19 *The English Reports*, vols 1–178 (Edinburgh: W. Green and Sons, 1900–1932), vol. 79, p. 382.

20 *English Reports*, vol. 77, pp. 816–822.

21 *English Reports*, vol. 77, pp. 816–822.

22 *English Reports*, vol. 123, pp. 1155–1156.

23 *English Reports*, vol. 123, pp. 1155–1156.

24 *English Reports*, vol. 123, pp. 1155–1156.

25 *English Reports*, vol. 79, pp. 1039–1040.

26 *English Reports*, vol. 83, p. 1134.

27 *English Reports*, vol. 83, p. 1134.

28 *Calendar of Assize Records. Surrey Indictments. Elizabeth I.*, ed. J. Cockburn (London: Public Record Office, 1980), no. 3116, p. 507.

29 *Somerset Assize Orders, 1629–40*, ed. T. Barnes (Frome: Butler and Frome, 1959), pp. 57–8, quoted in P. Slack, *From Reformation to Improvement: Public Welfare in Early Modern England* (Oxford: Clarendon Press, 1999), p. 73.

30 C. Fraser (ed.), 'Durham Quarter Sessions Rolls, 1471–1625', *The Publications of the Surtees Society*, vol. 199 (1987–8), pp. 262–263.

31 *Court Leet Records, 1603–1624*, ed. F. Hearnshaw and D. Hearnshaw (Southampton: Southampton Record Society, 1907), p. 395.

32 Barnes, 'Environmental control', pp. 1334, 1343, 1345, 1360.

33 Barnes, 'Environmental control', pp. 1361–1362.

34 Cavert, 'Coal smoke', p. 331.

35 Cavert, 'Coal smoke', pp. 311–312.

36 Cavert, 'Coal smoke', p. 312.

37 Palliser, *Tudor York*, pp. 23–25.

38 Palliser, *Tudor York*, pp. 23–25.

39 C. Cross, 'Tudor York', in P. Nuttgens (ed.), *The History of York: From Earliest Times to the Year 2000* (Pickering: Blackthorn, 2001), pp. 141–176; A. Dickens, 'Tudor York', in P. Tillott (ed.), *A History of Yorkshire: The City of York* (London: Victoria County History, 1961), pp. 117–159; W. Sheils, 'Seventeenth-century York', in

P. Nuttgens (ed.), *The History of York: From Earliest Times to the Year 2000* (Pickering, 2001), pp. 177–211.
40 Palliser, *Tudor York*, p. 82.
41 P. Withington, 'Views from the bridge: revolution and restoration in seventeenth-century York', *Past and Present*, 170 (2001), pp. 121–151, on p. 126; P. Addyman, 'The archaeology of public health at York, England', *World Archaeology*, 21 (1989), pp. 244–257.
42 Palliser, *Tudor York*, p. 60.
43 Palliser, *Tudor York*, p. 61.
44 York City Archives [hereafter YCA], B37, York Corporation House Book, 1650–1663 (03/02/1652).
45 P. Halliday, *Dismembering the Body Politic: Partisan Politics in England's Towns, 1650–1730* (Cambridge: Cambridge University Press, 1998), p. 7.
46 Halliday, *Dismembering the Body Politic*, pp. 4, 7.
47 Withington, 'A view from the bridge, p. 129.
48 Withington, 'A view from the bridge, p. 129.
49 Palliser, *Tudor York*, pp. 62, 79.
50 *Court Leet Records* [of Southampton]; W. Hudson (ed.), *Leet Jurisdiction in the City of Norwich in the XIIIth and XIVth Centuries* (London: Quaritch, 1892).
51 S. Webb, *The Manor and the Borough*, p. 4.
52 YCA, B27: York Corporation House Book, 1577–1580 (13/04/1580).
53 YCA, B27: York Corporation House Book, 1577–1580 (21/10/1580).
54 YCA, B37: York Corporation House Book, 1650–1663 (27/09/1654).
55 Edinburgh City Archives [hereafter ECA], SL1/1/8: Edinburgh Town Council Minutes, 1585–1589 (14/04/1590).
56 *The Register of the Privy Council of Scotland, 1545–1625*, 14 vols, ed. J. Burton and D. Masson (Edinburgh: H. M. General Register House, 1877–98), vol. 11, p. 311.
57 *Register of the Privy Council of Scotland*, vol. 11, pp. 530–531 (04/03/1619).
58 A. MacDonald, *The Burghs and Parliament in Scotland, c.1550–1651* (Aldershot: Ashgate, 2007), pp. 6–8, 186.
59 MacDonald, *Burghs and Parliament*, pp. 186–187.
60 MacDonald, *Burghs and Parliament*, pp. 6–8.
61 Clark and Slack, *English Towns in Transition*, p. 15.
62 *Records of the Convention of the Royal Burghs of Scotland with extracts from other records relating to the affairs of the Burghs of Scotland, 1295–1711*, 4 vols, ed. J. Marwick (Edinburgh: Scottish Burgh Record Society, 1876–80), vol. 2, p. 254 (06/07/1608).
63 *Records of Glasgow*, vol. 1, p. 285 (16/07/1608).
64 *Records of Glasgow*, vol. 1, p. 285 (16/07/1608).
65 *Records of Glasgow*, vol. 1, p. 285 (16/07/1608).
66 *Records of Glasgow*, vol. 1, p. 285 (16/07/1608).
67 *Extracts from the Records of the Burgh of Edinburgh, 1589–1718*, vols 5–13, ed. M. Wood, R. Hannay and H. Armet (Edinburgh: Scottish Burgh Record Society, 1927–67), vol. 6, pp. 45–46 (21/10/1608).
68 *Records of Stirling*, vol. 1, p. 120 (25/07/1608).
69 National Archives of Scotland, PA2/32: 'Act for cleansing the streats of Edinburgh', at Scottish Parliament in Edinburgh on 29/04/1686, (Legislation 08/06/1686), f. 235.
70 L. Stewart, *Urban Politics and the British Civil Wars: Edinburgh 1617–1653* (Leiden: Brill, 2006), p. 2.
71 Dingwall, *Late Seventeenth-Century Edinburgh*, pp. 13, 16–21; Makey, 'Edinburgh', p. 205; M. Lynch, *Edinburgh and the Reformation* (Edinburgh: John Donald, 1981), p. 10.
72 D. Buchanan, 'A description of Edinburgh', in P. Brown (ed.), *Scotland Before 1700, from Contemporary Documents* (Edinburgh: David Douglas, 1893), pp. 313–318 on p. 314.

73 M. Lynch, 'The Scottish Early Modern Burgh', *History Today*, 35, (Feb, 1985), pp. 10–15, on p. 11.
74 Dingwall, *Late Seventeenth-Century Edinburgh*, pp. 12–13; ECA, SL1/1/18: Edinburgh Town Council Minutes, 1653–1655.
75 Stewart, *Urban Politics*, pp. 1–2.
76 J. Colston, *The Incorporated Trades of Edinburgh* (Edinburgh: Colston & Co., 1891).
77 Kennedy, 'Inverness', p. 44.
78 Kennedy, 'Inverness', p. 34.
79 Kennedy, 'Inverness', p. 34.
80 D. Walker, *A Legal History of Scotland*, 6 vols (Edinburgh: T & T Clark, 1988–2001), vol. 4, pp. 324–325; H. MacQueen, and W. Windram, 'Laws and Courts in the Burghs', in M. Lynch, R. Spearman, and G. Stell (eds), *The Medieval Scottish Town* (Edinburgh: Donald, 1988), pp. 208–226.
81 At least one Dean of Guild Court Decreet survives: Innes vs. Paterson, 15/06/1692, see National Archives of Scotland, RH0/14/68: 'Edinburgh and Leith Papers, 1329–1851 – Decreet of Guild Court in favour of Robert Innes against John Paterson, for obstructing vennel with middings'.
82 R. Rodger, 'The evolution of Scottish town planning', in G. Gordon and B. Dicks (eds), *Scottish Urban History* (Aberdeen: Aberdeen University Press, 1983), pp. 71–91, on p. 86.
83 H. Dingwall, 'The importance of social factors in determining the composition of the town councils in Edinburgh 1550–1650', *The Scottish Historical Review,* 65:179 (1986), pp. 17–33, on p. 22.
84 Dingwall, 'Social factors', p. 23.
85 Dingwall, 'Social factors', pp. 22–23.
86 ECA, SL1/1/7: Edinburgh Town Council Minutes, 1583–1585.
87 M. Wood, 'The neighbourhood book', *The Book of the Old Edinburgh Club*, 23 (1940), pp. 82–100, on p. 89.
88 Rodger, 'Evolution of Scottish town planning', p. 76.
89 For example, Stevensone vs. Rutheid and Huntar, 1662: ECA, SL1/1/21, Edinburgh Town Council Minutes, 1661–1662.
90 Rodger, 'Evolution of Scottish town planning', p. 77.
91 ECA, SL1/1/11: Edinburgh Town Council Minutes, 1600–1609.
92 ECA, SL1/1/30: Edinburgh Town Council Minutes, 1681–1684.
93 Van der Heijden, 'New perspectives', pp. 272–273.
94 ECA, SL1/1/30: Edinburgh Town Council Minutes, 1681–1684.
95 Reed, 'Urban landscape', p. 313.
96 Jorgensen, 'Sanitation and civic government', pp. 301–302.

3 Civic-funded sanitation services

Waste disposal, street cleaning and drainage

Introduction

In 2011, the UK's Communities Secretary, Eric Pickles, went as far as to term residential weekly bin collections in Britain as a 'basic right'.[1] However 'basic' a right sanitation provision is perceived as today, the situation was certainly understood in markedly different terms between 1560 and 1700. If, today, local councils began to introduce publicly funded window cleaning operations, would our descendants in the year 2500 describe having their windows cleaned by their local governors as a basic British right? In the period 1560 to 1700, householders still held a relatively high level of responsibility over disposing of their waste and over keeping streets and other outdoor public areas clean. Although some civic-funded rubbish collection services were provided, this was by no means perceived as a basic right, the exclusive responsibility of one's civic government. Nevertheless, corporations and councils did finance, oversee and regulate certain elements of the work involved and the extent and manner of such provision varied considerably from one settlement to another. Undoubtedly, inhabitants understood that street cleaning and the removal of waste from the urban landscape was integral to the 'commonweal', and they understood theirs and their families' and servants' roles within that system. That contemporaries were obliged to maintain the cleanliness of their forefronts (the area directly before their doors), often under the threat of a fine, explains why most people were so careful when disposing of their household, agricultural and industrial waste. In order to avoid being presented at their local court, and having to pay a monetary fine, contemporaries were necessarily motivated to keep their forefronts clear and devoid of filth. It was simply not in townspeople's interests to have poured their chamber pots directly onto their forefronts as a matter of course, day after day, because this would have increased the time they subsequently had to spend cleaning them. Furthermore, householders were interested in keeping the area around their homes clean and sweet-smelling to protect theirs and their family's wellbeing against perceived dangerous airborne miasmas which, they believed, carried disease. Many urban dwellers were also motivated to contribute to neighbourhood and wider civic pride and to perform their duties in terms of mutual neighbourly obligations. It would be misleading to assume that all neighbours came out willingly to sweep their forefronts and to scrub their sections of street sewers in a harmonious, communal and idyllic fashion, and it is important to bear in mind that a minority of householders neglected their duties in this respect. However, as this chapter demonstrates, the majority of householders did not have to be coerced into keeping their forefronts clean and disposing of their waste efficiently; most performed these duties willingly and unproblematically in harmony with top-down sanitation provision and regulation from their local governors. This chapter outlines which elements of street cleaning and waste disposal duties tended to be undertaken by civic employees and overseen by local governors in a range of British towns and cities, but no two settlements maintained precisely or even roughly similar sanitation arrangements. It explains: the line between the governors' and inhabitants' responsibilities, which differed from town to town; how and why these systems were modified over the course of fourteen decades in various settlements across Britain; how far the respective systems differed from one another; and how different systems shaped the efficacy of waste disposal and street cleaning on the ground. The chapter discusses how street cleaning and the disposal of waste functioned in settlements across Britain with different functions and characteristics, before focusing on Edinburgh and York, respectively, in significant depth.

English towns and Scottish burghs

The various civic-funded systems and processes which functioned in each town or city to maintain a relatively clean outdoor environment were not invented in 1560. Both English and Scottish medieval governors had been tackling urban sanitation problems for centuries; by 1560, long-established and well-considered systems and processes were already in place. In most towns, householders were expected to keep clear, to sweep clean and to pave the area before their property to the middle of the street (the forefront) once weekly, usually on Saturday nights after the weekly market and before the Sabbath. In 1578, Sheffield's Court Leet Jurors threatened 'a paine that everye persoune inhabitinge within the Towne of Sheffeld shall have the strete againste his dore where it hath bene accustomed to be paved before Michelmasse next' under the pain of 6s 8d.[2] Such orders were passed by numerous different urban courts using strikingly similar wording. In 1636, Salford's Portmote Court ordered 'inhabitants ... shall cause their streets to be swept every Saturday and cause the dunge to be caryed away that night', warning that contraveners would have to pay 6d for each offence.[3] Urban inhabitants were well aware that sweeping their forefronts was their own responsibility; by 1560, this practice was centuries old. However, there was an important difference between forefronts above and below the Anglo-Scottish border. In England, major thoroughfares were referred to as 'the King's highway' or 'the King's street'. The streets themselves were crown property and not the private property of the inhabitants, but English householders were still responsible for cleaning and paving the section of the street between their house front and the centre of the thoroughfare, known as the crown.[4] For example, in Bristol, in April 1635, Mr

William Jones, a merchant, was presented at the Court Leet for 'suffering a dungmixon to bee made under the wall by his house at the upper end of Martin Lane and for the offendor they know not'.[5] Even though Jones did not deposit the dunghill himself, he was nevertheless held responsible for it because it was his duty to maintain a clear and clean forefront. English householders were also responsible for maintaining their section of the street drain or sewer which ran either down the crown of the street or down both sides of it in front of the properties. In Scotland, however, the forefront, or foreland, was an area of private property fronting the burgage plot which extended only to the edge of the *Via Regia* proper, which was crown property. A burgh council could still order inhabitants to clean the section of the causeway running past their property, but the householders' forefronts or forelands between their house frontages and the edge of the causeway were private property, not the property of the Crown.

While inhabitants were expected to sweep their own forefronts, in many towns civic employees were paid to sweep public areas around wells, market places, bridges, docks, harbours and gates. In February 1579, Berwick Council allotted to a widow enough pasture on which to keep forty ewes for 'kepinge the cawsey [i.e. causeway] withoute St Marygate nowe done by widow Joweye'.[6] In Carlisle, various individuals worked on a casual, and sometimes long-term, basis to complete small-scale hygiene tasks, without liveries or contracts. In 1653–1654, William Murhouse earned 8s 'for swipping Caldew Gate' for one year, and in 1672–1673, Widow Wilson also earned 8s for doing so, but these arrangements only lasted for one-year periods.[7] Widow Elizabeth Threlkeld, however, was paid 8s to sweep Richard Gate every year between 1653 and 1660.[8] Subsequently, after 1660, Widow Amy Wallas took over from Widow Threlkeld, and she, too, earned 8s annually until 1673.[9] Sheffield Burgery also made such *ad hoc* payments for street cleaning, such as a payment of 4s in 1623 'for sweeping the Bridge and pavement att the churchgates'.[10] Such *ad hoc* tasks, carried out using casual labour, often co-existed alongside more centralized and regular sanitation systems. Some towns employed full-time street cleaners. In Bristol, in October 1628, the city scavenger, John Brodway, was presented to the Court Leet for 'not keeping cleane the streete betweene the Dolphin and Newgate and suffering great heapes of durt to lie in the streete on the sabath day'.[11] Similarly, in October 1635, they presented a city 'raker', Sammuell Moggs, for not 'carrying away the soile lying in severall places from the key pipe unto the marshe gate'.[12] At the same court session, Bristol's 'City Scavenger', who might well have been related to the raker working under him as he was referred to as 'Moggs', was presented for 'goinge with waine wheeles shodd with great dowles of iron which doth shake the streetes and houses on the bridge at all houres of the night'.[13] This suggests that he collected at least some of the muck during the night. Indeed, Mark Jenner terms the carrying away of privy waste by nightwalkers in early modern London as 'deeds of darkness'.[14] Elsewhere, in Berwick, a scavenger was appointed in 1568, to carry 'all the dunge, filthe and ashe' to 'suche ordinarye places at the Rampiers [i.e. defensive ramparts]' and 'to have his wadges ... and suche other Livinge and Wadges as were sufficientt for that service'.[15] With reference to Norwich and

Coventry, Dolly Jorgensen identifies the appointment of such junior officials, such as scavengers and conduit keepers, increasingly between 1400 and 1600, as part of a wider process of 'specialization' which she calls 'a transition from a top-heavy medieval structure that put sanitation in the hands of the highest civic authorities to a dispersed model of responsibility with involvement at site-specific, local levels'.[16] Appointing a full-time town scavenger, however, did not obviate the cleaning of forefronts by Berwick's householders. In October 1594, for example, the following complaint was recorded at the Bailiff's Court:

> it is a great abuse & faulte in servants that they are suffered in time of raine to swepe downe the myre & filthe from one to another for they ought everye one to clense up & lay it together within themselves & soe to carye it awaye.[17]

The communal aspect of the suggested solution to this problem is striking; working 'together' to maintain street cleanliness was not merely an imaginary ideal, but it occurred in reality. Dunfermline Burgh Council did not provide any help towards street cleaning and, in 1628, ordered every street 'and in special' the streets under the Abbey walls to be 'clengit & keepit clene'.[18] Significantly, inhabitants had not only to clean the streets, but they also had to keep them clean henceforth. Whereas in Oxford, a town scavenger was appointed in 1541 and again in 1578; in 1621, in league with the university, yet another was appointed.[19] The amount of assistance, and the style and manner of such assistance, which townspeople received from their urban government towards the removal of muck and rubbish varied considerably from settlement to settlement.

While Sheffield Burgery did not employ any street cleaners, it did provide an ingenious mechanism to aid inhabitants' street cleaning. A small, manmade reservoir, called Barker's Pool, situated at the highest point in the west of the town, near the market place, was fitted with sluice gates which opened into each of the main, salient streets descending from it. During dry weather, when sweeping the streets became difficult and dirt started to accumulate, these sluice gates were opened and water flowed down the streets to enable householders to sweep their forefronts. The water came down Fargate, High Street, Market Street, Water Lane and then down into the River Don.[20] Barker's Pool was cleaned out, kept watertight and repaired at the Burgery's expense throughout the period. In 1572, for example, 6d was paid 'to Thomas Creswike for a shotle [i.e. shuttle or sluice gate] to Barkers Powle'.[21] And, in 1636, 1s 6d was paid 'to James Hodgson for feying [i.e. cleaning] and keeping of Barkers Poole'.[22] This unique mechanism is an insightful example of town authorities' endeavours to keep the urban landscape clean. Perhaps it was Barker's Pool which caused the Earl of Oxford's Chaplain to comment in 1725 on 'the health of the place, which few towns so populous enjoy with such constancy as they do'; he specifically mentioned Barker's Pool, noting the inhabitants' 'opportunity of sweeping into it all their uncleanly encumbrances'.[23]

The removal of waste from the urban landscape was not always a task for which a scavenger was paid a wage because dung was a valuable fertilizer, which could be sold to local farmers. In Stirling, one man was awarded the contract to arrange for the removal of waste from Stirling's streets, known as the 'Gait Dichtings', for the priviledge of which he paid Stirling Burgh Council 140 pounds Scots annually. In November 1599, Stirling Council recorded: 'Gait Dichtings Set to Archibald Smith for seivin scoir punds'.[24] Inhabitants could accumulate their own private dunghills on their forefronts and sell them privately, but Archibald Smith was responsible for arranging the collection of the muck and rubbish which accumulated in the public causeways, such as manure from horse traffic, muck and other waste which was deposited on the streets by inhabitants and dung and other materials which dropped from the carts. It is unlikely that Archibald would have removed the waste himself; clearly a man of substantial means, he probably employed others to collect it on his behalf in exchange for wages. Archibald would have benefited from either applying the fertilizer to his own crops or selling the muck to local farmers for a higher price than the combined sum of buying the contract from Stirling Burgh Council and paying men to remove the muck from the streets. He could also have used some of the muck on his own land and sold the remainder to local farmers, but what happened to the muck after it left the burgh has been lost from the written record.[25] It is possible that although Berwick Corporation paid a scavenger to carry waste from the streets to the ramparts, the town council then sold the muck to farmers themselves; however, if this was the case, the receipt of money from the sale of muck was not recorded in the town accounts.

In Ayr, inhabitants' muck was removed at the burgh's expense without any effort required from householders themselves. Between 1551 and 1610, Ayr Council arranged to remove muck and rubbish to the surrounding countryside irregularly, presumably if and when it accumulated to intolerable levels or a prestigious occasion was approaching, using casual and temporary labour such as 'the boys' or particular townsmen. The occurrence of intermittent, large-scale cleans requiring, as in 1593, 160 horses to heave the muck into the countryside on sledges, suggests that dirt was allowed to accumulate in sixteenth-century Ayr for substantial time periods. From 1611, however, Ayr Council paid particular employees annual salaries to keep the streets clear. Between 1611 and 1616, different individuals were employed for one-year periods, but between 1616 and 1624, David Huntar was employed successively for 6 li Scots annually. There is no reference to Ayr Council receiving money either from the men whom it paid to collect the muck from the streets or from any local farmers to whom the muck was undoubtedly sold. If Ayr Council paid an annual salary to an employee to collect the muck, one would expect that the council would then have claimed the full amount of money from the sale of that muck to local farmers. If the council received money from these transactions, they should have been recorded in the accounts, but they were not. Notably, these accounts suggest that Ayr's inhabitants yielded their valuable muck to their burgh council without receiving any recompense. There are no references to the council having bought the muck from inhabitants, but the muck removal was funded by the civic purse, which could well mean that the inhabitants exchanged the value of their muck for the cost of its removal.[26] While what happened to the muck after it left town has been lost from the written record, the system was efficient in terms of street cleanliness because after 1611, irregular public hygiene tasks disappear from the accounts.[27] Ayr's accounts reveal an unmistakable attitudinal change among the burgh councillors, who regularized civic-funded waste disposal increasingly from the sixteenth into the seventeenth century. Notably, this attitudinal change, in 1611, followed the order discussed in chapter two, issued in July 1608 by the Convention of Burghs on King James VI and I's behalf, stipulating that in each burgh 'particular actis and statutes are sett doun for removeing of all … filth' and that each burgh shall 'put the samyn to dew executioun mair cairfulle and delegentle' than they had done previously under the pain of forty pounds Scots.[28] Although the English Parliament could issue and roll out nationwide Acts, in England there was no equivalent representative urban assembly to tackle specifically urban issues.

In many towns, civic employees or casual labourers were paid to maintain primary drains which served entire streets and wards at the expense of the civic purse. In the financial year 1605–1606, Berwick Council paid 3s 6d to 'Edward Morton and to the Plumers boy and to women which wear gott in to make cleane the diches for the pasage of the water att severall times'.[29] By June 1631, Perth had developed a more regular system by which David Thomson was paid an annual salary to scour a particular sewer. Perhaps this is why by 1689, Thomas Morer observed there 'two long spacious streets … which being well paved, are at all times tolerably clean'.[30] Perth Burgh Council paid 33 li 9d Scots to David Thomson 'from the town yeirlie' for 'redding [i.e. cleaning] of the watergang beneath Tullitoun'.[31] In 1682, Sheffield Burgery paid 6d for 'mending the Truelove gutter with Lime and sand'; but by 1688, it had been 'then agreed by the Trustees present that John Webster shall have allowed him 30s for money laid out for scoureing and repering the Truelove gutter'.[32] Gradually, many different towns moved towards a more regularized and longer-term, less reactive and less informal, system of maintaining the sanitation infrastructure. In some towns, particular civic officials were held responsible for arranging such maintenance. At the Sheriff's Tourn in Scarborough, in October 1640, the town Chamberlain was apprehended for neglecting his civic responsibility to arrange and fund the maintenance of 'one sinke or comon watter suer nere ajoininge to Mr John Herysons noisome to the kings people'.[33] Building and maintaining sewers was quite a complex operation, requiring fiscal and material resources as well as skilled labour. A record made by Stirling Burgh Council in 1671 demonstrates the complexity of installing a drainage system.

> The hoill [i.e. hole] … wherthrow the said gutter runs presentlie be built upe with stone & lime and a … breastwark of stone be built therat for stopping the current of the said gutter and that a syver [i.e. sewer] be made therat throw beneath the calsey to convoy the same to the meikle dub [i.e. cess pit into which the burgh's sewers drained] and that the said syver … be mendit at the mouth and an Iron grait put theron as was of old, and to be mendit alsoe in the midle wher it is decayed and layed with flags.[34]

Although many sewers in this period were open channels, this drainage system at Stirling featured a 'syver' which was to pass 'throw beneath the calsey' and would have been covered and therefore less noxious.[35] A sewer not only required investment when it was initially constructed. Substantial sums for materials and labour were required to repair and maintain it to ensure that it continued to function efficiently for the benefit of the population. Such sanitation infrastructures were established and maintained throughout the medieval period too, and many communal sewers which helped to drain early modern towns had been installed installed under medieval corporations and councils.

Carlisle Corporation maintained a drainage system of open sewers which ran around the inside of the city walls and down the crown of the main streets to carry liquid waste and rainwater away from dwellings and businesses.[36] Seventeenth-century Carlisle's inhabitants inherited this long-established drainage system from their medieval ancestors. H. Summerson noted that 'conduits' functioned 'to keep the streets clean' throughout the medieval period, having been initially introduced to the city in 1292 by Carlisle's Dominican friars, who 'were licensed in 1238 ... to bring a water conduit under or through the city walls to their house'; by 1292, the friars had successfully 'built "a gutter enclosed in stone" which carried away their refuse'.[37] Indeed, Summerson goes as far as to state that friars were 'in many places ... pioneers in the construction of drainage systems'.[38] Although the Dominicans of Carlisle were required to obtain a licence in 1238 to bring a water conduit through the city, this is unlikely to have marked the construction and installation of the drainage system itself, given that there had been a major Augustinian community attached to Carlisle Cathedral since the 1130s complete with a large-scale water-flushed latrine and drainage system of its own. The need to obtain a written licence in 1238 is far more likely to have resulted from the Dominicans' late integration into the rest of the built environment and the urban infrastructure of the city around this time, at which point they had to bring water to their site through urban dwellers' private land, hence the need for a licence. W. Hutchinson's description brings seventeenth-century Carlisle's watercourses to life vividly.

> The kennels or gutters were deep trenches, and stone bridges were placed in many different parts for the convenience of passing from one side of the street to the other. These gutters were the reservoirs of all kinds of filth, which when a sudden heavy rain happened, by the stopping [of] the conduit of the bridges, inundated the streets so as to render them impassable on foot.[39]

The watercourses had bridges to facilitate pedestrians' clean passage. In 1628, for example, Thomas Barnefather and John Merlan were ordered to 'lye noe more dung or rubbish on the forestreete neare the bridge of Michaell Bleablocke whrebye the water may have passage'.[40]

While major watercourses and sewers were maintained by most town councils, however, a substantial proportion of urban householders were responsible for scouring the section of the street watercourse which flowed before their property, especially those served by the minor channels in lanes and closes. A minority of neighbours neglected to perform this duty and when channels became blocked with sediment, householders had to be prompted to scour them. A formal street inspection of Sandgate in Berwick on Tweed highlighted 'there is a greate slacknes in the officers that sufferithe suche a fowle and noisome Channell to remaine so filthye all alonge Sandegate extendinge frome Bartholomew Bradfurthes house down Thomas Jennysons'.[41] In the spring of 1670, moreover, a Subsidiary Manorial Court held in the small township of Newbottle, County Durham, fined an inhabitant 10s for blocking a sewer.

> We present [Robert Chilton] for altering of the Cundich [i.e. sewer] which formerly went through a barne … through which cundich all the newsencis goe, which now hee hath stopt, and hath turne it into the town street, and then into the Common burne whereby the people of the townshipp cannot take upp cleane water for the use of theire familys without great danger.[42]

Presumably, numerous families complained to the court about Robert's inconsiderate actions, which they perceived as a failure to contribute to the commonweal. These families were bearing water for their family's use, perhaps even to be used for their drinking water, from the burn. In April 1609, Sheffield's Court Leet Jurors made a record which confirms they made householders responsible for maintaining some, if not all, of the town's drainage infrastructure. They recorded:

> a paine laid that Thomas Horner shall scour his ditch after Sisottfield side and keepe the water in the right course that that breake not into the laine at Upperthorpe gate before Penticost next and so to keep the same at all times under pain of 10s.[43]

Similarly, in Macclesfield in 1601, Richard Tayler was presented at the Court Leet because he 'made a diche in Gowsland within this borroughe upon the Queen's Highe Waye to the great annoyance of Leonarde Pott his neighboure, contrary to all goode consiens & equitie'.[44] The use of the words conscience and equity allude to the communal, neighbourly and mutual obligations which underpinned the maintenance of the sanitation infrastructure in the micro-scale urban landscape. In 1606, the Macclesfield Court Leet Jurors presented a father and son, James and Edward Smethweston, 'for turning the water out of the right course and delving downe the water bankes'.[45]

Inhabitants could also be fined for deliberately blocking sewers with solid waste. At Scarborough's Sheriff's Tourn in 1623, for example, Lawrance Welbank was apprehended for 'casting his … fish, beanes, fish gutts & flecher [i.e. butchery] shells in the gutter against Mr Baliff Thompson his garden in the street very noisom to all passers by'.[46] A similar offence was presented at Berwick on Tweed's Bailiffs' Court, in 1593,

We finde and presente a faulte in sufferinge the water and filthe to issue downe frome Castlegate into the ditches without the newgate, for therbye the said ditche is stuffd and gorged upp with mire and filthy gorr to the greatte annoyance of the towne.[47]

Although this offence was presented as a great annoyance of the town, no individuals' names were cited; it was directed as a communal warning to all of the neighbours living in the vicinity of, and therefore contributing to, this nuisance. In 1655, some Glaswegians had to use stepping stones to enter their homes because 'a great abundance of red [i.e. rubbish] ... had fallin in the guitter and stoppit the current of the water'.[48] Glasgow Council ordered the blockage to be cleared to enable clean access to buildings, but again no individuals were named in the presentation of this nuisance. Similarly, in April 1667, Whitehaven's Court Baron threatened a fine of 3s 4d to

William Atkinson and William Grayson or any other persons that hath laid any ashes or Rubish or any sort of durt at Mr Craisters shop ... in or neare the water course that they carrie it away before the 25th day of July next.[49]

Detection of those responsible for creating insanitary nuisances was clearly not always possible.

It is important to appreciate that the majority of householders did not have to be forced to clean their sections of private sewers. Indeed, in October 1668, an inhabitant of Whitehaven approached the Court Baron to reclaim her right to do so.

Elleanor Harris widdow pleintes Ann Lawrence the wife of George Lawrence for hindring and stopping the said Elleanor to goe unto a certaine place on the backside of her house to cleanse the gutter or conduit of water & rubbish as she was anciently accustomed, the stopping whereof is of great annoyance to the said Ellen Harris as she is ready to prove.[50]

It was then 'ordered that Elleanor Harris have liberty to goe through the house of the said An Lawrence to cleanse the water course on the backside of her house'.[51] This case demonstrates explicitly that public sanitation was important to inhabitants, who did not always wait for civic authorities to provide services for them, and that contemporaries were prepared to take action, bottom-up, to uphold the sanitary condition of outdoor spaces themselves. Elleanor's attitudes towards sanitation were only preserved in the documentary record because a problem occurred: she was unable to access the sewer. However, Elleanor represents the majority of urban inhabitants in the period, people who completed their own sanitation duties day after day and did not cause problems for either their urban governors or their neighbours by flouting sanitation bylaws or neglecting communal sanitation duties. Elleanor represents thousands of her counterparts who neither caused nor encountered significant problems in this area of their urban lives, and therefore never entered the records in relation to sanitation. Their steady and uneventful compliance with sanitation bylaws, customs and duties, both formal and informal, underpinned the foundation of sanitation systems as they functioned throughout the period.

In most towns, a minority of residents stored rubbish and muck in inappropriate areas and neglected to remove it regularly. Some town councils provided rubbish dumps for inhabitants to reduce such irregular deposition. In 1673, Bideford's local governors provided thirty 'tobacco hogsheads strongly looped, or some other fit vessels' to be situated around the port to be emptied by the town scavenger.[52] A whole century earlier, Berwick Council, 'for the more comly and cleane kepinge aswell of the stretes as the walles & Rampiers of this towne', ordered inhabitants not to,

> laye or bestowe any of the compost, dust, ashes, or uncleane thinge in any [of] the stretes, or uppon the walles, neither should [they] cast any therof over the walles, but leade or carrye away the same unto suche places as was or shoulde be appointed for the bestoweinge therof wheras poles with baskettes on them have and shoulde be sett.[53]

Presumably, once full, these baskets, erected on poles, which were effectively public rubbish bins, were transported out of town at the corporation's expense. This system continued throughout the seventeenth century. Some burgh councils, while not actually employing street cleaners, still attempted to enhance long-term street cleanliness by placing increasing responsibility upon householders themselves. Councils and corporations tended to work with inhabitants as much as possible towards mutually beneficial ends. Aberdeen's council designed an especially ingenious long-term plan in 1639:

> If any privie be castin doune on the streits or under forestaires, the indwellar in the houssis nixt adjacent thairto salbe obleist [i.e. obliged] to remove the same befoir aught [i.e. eight] houres in the morning, under the paine of foure merks ... and the hous ... out of ... [which the] privie is brocht [i.e. brought], the awnar thairof sall pay ten merks ... the half to the maister of the house wha salbe wrongit, and the other half to the deane of gild.[54]

Aberdeen's system had the potential to be highly effective. To avoid a fine, inhabitants cleared waste which their neighbours deposited carelessly. They were then rewarded for doing so with half of the fine subsequently exacted from the offending neighbour. This system was ingenious because it forced inhabitants to aid the council's endeavours towards enhancing street cleanliness by both removing waste from the streets and informing on careless neighbours. In this order there is a clear sense that maintaining a sanitary standard around one's property was integral to the whole town's commonwealth and to good neighbourly obligations within one's immediate environs. If neighbours had not been concerned about outdoor sanitation, they would have been disinclined to participate in this regulatory system, and indeed the council would probably never have designed it in this way in the first place.

In 1578, at Sheffield Court Leet, it was recorded that Lawrence Shemeld, the wife of Sawood, Thomas Harison and Robert Stanyfurth, a painter, had laid 'certeine Mainor [i.e. manure] or dounge in the hie stretes contrarie to a paine laid' for which they were each fined 4d.[55] That four people were fined in unison suggests that they contributed their respective waste to a common dunghill which they accumulated in one location. Although neighbourhood dunghills could be quite large-scale features used by a large number of households, they could also be much smaller products of only a few people's waste. In June 1612, Perth Council ordered 'the persones … that lies fulyie [i.e. muck] in the north inche [i.e. the burgh muir] to be waidit [i.e. punished]'.[56] If muck was laid in any areas which had not been formally sanctioned as common dunghills, inhabitants were vulnerable to being punished, usually either by the means of the confiscation of their valuable muck or a monetary fine. In 1556, Peebles' councillors ordered 'the middinns to be clengit of the gait' within eight days and, in 1578, Glaswegian councillors ordered 'the haill middins be removit of the hie gait'.[57] Similarly, in 1590, Lanark's council ordered 'all that hes midins' on the street, the market cross, around the market weighing beam or on the tollbooth stairs to arrange for it to be removed.[58] Similarly, in 1677, Inverness Council ordered,

Intimation to be make be towk [i.e. sound] of drum at the mercat cross be two hours this afternoon requiring [and] comanding all the inhabitants that have any middings & dunghills on the Kings hie way betwixt this & the milne burn sall remove the samen within fourtie eight hours under the pain of confiscation of the middings & fineing of the contraveiner at the Magistrats discretion.[59]

Notably, 'confiscation of the middings' often represented a significant amount of monetary value to the owner. That householders were presented at court for neglecting to remove their rubbish from town confirms that in some early modern British towns, even in the late seventeenth century, this task was still explicitly their own responsibility.

What is clear from the above extracts is that cleaning forefronts, removing rubbish and scouring the sewers which coursed along the crowns of thoroughfares was very much a part of everyday urban life in sixteenth- and seventeenth-century British towns. While early modern sewers were sophisticated and useful facilities, their efficiency depended on inhabitants' compliance and care not to place solid waste and rubbish into them and not to interfere with their courses. Each urban settlement developed its own unique arrangements for maintaining a sanitary standard in the outdoor environment, with very different proportions of work carried out by householders and local governors in different urban settlements. Although broad patterns can be discerned, each town's particular systems and processes must be appreciated in their own right in order to understand how they functioned on a daily basis.

York

Introduction

York Corporation also took public sanitation seriously and although the corporation members discussed sanitation issues alongside and in between discussions about other urban issues, they still devoted significant amounts of time, resources and effort into designing, implementing and maintaining processes and systems to keep the streets clean and to remove large volumes of waste and dung from the city. Most of the historians who have studied and commented on York's sanitary condition during the late medieval and early modern periods have tended to paint an unsavoury picture. In 1913, for example, T. Cooper wrote a damning account of the inadequacies of York's public hygiene infrastructure in the medieval period, noting that

> the thoroughfares and byways ... were loathsome and deep with offensive matter ... [the] Corporation delegated the duty of keeping the streets clean to the citizens at large, but as they failed to perform this necessary duty, the streets remained dirty and unkept.[60]

Cooper assumed, on the basis of repetitive sanitation bylaws recorded in York's House Minutes, that all citizens neglected their civic duty to maintain clean forefronts and to remove their rubbish from the city. In 1979, David Palliser offered a similarly vivid and damning, but ultimately imaginative, depiction.

> Cheek-by-jowl with the castle, cathedral, churches, and city walls were narrow, filthy streets of huddled houses and cottages ... The lesser streets and lanes were even narrower, and probably lined with one- or two-roomed hovels ... Both streets and lanes were also much more squalid than can easily be pictured. Repeated corporation orders to cleanse the streets, remove garbage heaps, and drive out scavenging pigs are eloquent enough of normal conditions, and passers-by risked being spattered as chamber-pots were emptied.[61]

Palliser has elaborated on the facts in relation to the government of Tudor York in order to create an artistic, heavily biased and entertaining image for the reader. Palliser's pessimism when describing early modern York as a historian in the late 1970s could well have stemmed from the general urban decay prevalent across the UK and the USA in his own time. In a similar vein, Carole Rawcliffe suggests that the generally negative perspective of the Victorians towards medieval sanitation could have resulted from the 'very poor' conditions which they witnessed in their own contemporary urban slums which had resulted from eighteenth- and nineteenth-century urbanization.[62] Rawcliffe also suggests very convincingly that as the Victorians were 'firmly wedded to the ideals of Empire', they might have 'felt a similar affinity with the Romans, whose achievements in the fields of hygiene and urban planning appeared to cast the limitations of their medieval successors into even sharper relief'.[63]

In 2004, Pamela Hartshorne's in-depth study into York's public spaces between 1476 and 1586 contributed a more realistic interpretation of York's pre-modern sanitation provision, offering a distinctly more sophisticated and professional academic analysis of contemporaries' attitudes towards the sanitary standards of the urban landscape. While waste disposal and insanitary nuisance was not the primary focus of her study, and her research concerns a period which largely precedes this book's chronology, she nevertheless offers some useful and apt observations regarding contemporary conceptions of street cleanliness in the city.

> In streets which were narrow at the best of times, the problem of waste, rubbish and clutter was a perennial one … Contrary to popular belief about the squalor of pre-modern cities, York had an established system for removing filth from public space. The House Books record a consistent concern on the part of the civic authorities to ensure that human and animal excrement, carcasses and butchers' refuse, house and garden rubbish … were removed from public space. The wardmote juries frequently described dunghills as a nuisance, and tried to ensure that they were removed.[64]

Using a markedly different approach to this topic, Hartshorne focused not on the failures of the city's hygiene infrastructure, but rather on the corporation's efforts to improve conditions in the context of simple technology and necessary urban agriculture, and she paid close attention to York's long-established medieval processes and systems for street cleaning and waste disposal.

In 2008, moreover, Dolly Jorgensen conducted an analysis of the management of street cleanliness and drainage in several Scandinavian and English medieval towns, including York, between 1350 and 1550, in which she emphasizes the necessarily co-operative element of managing outdoor sanitation and waste disposal in the context of relatively rudimentary technology, on a practical and daily basis during the period. She argues quite rightly that urban governors' top-down orders could not have functioned successfully without considerable compatibility with inhabitants' bottom-up concerns, and highlights that 'managing uncomplicated technology can be complicated' when its effective functioning relies on householders' daily compliance.[65]

> The effectiveness of medieval sanitation was contingent upon *both* physical maintenance of the technology and cooperation from residents. During the late medieval period some waste in the streets may have been a daily reality, just as littering is today, but streets covered with several inches of refuse do not appear to have been a regular part of urban life. Because of the primitive technologies available … waste disposal had to become a highly social activity in the medieval city, with responsibility for sanitation divided between the government and citizenry.[66]

Jorgensen makes it clear that a positive attitude towards this area of city government and the deep sense of value which contemporaries attached to keeping their cityscape clean, both among York's governors and inhabitants alike, were already well established in the medieval period. This was the inheritance in 1560, not the condescending pictures imaginatively, but unhelpfully, drawn by Cooper and Palliser.

1560–1599

Between 1560 and 1599, York Corporation recorded bylaws and discussions of issues pertaining to waste disposal and environmental regulation in its official house minute books a total of fifty-five times, compared to eighty-two in the first half, and forty-eight in the second half, of the seventeenth century. Such references to this area of city government range from as few as six to as many as twenty-two times in one decade, compared to as few as four and as many as thirty-one per decade in the first half of the seventeenth century, and as few as three and as many as twenty-one in the second half of the seventeenth century. Between 1561 and and 1599, the two largest priorities for the corporation in this area of city government were street cleaning and the disposal of solid waste. The traditional medieval forefront system, whereby householders were required to clean the area before their properties up to the crown of the street, had survived intact throughout the medieval period, and in 1560 it was alive and well. At the beginning of this period, householders were still responsible for arranging the removal of their own rubbish and the removal or sale of their manure from outside their properties as well as for keeping any open sewers and drains pertaining to their properties scoured and flowing efficiently by sweeping them out frequently with water, using simple brooms made from a dense bundle of twigs tied around a central pole which were known as besoms. The constables were responsible for ensuring that all inhabitants carried out this duty with respect to their own property within the bounds of their own parishes at least twice weekly, and this duty applied to private householders, business-owners and guardians of public buildings and institutions, such as the churchwardens of York's many parish churches. In June 1564, for example, the corporation issued a reminder 'to every constable in the Cite and suburbs' of their responsibility to oversee 'the streets and chanells every of theym within ther rowmes [i.e. bounds] cleane swept and clensed with water and besoms' and also that 'all the dung and filth' should be removed every Wednesday and Saturday, ensuring that the constables presented anyone failing to comply under the threat of imprisonment.[67] Those who were presented for failing to carry out those duties in particular were to be fined 10s for the chamberlain's use and this fine was to be exacted from the occupier, whether they owned or rented the property concerned. While the medieval forefront system was clearly still operational, the obvious need to issue reminders to the constables who implemented and maintained this system on the ground out in the parishes suggests that it was perhaps under some strain and in need of modification.

In April 1580, the corporation made an important decision to appoint four scavengers, one for each ward, to clean and remove waste from the streets on Tuesdays, Thursdays and Saturdays, 'all that every man will putt owte at there doores', and to charge inhabitants for this non-negotiable, citywide service.[68] Later in 1580, in October this heavily centralized and markedly different street cleaning and solid waste disposal system, which was designed to reduce the city's reliance on householders' compliance, was developed even further – albeit running alongside rather than actually supplanting the forefront system. It was decided that the 'constables of everie parishe shall collecte and gather the money assessed upon the inhabitants within ther severall parishes for the skavengers', and that this money would be collected twice yearly at the Annunciation and Michaelmas, from 1581 henceforth. In addition to the scavengers receiving 'all the donge and filth for their paines', the constables were 'to pay the skavengers wages'.[69] The scavengers were called John Jackson, William Drinkall, Oswald Chambers and Robert Shearshaw, for Walmgate, Monkward, Bootham and Micklegate wards, respectively, and they began work cleaning the streets and removing rubbish and dung from the streets the following Saturday, before the Sabbath. This marked change in the city's waste disposal was promulgated and explained to inhabitants through the medium of their parish churches.[70] However, this does not mean that York's environmental regulation had a religious dimension. Rather, the parish churches were utilized as practical administrative facilities for the dissemination of important information because large numbers of inhabitants were gathered in these places at one time. Moreover, the use of parish churches as a medium for promulgating regulations reflects the overarching nature of early modern local government and urban management more generally. Today, the announcement of the council's sanitation plans in a church service might seem very obviously incongruous, but these aspects of urban life would have seemed far more complementary in the sixteenth and seventeenth centuries when all aspects of urban life blended together in one overarching melting pot of the 'commonweal'.

The street cleaning system was established with the expectation that inhabitants would leave their rubbish and agricultural dung out at their own doors to be collected by the scavengers on Tuesdays, Thursdays and Saturdays. This method of disposing of most sources of solid waste seems to have been working well. However, it is clear that inhabitants regarded the disposal of human waste in a different way, tending to dispose of it separately and in a very different manner. In May 1583, for example, the corporation issued an order forbidding inhabitants to 'lay, cast or empty any tubbes or other filth in any place within this cittie, but to bury the same in ther owne ground' under the pain of 2s 4d.[71] The 'wardens of every ward' were ordered 'to appoint a convenient place without every barr ... wherein the inhabitants of every ward may lay and put ther tubbes and filth', and in the meantime inhabitants were to be instructed to deposit it at St George's Close.[72] The use of the term 'filth', rather than 'muck' or 'dung', suggests that this pertained to human waste rather than dung or rubbish, but it is impossible to say for certain. Most inhabitants would have deposited their own bodily waste into dry privy pits, hence the reference to burying it on their own ground, but clearly a large number of inhabitants had no such facility and as this was not collected by the scavengers, they must have deposited it in various public places instead. No further records were made in relation to the eventual location of such disposal points, but it is possible that the disposal of human waste in particular was not perceived as a fitting subject for the corporation's official house minute books. The details might well have been decided unofficially between the corporation and the wardens, but not recorded. This would also explain the somewhat ambiguous and implicit references to 'filth' rather than explicitly explaining the difference between the waste collected by the scavengers and the tubs of 'filth' deposited in public places around the city by inhabitants.

Similarly, the house minutes contain minimal references to the provision of public privies, maintained by civic employees. In January 1601, the corporation recorded that 10s 'shalbe given forth of the Chamber to Mr Sheriffe which they paid for clensing of the lowe grate or privie in the womans kidcote'.[73] The women's kidcote was the name of the women's prison in the city, which was situated on Ousebridge and for which the Sheriff was responsible. There was also a public privy in the King's Wall, which was funded by the corporation, but a reference to it in June 1664 suggests that they were trying to prevent 'common' access to it: 'the Company of Tailors and Drapers have liberty to make upp a Crosse wall on the Cittyes ramper to prevent the passage of late made comen to the house of Office in the Kinges wall'.[74] Sixteenth-century Exeter had four public privies: one over the leat channel outside of the West Gate which was established in the fifteenth century, and three more, built in 1568.[75] Although there are minimal references to public privies in the written records, it is highly likely that there were many more private, semi-private and perhaps even fully public privies in the city which never entered the written record. Dry privy pits in backlands might well have been shared in the same way as wells, between designated pairs or larger groups of families who maintained the facilities communally.

Despite the advances made in York's sanitation provision by appointing centrally funded scavengers to remove waste, and despite the constables' efforts to ensure that householders continued to maintain their own forefronts, some locations continued to be used as dumping grounds. In February 1587, for example, an order was issued against dumping waste at the Staith, and Hugh Jenkins was appointed to present and fine anyone who dumped waste in this strategic area henceforth 3s 4d.

> No maner of person ... shall lay ... anye maner of donnge or filth at the Puddinge Hooles or staith or any other place but onelye at the Castle Milnes at the bancke their upon the paine of iij s iiij d to be forefacted for everye offence, thone [i.e. the one] halfe to the Common Chamber, and thother [i.e. the other] halfe to the presenter and that the keeper of the said staith shall present here after from time to time all defaultes which he canne learne of contrary this order upon like paine. And nowe Heughe Jenkins is appointed to present thes offences, and to have the ... fines.[76]

Hugh Jenkins was trusted to enforce this regulation as an informal representative of the corporation, for which he received half of the fines received. In the financial year 1585–1586, moreover, the Chamberlain paid James Allanby and Ralph Magham 5s for 'keping clene the stath & for bringing in coles & turves to the common chamber'.[77] In February and December 1590, and again in February 1593, the corporation issued orders against dumping rubbish in Hungate, seemingly a particularly problematic hotspot for such inconsiderate disposal.[78] Hungate's cleanliness would certainly have suffered from inhabitants' preponderance to drive their cattle down that particularly straight thoroughfare running down towards the River Fosse to allow the cattle to drink from the riverbank at its base. Indeed, the corporation ordered Hungate to be 'clensed by comon dayes worke of the parishes next adjoyning' because 'the inhabitantes have enformed the place to be most convenient for watering ther cattell'.[79] That some individuals continued to dump waste in numerous convenient locations across the city, despite the corporation's efforts to provide citywide systems to remove the potential for this kind of behaviour, demonstrates that there was room for improvement in York's environmental regulation and sanitation systems.

The scavengers continued to clean the main thoroughfares and remove rubbish and dung which had been deposited onto the streets, and the corporation continued to respond to problematic accumulations of waste by making special arrangements to have particular areas cleaned. In November 1590, for example, the inhabitants of two parishes, Allhallows and St Michael's at Ousebridge, were asked to contribute 'towardes the clensinge of the dongehill at Castlegate posterne and the donge in the laine betwene Castlegate and the posterne'.[80] The dung was then taken to the previously appointed place in St George Close. Similarly, in September 1594, the parishes of Monk Ward were ordered by the corporation to remove 'the donge which is laid in the hie waye without monckbarre' and 'the donge in hungat' by means of common day work by all able-bodied people over the age of sixteen years living in the relevant parishes.[81] York Corporation made significant advances in the areas of solid waste disposal and street cleaning, and the appointment of four scavengers surely alleviated much of the burden which had previously been placed on householders' shoulders, but while it certainly helped, it was by no means a comprehensive system and householders' and respective neighbourhoods' responsibility for the cleanliness of streets and other outdoor public spaces continued alongside it. Indeed, a lease on a house, garden and orchard without Monk Bar, issued in 1590, a whole decade after the appointment of scavengers to clean the main thoroughfares three times a week, stipulated that the tenant had 'to maintaine the fences and to repaire and keepe cleane the hiewaye which [is] joininge upon the said gardin and orchard'.[82]

Even if the main thoroughfares were to be cleaned by the scavengers, the responsibility for cleaning smaller lanes and streets rested firmly on householders' shoulders. In June 1593, for example, householders were again reminded of their obligation under pain of 3s 4d to sweepe their dores twise everye weeke viz Satterdaye at night and tewsdaye at night weeklie and that everye one after everye swepinge shall cast downe a soo [i.e. bucket] full of water upon their pavinge and in the guttors to washe and cole the same withall.[83]

Manually flushing the gutters with water was an integral part of cleaning one's forefront, but sweeping solid waste into the gutters was unacceptable, as the corporation emphasized in a forefront order in September 1594 under the pain of 12d.

To clense all the stret myer & other such like annoyances forth of the stret & channells every one so farr as his tent [i.e. property front] extendith & not [to] swepe any of the same either in or after any shoure [i.e. shower] or at any other time downe the chennell towardes the grate at the southend of Fossebridge nether to suffer any thing to discend downe the said chennells towardes to [the] said grate but only water.[84]

In July 1598, the corporation ordered the city's constables to pay workers to sweep inhabitants' forefronts for them, if they refused to do so, after 'haveinge reasonable warninge to doe the same' and to charge them for the work done.[85]

The next most frequently discussed issue pertaining to environmental regulation was the problematic and perennial public nuisance of free roaming livestock. In July 1565, for example, the corporation renewed an ancient ordinance 'ageinst keping of iiij foted bestes upon the common moates', by which they meant the moats which ran inside and outside of the city walls which were dry for most of the year, thus providing an open space on which livestock could be grazed.[86] In December 1575, the corporation passed the following bylaw ordering householders to bind their swine securely in direct response to this nuisance having arisen as a significant issue at the recent wardmote court and sessions of the peace:

Diverse citizens that kepith swine and lets them run abroade in the streets not onely to the great noysance, but also against the speciall charg geven at the Warde Mote Courts and Sessions holden within the said Cittie; for reformacon wherein it is now agreed that it shalbe lawfull to anie the officers at mace to my Lord Mayor and to the Sheriffs sergiants and also to the constables to take anie swine of anie citizen that they finde abroade in the streets except they be or goe to the market place to be sold and the same swine so taken they shall impound in the common fold of that ward wherein the said swine shalbe taken.[87]

Once the swine were confiscated, they were 'saiflie kept unto suche time as he or they the owners' paid the officer 6s 9d.[88] In June 1589, the corporation delegated the responsibility of punishing inhabitants who failed to bind their swine properly to the Searchers of the Occupation of Butchers, who were allowed to retain half of any fines received.[89] Similarly, in October 1598, the

Tipstaves were given authority to punish those whose swine roamed freely through the city and in the suburbs.[90] The successive efforts taken by the corporation to curtail and regulate the nuisance of free roaming livestock in the late sixteenth century suggests that unbound livestock was causing significant problems in the city during this period.

Dirty trades did not cause particularly significant problems in late-sixteenth-century York. The references to dirty trades in this period are to soap-boiling, butchery and lime-burning. In January 1584, Giles Howland was admitted to perform the craft of soap-boiling in the city, with the preventative warning that if Giles 'shall happen to do any act or thinge in or by selling and boiling the said sope that shall by any meanes be thought and judged by the Lord Mayor and Aldermen to be hurtfull to the cittizens' then the act was to 'be void and of none effect'.[91] This is evidence of a distinctly proactive, rather than reactive, approach to environmental regulation and to limiting the negative impact of dirty trades on inhabitants' life quality. The use of the word 'hurtfull' is revealing in that it suggests a link between regulating dirty trades and protecting inhabitants' health and wellbeing, almost as if malodours could physically hurt a person's body. In August 1585, to reduce the malodorous impact of butchery, one location in each ward was set aside specifically for the burial of butchery waste: the lane beside Bowbridge in Micklegate ward; the street without Fishergate in Walmgate ward; at Fosse side beside Monkbridge in Monk ward; and in 'some owte corner in the Horsefair' in Bootham ward.[92] This is evidence of a proactive attempt to organize how the city disposed of its waste on a practical level in order to make it more efficient.

The overwhelming majority of references to this area of city government recorded in the house minutes between 1560 and 1599 were recorded in the 1580s and 1590s (73 per cent), and far fewer were recorded in the 1560s and 1570s. Of course, the waste disposal systems and processes referred to during this period were not designed from scratch in 1560, by which point many long-established systems were already in operation, and had been functioning efficiently in the city for centuries. But in the last four decades of the sixteenth century, these traditional, inherited systems were modified and became increasingly organized, more centralized and less reliant on inhabitants' compliance. The corporation seems to have instigated these improvements intentionally as a direct response to the modest population rise strongly indicated by the estimates in Figure 2.

1600–1650

Between 1600 and 1650, issues pertaining to waste disposal and environmental regulation were recorded in the house minutes a total of eighty-two times, ranging from as few as four to as many as thirty-one in one decade. Most references were made in the 1610s, 1630s and 1640s and far fewer were made between 1600 and 1610 and in the 1620s. The corporation discussed this area of city government significantly more than they did either in the last four decades of the sixteenth century or in the latter half of the seventeenth century. During this half century, waste disposal and environmental regulation attracted significant levels of focused attention from York's local governors. As in the late sixteenth century, the most frequently recorded issues within this area of city government were the disposal of solid waste and street cleaning. During this period, the corporation began to discuss such issues in a distinctly far more serious tone, and in relation to matters of public health, explicitly connecting the constables' failure to ensure inhabitants carried refuse and dung away and swept their forefronts, and the consequent accumulations of waste and dirty streets in the city, with the increased threat of plague epidemics. This is an important discontinuity in the corporation's attitude towards environmental regulation and waste disposal and surely resulted from the fact that York suffered from three plague epidemics, in 1604, 1631 and 1645. That this area of city government was not only discussed more frequently at council meetings but also in a far more serious tone in the early seventeenth century was a direct response to the plague epidemics.[93]

In March 1600, the corporation called 'diverse Constables' into the Mayor's court 'for not causing ther persons to swepe ther dores wekely & to cary the heapes & myer away'.[94] The constables responded to the accusation that they were failing in their duty by explaining 'that they have sundry times given warning which hath bene lightly regarded and that they cannot get them to clense the same in dewe time'.[95] Nevertheless, the corporation 'feared that if the same be no better clensed when warm wether comes [in] June then it hath bene this winter time that infeccion maye growe therby', and issued harsher warnings that defaulters of this obligation would be referred to the wardens of their ward and committed to ward and 'ther so remaine till the same be clensed & during the pleasure of the said wardon'.[96] If, however, it was found that the constable was at fault, rather than the inhabitant, he would have been committed to ward instead. This record is distinctly different from those of the late sixteenth century. There is an unmistakable fear of infection and an unambiguously serious tone and sense of panic. Clearly, impending hot weather and the perceived fear of malodours and miasma was a major motivating factor in passing this bylaw.

Only one month later, in April 1600, the corporation recorded a similarly serious order regarding accumulations of waste and dung in Hungate. The Sheriff made arrangements for Hungate to be cleaned, yet again, but they were not simply reacting to the problem; this time, they attempted to prevent its recurrence in the future proactively. They threatened to fine inhabitants who disposed of waste in Hungate henceforth 5s for 'every soofull or tubbe full' and even threatened that inhabitants who flouted the prohibition of dumping waste in Hungate would 'be ponished in the pavement stockes'.[97] This order was promulgated through the medium of the constables and the parish churches, emphasizing to the constables 'to go thorowe your parish from howse to howse and give particuler notice herof to all housholderis in the same parishe' and to 'deliver this note to your Curate whom I require to publishe the same to thair parishioners in yor church on sondaye next when most resorte of the same shalbe ther'.[98] Again, the serious tone and the harsher punishments resulted from the threat of plague, as they elaborated that Hungate's insanitary condition is not onlye verye noysome to the quenes subjectes … aswell in ther passage by filth under fote as by straitininge ther waie but also the same is greatlie to be feared to brede infeccon in that parte of this Cittie when the wether shall growe warmer.[99]

The corporation realized that by prohibiting waste disposal in Hungate, they would simply transplant the problem to another location, so they planned instead to find another place in which inhabitants could dispose of their waste, and to use the Postern Close in Lathrop until a suitable location could be found.

In March 1603, in preparation for James VI and I's visit to the city in April as he united the English and Scottish Crowns by travelling from Edinburgh to establish his new combined Anglo-Scottish court in London, the corporation ordered a general clean up 'for the more Bewtefyinge of this Cittie'.[100] This included the removal of all dunghills and filth and the constables were ordered to make a special effort to ensure that inhabitants cleaned and paved their forefronts. During the plague epidemic of 1604, there is no record of any extra street cleaning or waste removal in direct response to it, but inhabitants were warned either to kill or to confine to their houses all dogs and cats, which were believed to be instrumental in spreading plague between humans.[101] Despite previous repeated efforts to deter inhabitants from dumping rubbish at 'the staith', the corporation still had to appoint a man called James Sidgewick 'to watch and loke unto all suche as do lye anie filth or donge at the staith and to present unto my Lord maior for the time beinge all such as shall offend therin'.[102] As chapter four demonstrates, this particular location was a very popular place at which to dump one's waste.[103] The picture conjured up by the repeated orders against dumping rubbish in public places is one of flagrant disregard for the urban environment by the majority of inhabitants and a chaotic urban landscape in which there was a distinct lack of organization in relation to waste disposal. However, while a minority of inhabitants dumped their rubbish in inconvenient places and caused significant problems for the corporation by blocking thoroughfares with waste and creating insanitary nuisances which reduced the quality of their neighbours' daily lives, many more disposed of waste in an organized and careful manner. Had this not been the case, the city could not have functioned.

Dung was an incredibly valuable asset in this early modern city and inhabitants went to great lengths to preserve it for sale. Within each neighbourhood, there were informal, small-scale systems for disposing of waste, which functioned from the bottom upwards. In October 1610, for example, the corporation discussed the future of a communal midding in Bootham Ward because its previous owner, Percival Wilson, had died. For permitting his neighbours to pile their dung on his land, the city had paid him 3s 4d each year, 'be sides the dunge' which could be sold.[104] Unfortunately this council record does not detail how long this arrangement had been in existence, but it seems to have been quite a long-established system, which undoubtedly was replicated across the city, and it only features in the council record as a result of his death and the need to renew this contract for the future. Seemingly, Percival's widow was unwilling to continue the contract:

wheras the saide percivall wilson wife after her husband death refused to kepe the same in suche sorte and upon suche Condicons as Mr Thomas Jackson and Mr Robte Askwith Aldermen two of the wardons of Bowthome warde did thinke fitt.[105]

Therefore the contract was passed to 'George Chapman officer of the same warde' who was 'from hensforth dureing the pleasure of this Court [to] have all suche dunge as shall hereafter be laide on the same place', under the provison that

he do cause the strete or Cawsey ther to be Clean kept and do repaire from time to time the Cawsey or strete from thend of the buildinge of Sir William hildyard knight howse unto the river of Owse and also do kepe Cleane the Comon hall layne.[106]

This dunghill contract renewal, which only entered the record unusually due to Percival's death and his wife's subsequent refusal to continue the arrangement with the corporation, provides a fascinating insight into the ways in which dunghills functioned in the neighbourhoods of York at this time. There were surely many other similar arrangements made across the city, such as the arrangement made by the corporation in September 1627 with George Chapman, to have 'the benefit of a peece of ground lying without Munckbar beyond a garden of Tristrams langwiths for manure to ly in the same'.[107] Very similarly, in October 1649, Cuthbert Carr, a Gentleman of Hexham in Northumberland, granted to Mathew Armstrong, a Chapman also of Hexham, eight yards of ground 'now used for a dungehill', situated next to a house belonging to William Hutchinson on the east and a 'channel or gutter upon the north and south', which was known as a 'middinge steade', at the annual rent of 6d.[108] Such arrangements suggest that the disposal of dung was not always as chaotic as the repeated orders in the council record suggest. Such orders concern only the minority of inhabitants who disposed of waste inconsiderately; the majority of informal, micro-scale waste disposal systems were not written into the record, so long as such arrangements continued without problems.

Similarly, the equipment used to clean the streets is rarely mentioned in the records. The corporation recorded that they were considering whether 'it be ftting to hang a doole [i.e. shovel] at the end of the land adjoyning to Mr Hudsons house leading out of fossegate into hungate or to hier one to sweepe the same'.[109] This suggests that the provision of communal equipment with which to clean the streets, even an item as simple as a shovel hanging on a wall, may well have been common in the city. Clearly, such equipment could be costly, hence the corporation's debate over whether to hire or purchase the shovel. This perhaps explains why it was provided on a communal basis. Both the ephemeral nature of items such as besoms, essentially a collection of twigs attached to a central pole, and the potentially widespread provision of communal items such as shovels would explain the lack of such equipment in the inventories of individual households. Clearly, inhabitants had the means to clean their houses and streets, but they may well have used ephemeral or communal equipment to do so.

Much of the city's dung was transported out to the surrounding rural areas to be used as fertilizer. Not all such dung was transported out of the city by the scavengers and by individual householders, however, because some local farmers found it worthwhile to travel into the city to collect the dung and transport it to their arable lands themselves. However, in September 1632, the corporation prohibited the practice of transporting dung out of Monk Bar because 'the waines coming for & carrying away the same doe much breake downe & hurt the causeys leading betwixt the same barre & monck bridge'.[110] Presumably the corporation perceived the consequent disposal problem as having been easier to deal with than the damage caused by the transportation of the dung out of the city. However, in December 1644, proper arrangements were made for the transportation of the city's muck to the surrounding countryside. Several aldermen were ordered to meet and

> sett downe what waines [i.e. carts] they thinke fitting to come in from every Towne about the Citty to fetch and cary away the manure in the severall places of the Citty and at what times & to what places and to appoint some to see them leaden.[111]

What was decided at this meeting, presuming that it did take place, was never recorded in the house minutes, but the plans were not necessarily scrapped. A plan may well have been confirmed unofficially and deliberately left out of the records due to the unsavoury nature of the topic.

Instead of continually repeating top-down orders to deter inhabitants from dumping rubbish in particular public areas, and threatening increasingly severe punishments and fines, the corporation was receptive to inhabitants' suggestions to take proactive action to prevent such problematic waste disposal in the future. In August 1633, for example, Mr Blanshard requested that he have a lock and key for the door of the lane adjoining his house in Coney Street, in which inhabitants were continually dumping their rubbish, so that he could control who entered the lane and thereby reduce the accumulation of waste next to his home, which was 'very noisome to the neighbours & passengers that way'.[112] The corporation granted him this request.

> The request of the said Mr Blanshard that he the said Mr Blanshard shall have a lock and key of the doore of the said lane, and shall every day open the same at sunrising and keep the same open till sun setting for the Citizens and neighbours to have egresse and regresse to carry and recarry water and other things (except dung and manure). And that if any of them doe marr or spoile the same at any time with Carriage of any thing through the same, then the same persons to dresse and make the same cleane againe. And that nether Mr Blanshard nor any other shall ly any dung or manure there att all.[113]

This is an insightful example of an inhabitant's concern about the cleanliness of his micro-scale environment and it proves that inhabitants did not wait passively for the corporation to take action to improve the sanitary condition of their neighbourhoods, but that they were prepared to approach their local governors with suggestions to make well-considered changes which would improve the quality of their daily lives. This arrangement was modified slightly in September 1638, however, when the Mayor had a key cut for himself.

> There shalbe another key made for the lock of the doore of the same lane and allwayes left in my lord Maiors custody that hee may give leave in his discrecon to Cittizens or others to carrie dung or manure or any thing els downe the same lane to lead into catches or other vessels to carrie the same away by water soe that they make the lane cleane againe when they have done.[114]

Clearly, the mayor did not take this action exclusively to undermine Mr Blanshard's independence in this matter, and he was not trying to overturn his idea completely, but rather he was ensuring that inhabitants could still access the boats which carried their waste away, in order to ensure that inhabitants did not instead dump their dung elsewhere.

It is clear that some of York's dung left the city by water. Indeed, a record made in January 1640 noted the arrangements made for 'getting the manure in Hundgate removed and carried to the Taighall and there spread and provide men and boates for carrying the same away'.[115] Hungate continued to function as a magnet for the city's manure. In January 1641, arrangements were made, yet again, to clear the manure away by means of common day work by Walmegate and Monkgate wards. In February 1644, moreover, a party was sent to 'veiw hungate and also the garthes and grounds thereabouts and Consider of sume good Course for removing the manure in hungate into some of those grounds or otherwayes as they thinck fit'.[116] The following month, two orders were issued prohibiting dumping dung in Hungate under the pain of 5s.[117] By June 1646, the problem had still not been resolved, and yet another party was sent to 'view the lane leading from Hodgerlane to Hungate and advise with the inhabitantes adjoining upon that lane and take order either by hanging a doore or otherwise how it may be kept cleane'.[118] Physically barring inhabitants from entering the area was far more proactive, and seems to have been the only means of solving this particular problem in the context of ineffectual fines. The Mintyard was also a problematic area in which inhabitants tended to dump waste and in May 1645 the wardens of Bootham Ward were sent to

> see what fulture & dung lyes in the Mintyard & Consider of a way for removing theireof & for the preventing of the lyeing any more theirein … the same being very noisome to the inhabitants neare that place & of daingerous consequence in respect of the smell theirof to the citty.[119]

The smell of the dung was clearly a major motivating factor for removing it. That they used the word dangerous implies that the councillors literally feared the consequences of inhaling such malodours.

It is important to remember that the nuisances which appeared in the house minutes were by definition noteworthy and unusual and the great majority of inhabitants disposed of their waste carefully and conducted their crafts and trades considerately in the city without ever attracting the corporation's attention. Moreover, the scavenger system functioned efficiently throughout the early seventeenth century, at least to the extent that no problems were recorded in the house minutes, and the scavengers continued to be appointed in each ward and paid by the chamberlain. However, inhabitants continued to be held responsible for their own forefronts and this medieval and early modern system continued alongside citywide, centrally funded street cleaning efforts. Churchwardens were similarly responsible for the street before their church, their forefront, and they could be fined in the same way as householders could be fined, for neglecting their obligation to clean their forefront and to remove waste from it. In 1643, for example, the churchwardens of St Michael's Church paid Matthew Lealman 1s 8d for 'sweeping & caring away the manure in the Church yeard'.[120] In the disbursements of 1644 for the parish of St Trinity's parish in Goodramgate, moreover, constables James Wilson and Thomas Fawcitt paid 1s 6d 'to two men for burying of dead horses & for aile to them before they went to bury them' and they paid 1s 4d 'to two men to helpe clence the bar steed'.[121]

While most householders did not keep detailed account books as churchwardens did, and private homes were not as large and therefore had much smaller forefronts, some householders might well have paid someone other than their own household servants to clean the street for them, especially wealthier, high status householders. The duty was to ensure that the forefront remained clean, not to actually clean it oneself. A Newcastle upon Tyne bylaw, passed by the River Tyne Court appointed by Newcastle Corporation in 1613, stipulated that all servants living very close to the river, in Gateshead, Sandgate and the Close, had to swear in court annually that they would not cast rubbish into the river.[122] For example, in February 1647, 'the inhabitants of Pipewellgate [in Gateshead] sent in their servants' who were sworn in court 'not to prejudice the river [Tyne] with solid waste'.[123] Servants were typically responsible for waste disposal in most other towns too, but most of them, certainly servants living in contemporary Carlisle, Edinburgh, Berwick, Bristol and York, were not presented in court for contravening waste disposal bylaws in their own right; their heads of households were presented and fined on their behalves. For example, in April 1629, the Bristol Court Leet presented Richard Balman, a brewer, 'for suffering his servants usually to bringe forth much durt and throwing it in the channel to the offence of his neighbours'.[124] Balman's rather dubious defence of this presentment was to make an accusation that 'the jurie went about like rogues and fooles to present they know not what'.[125] Unusually, then, servants living around the Tyne estuary were made responsible for their own actions, which must surely have improved the efficacy of environmental regulation. Notably, households lacking servants were represented by either the householder's wife or widow who swore the oath alongside neighbouring servants. This proactive bylaw demonstrates that proactively protecting the River Tyne from rubbish was the priority and raising fines was merely a resultant byproduct of that regulation.

In York, while the nuisance of free roaming livestock was not as much of an issue between 1600 and 1650 as it had been throughout the previous four decades, it was still discussed. In March 1614, for example, the corporation discussed the city's fortnightly sheep and cattle market, which had traditionally been held in Walmegate 'for divers yeres past', but significant obstruction problems were caused by

> the great inconvenience of that place, for all the somer season, not onely be reason of the want of feldes and convenient roomes to place sheep and Cattell in, but also the strait waies and passages through which ... droves of Cattell must of necessity have ther waye.[126]

Notably, the waste produced by the standing sheep and cattle is not mentioned in the minutes; rather, the physical obstruction in Walmegate seems to have been of utmost concern. Despite complaints from 'Lord Wharton and other the knights gentlemen & substanciallest inhabitants' that the 'cattell that are brought unto the same faire do come from the forrest side and of that parte of the countie which to drive through this citty wold be verie troblesome', the corporation decided to continue holding the fair in Walmegate, 'being a large strete wher many poore cittizens do dwell which is a great benefitt unto them'.[127] Perhaps the waste produced by these animals was also an issue, but it was omitted from the minutes. Despite the obstructive nuisance caused by this market, the corporation decided to allow its continuance because of its economic benefit to poor city dwellers who relied on it for their livelihoods.

In March 1616, moreover, the corporation issued an order reminding inhabitants to keep their 'kine, swine and masty [i.e. mastiff] dogs ... upp in ther howses and not suffer them to goe into the strets dureing the time of the King his highnes being in this citty'.[128] This order confirms that free roaming livestock was still a nuisance, but also that King James I and VI's forthcoming visit to the city was the major motivating factor for this effort to suppress the nuisance, rather than inhabitants' daily life quality and the salubrity of the city's environment. Another very similar order, passed in May 1633, forbidding inhabitants to allow their 'kine swine or mastive dogs to come within the streetes of this Citty' was passed in preparation for Charles I's visit to the city.[129] This does suggest that suppressing the nuisance of free roaming animals was motivated more so by the desire to impress prestigious visitors rather than by the aspiration to improve public health. Free roaming animals threatened to undermine the image of a civil and well-governed city, and could not be permitted to pollute the pageant of civilized urban life in front of the reigning monarch.

The movement of livestock from within the city to places where they could be pastured was managed closely, and this task was delegated to four pasture masters, one for each ward. In September 1627, for example, it was ordered that the pasturemaister of Micklegateward shall veiwe what passage is made for the cattell of that warde to passe thorough a little close of Alder Heinsworth … and if there be not a sufficient way then to take downe one of the railes that goe through.[130]

And, in September 1631, the following order was passed.

The kine that goe to the Common shall continue to goe still, and that the owners shall carry them themselves to the barr, and that then a hirde [i.e. herdsman] to be chosen at St Micheles shall drive them to the Comon and bring them back againe to the barr at night & then leave them that the owners may fetch home every one his owne. And all the milk maides to be stained and stopped at the barr that they goe not forth to milk.[131]

It is clear from this order that while a minority of livestock, especially swine, did cause a nuisance when they broke free and wandered at large through the city, the movement of the majority of livestock, especially larger beasts such as cattle, was closely managed. The corporation employed junior officials such as pasture masters and herds to manage this aspect of daily life in the city.

Dirty trades were also much less of an issue in this period than in the preceding four decades, though cloth-bleaching, soap-boiling and butchery waste were all raised and discussed briefly in council meetings during this period. Waste disposal and environmental regulation were discussed significantly more frequently in the early seventeenth century than they were either in the preceding four decades or in the subsequent half century. Both the distinctly more serious tone of the discussions which took place in the first half of the seventeenth century and the link between dirt and public health indicate that the heightened concern and increased efforts on the part of the corporation resulted from the three plague epidemics which occurred in the city in 1604, 1631 and 1645.

1651–1700

Between 1651 and 1700, issues pertaining to waste disposal and environmental regulation were recorded in the house minutes a total of forty-eight times, significantly fewer than the number recorded in the first half of the seventeenth century. This does not necessarily imply, however, that concern over the environment decreased after the threat of plague had receded. It may well have simply required relatively less attention because the systems and processes in place were functioning more efficiently. Furthermore, while plague was not to strike the city again, the overhanging threat that it would remained present throughout this period.

Street cleaning dominated the corporation's discussion of this area of city government during this period, though waste disposal was also discussed quite frequently. The threat of plague shaped environmental regulation and the corporation's discussion of sanitation well into this period. In February 1652, for example, a preamble to a reminder to inhabitants to sweep their forefronts is dominated by the threat of plague and the link between dirty streets and disease is explicit.

> For the better preventinge of sicknesses & diseases occasioned by the noysomnes of streets; it is ordered ... that the inhabitants of this citty doe cause the streets before there houses yards and orchards to be swept once at the least every weeke, and the durt to be fourth with removed and the church wardens to doe the like against the church & church yards upon paine of 3s 4d.[132]

The corporation might not have understood complex germ theories, but their orders to rid the streets of noisome smells, which they believed spread disease, was positive, proactive and progressive in the minds of the men who designed them. In March 1655, moreover, the officers of the wards were ordered, yet again, to ensure that inhabitants swept and cleansed their forefronts every Saturday afternoon, and every Monday morning they submitted a report of everyone who neglected to perform this civic duty.[133] Another reminder of this bylaw was issued in December 1660.[134] The repetition of these orders over 140 years does give the impression that they were ineffectual, but they were bound to require repetition several times over the course of such a lengthy time period. The repetition once every five years or so of bylaws which ordered inhabitants to clean their forefronts on a weekly basis is not excessive. Rather than suggesting that the corporation failed to regulate the environment, such infrequent repetition actually proves the opposite. The fact that the mayor took the decision to manage this element of street cleaning weekly, by means of a report of contraveners every Monday morning, does not mean that the system was weak and ineffectual, but rather than the corporation was making significant efforts to monitor and manage the system much more closely and centrally.[135]

Just as in the period 1600 to 1650, many inhabitants took ownership of and responsibility for the disposal of their manure onto common dunghills conveniently near to their homes. Inhabitants continued to dump their rubbish and manure at places which were most convenient to them, even in explicit contravention of city bylaws. In September 1654, for example, a small party of three council officials were sent to survey 'the waiste peece of ground at staith', a particularly problematic area on the River Ouse near at which inhabitants continually dumped their waste, despite repeated bylaws against such behaviour. The solution to this continuing problem was simply to accept inhabitants' need to deposit their waste at this obviously convenient location, but to 'give order for making a wall aboute it for the inhabitants to lay there manure in'.[136] This does not infer that the corporation simply gave in to the inhabitants, or gave up on improving the city's sanitation, but rather that they accepted inhabitants' bottom-up influence in a mutually productive manner by officializing their informal actions. In this case, the corporation decided to work with the inhabitants, instead of trying to force them top-down to dispose of waste where they thought fit. In November 1664, the corporation allowed yet another informal dunghill to become an officially recognized one by building a wall around the area which inhabitants were already using as a common dunghill:

> the place where the manure lyeth neare Munckbarr ... be continued to that use for a comon dunghill and that the wardens of the ward ... doe bounder the same and George Francke officer of that ward is to take care that the dunghill there be kept ... upp and hee to have the benefit thereof.[137]

And in February 1667, the corporation decided that William Smalicker, whose job it was to clean the staith, was given the benefit of 'one halfe of the manure which is or shall be laid at the midden place at the east end of the staith ... provided that hee keep the high way cleane'.[138] In May 1675, moreover, a similar arrangement was made in Hungate where inhabitants had been dumping their manure for decades, if not for centuries. The corporation stopped fighting against the inhabitants' chosen waste disposal method and instead facilitated and accommodated it. In Hungate, the corporation ordered that a 'wall be built at the citties charge upon that part of ground lately bought of Mrs Slinger for lyeinge soile in, in Hungate'.[139] However, an order passed in March 1682, ordering the 'wardens of every ward doe meete and consider of convenient places for every ward for lyeinge manure compost & dirt in and make there report thereof', suggests that the several places which had been provided for the deposition of manure were not sufficient and that the facilities in place were far from comprehensive.[140] An order passed in December 1691 confirms that dumping rubbish and dirt in public spaces which had not been designated for waste disposal continued to be a problem towards the end of the seventeenth century. In December 1691, for example, it was ordered that

> Thomas Wilson be appointed to informe ... this courte of such persons as lay any dirt, gravell or rubbish in the highway out of Monkbarr without licence of the wardens and that my Lord Mayor appointe three other persons for the high wayes out of the other barrs. The penalty for soe doeing is twelve pence per loade.[141]

However, this order suggests that inhabitants at least showed a degree of consideration. Inhabitants might have perceived making the effort to carry waste to outside of the walls to dispose of it, or to locations such as Hungate or the staith, as having been less inconsiderate and potentially less problematic than dumping it in a narrow street or a marketplace nearer to their home. Contemporaries certainly did not dump their rubbish in a completely careless manner with no regard at all for the problems which such action might subsequently cause for their neighbours or themselves. It is clear from the existence of hotspots for waste disposal and from the tendency to dump waste outside of the walls that inhabitants put at least some thought into where they dumped their waste, even when it was in sharp contravention of a bylaw of which they had been made explicitly aware when it had been promulgated in their parish churches. It is possible that inhabitants bore in mind their economic interests in keeping the city thoroughfares flowing, presenting an unoffensive environment for prestigious visitors or not creating inconvenience for their neighbours, broadly conceptualized as the 'commonweal', when they purposely disposed of waste outside of, rather than inside of, the city walls or at disposal hotspots.

The transfer of valuable manure to local arable farmers continued to be closely regulated. In March 1655, for example, 'the Bailiffe of the Augistie' was ordered to

> give notice to severall husbandmen in the Augustie townes within 4 miles that they are desired ... to lead the manure out of the Hungate to their owne grounds which otherwayes [i.e. otherwise] is like to be noisome in hott wether.[142]

The corporation wanted to ensure that the muck was transported in March before the temperature increased subsequently, which would have increased the nuisance of the muck's malodour as it was transported by these local farmers. This infers that the maximum viable catchment area to which a farmer was prepared to carry manure from York was probably about four miles. Since the manure trade was conducted on a largely oral basis, details such as the extent of viable catchment areas have been effectively lost from history. The minutes recorded between 1600 and 1650 revealed that previously the city's manure had been carried, as a matter of course, to the riverside at the bottom of Hungate and piled onto boats to be taken down the river to arable land. Clearly, these arrangements continued into the latter half of the seventeenth century, alongside horse-drawn transportation out of the city by local farmers. In May 1673, it was 'ordered that Mr William Clarke have 4 li yearely abated him of his rent for Tenghall provided hee build a boate for carrying of manure to the said Ground'.[143] Tang Hall was a hall situated in parkland at Heworth, a village which was and still is part of the city of York. It is located only one mile to the north-east of York city centre and would have contained plentiful arable land in need of manure to be used as fertilizer. This area provided an excellent means of disposing of the city's manure, at the cost of 4 li per year in lost rent in return for William Clark's labour in building a boat for the muck's carriage along the River Fosse to the point where Heworth pastures met the river. In this case, York Corporation was effectively paying to have the city's manure removed, rather than selling it as a valuable fertilizer. Although fiscal investment was needed in order to build a boat to facilitate the transportation of the muck, this case underlines the fact that the urban to rural manure trade functioned in a variety of different ways from one urban settlement to another and that even within one town or city multitudinous arrangements could be used simultaneously. In May 1675, inhabitants were ordered to carry their dirt to 'such places only as the wardens of the severall wards ... shall thinck fitt' to allow for 'carrying the same away' to the surrounding countryside.[144] Aided by improved methods for removing muck from the city, the scavenger system continued to function well. Towards the end of the period, in February 1696, the corporation awarded 'William Cooke the Citys Scavenger' an extra 20s to his salary.[145] Unfortunately, it did not mention whether this was to compensate him for having taken on extra duties, but it can be safely assumed that the scavenger system must have been working well and that Wiliam Cook, at least, must have been doing a good job. Extra tasks continued to be assigned to various inhabitants, however, if and when extra work was required, such as in July 1674, when the Chamberlain paid 3s 4d to George Hobson 'for buyinge a shovell & skuttle [i.e. a dustpan and brush] for carryinge dirt from Botham Barr & clenseinge the same'.[146] And, in January 1674, 'the labourers imployed about carryinge away the manure in Hungate' were paid 3 li 10s.[147]

The issue of free roaming livestock was far less pronounced in this period than it had been previously, either in the late sixteenth century or, albeit to a lesser extent, than it had been in the first half of the seventeenth century. In February 1673, it was

> ordered that Mr Thompson shall not use the stable in the comon hall yard as a stable for the same appears to be noisome to the houses thereabouts & prejudiciall to the laine & if he shall make use of it as a stable he shall not be admitted to take a new lease of the house there.[148]

Despite the strategic importance of horse-powered transportation and the necessity of stabling horses in the city, the malodorous smell of stables had the potential to reduce the quality of inhabitants' daily lives. In this case, the rights of the inhabitants of the 'houses thereabouts' took precedence over Mr Thompson's need to stable horses in a previously empty stable in the Common Hall yard. In 1560, a similar request might well have been granted.

Dirty trades were far less of an issue in this period, but they still caused some problems which had to be discussed in council meetings. In November 1675, it was ordered that 'part of the pavement where rabbits are commonly sold be cleansed as the rest of the pavement is at the publiq charge and that such as doe sell rabbits there stand within the range of the markett'.[149] Similarly, in August 1689, the corporation ordered that the 'Searchers of the Butchers take care to sweep the Thursday Markett thrice every weeke where the calves stand or else the Court will take it into consideracon to remove the same into another place'.[150] Clearly, the waste produced by the calves was unpleasant and offensive. The waste, having accumulated to significant levels over the course of the market, had to be cleared away after the market and the ground had to be cleaned. Time and again, the corporation prioritized urban salubriousness over economic production. By the end of the seventeenth century, the city governors' environmental regulation was in a characteristically different league compared to that carried out by their forebears between 1560 and 1600. According to Peter Borsay, English provincial towns underwent a collective 'urban renaissance' in the eleven decades following the Restoration of the monarchy in 1660, which amounted to nothing less than a 'wider economic, social and cultural revival'.[151]

Although he admits that the English process was 'small fry' compared to the great Italian renaissance, he nevertheless asserts that 1660 marked the point at which the 'gloom began to lift' and when there was a 'widespread rise in living standards', leaving behind scenes of the mid-seventeenth century, when apparently 'the visual appearance of provincial towns must have seemed generally undistinguished and in some cases even shabby'.[152] In York, there was a substantially increased drive, between 1660 and 1700, to improve the efficiency of sanitation services, the organization of waste disposal and environmental regulation. Regarding urban problems such as sanitation, Borsay claims that although much of the progress achieved after 1660 was negated by 'mounting strain' that nevertheless 'substantial advances were made due to a new sense of inventiveness and purposefulness in tackling the problems that existed'.[153] While Borsay goes too far by suggesting that pre-1660 towns were visually 'shabby', the language of the minute books did change in the late seventeenth century, reflecting a different and more progressive attitude towards sanitation. The corporation appointed investigative committees more often and there is an unmistakable urgency in the language of discussions about environmental regulation. There were innovations and modifications throughout the period 1560 to 1700, as well as a significant numerical surge in the corporation's discussions about sanitation in the first half of the seventeenth century. However, increasingly towards the end of the seventeenth century, there was a distinctly different, increased motivation to eradicate insanitary nuisances quickly, which may well have been born out of the 'new wave of prosperity' and the atmosphere of 'cultural refinement and prestige' which Borsay has identified in the late seventeenth century.[154]

Conclusion

There were three main surges of discussion pertaining to sanitation and environmental regulation at corporation meetings: one at the turn of the seventeenth century, in the discussion of street cleanliness, and to a lesser extent in the discussion of dirty trades and solid waste disposal; another significantly larger peak in the middle decades of the seventeenth century in the discussion of street cleanliness and solid waste disposal, and to a lesser extent dirty trades; and a third peak around 1680 in the discussion of liquid waste disposal, street cleanliness and solid waste disposal. These peaks are not necessarily the result of dirtier conditions, or of a greater need to regulate the environment, but they could well have resulted from particularly fastidious mayors and councillors or greater pressure to keep the streets clean due to the heightened threat of plague and its perceived link with insanitary streets. The major peak in discussions relating to this area of urban management in the middle decades of the seventeenth century coincides with an influx of prestigious political visitors and military operations in and around York. In 1642, for example, Charles I broke with Parliament and held his court in York for a period of six months. During the British Civil Wars, York was a royalist city and in 1644 it was besieged by the Parliamentarians under Fairfax. The greater number of discussions in the 1650s could well have resulted from the establishment of the very fastidious Commonwealth.

York Corporation did not develop such dramatic changes and improvements to their sanitation systems and infrastructure as Edinburgh Council developed during the same period as we will see below. However, this does not infer that York Corporation was less concerned or less willing to improve public sanitation in their city; York's relative stagnation in comparison to the Scottish capital city was almost certainly a reflection of the city's relatively stable population, which did not increase substantially, and perhaps actually decreased, over the period. As in Edinburgh, the processes and systems developed to manage sanitation were not rolled out, top-down, from York Corporation to an unwilling population. Rather, the majority of inhabitants welcomed, and some even requested, such sanitation systems and some inhabitants actively shaped that area of urban management as true, historical agents in their city.

Edinburgh

Introduction

Only a handful of historians have written about early modern Edinburgh's sanitation. In 1940, for example, Margaret Wood wrote an important essay about the function of Edinburgh's Dean of Guild Court in the sixteenth century, in which she concluded that the system was a useful facility for the suppression of insanitary nuisances and that the court book minutes reveal a generally positive attitude towards sanitation by the inhabitants and their governors alike.[155] Much later, in 1994, Rab Houston wrote about Edinburgh's environment in the later period of 1660–1760, questioning how bad the sanitary condition of Edinburgh really was, and detailing many attempts by the city's governors and inhabitants to protect the environment against malodours and waste, concluding that 'keeping the city in a tolerable condition was a constant struggle'.[156] Between 2002 and 2005, archaeologists excavated beneath Edinburgh's Waverley Vaults, discovering the sites of some sixteenth- and seventeenth-century houses and backlands in what was formerly the separate burgh of Canongate. Soil micromorphology revealed 'a relatively rapid accumulation of domestic refuse and fuel to enrich the soil, consistent with a cultivation soil that had been deepened either by the deliberate addition of mineral material [such] as manure, or by the dumping of domestic waste'.[157] This efficient means of disposing of the types of household waste which increased soil fertility did occur within early modern Edinburgh. As well as removing manure from the city to local landward arable farmers, at least some of the city's waste was used to fertilize small-holdings and backlands within the city walls.

1560–1599

Edinburgh Council met every Friday morning in the Tolbooth on the High Street in order to discuss a diverse range of typically urban problems and areas of city government, from defence to gambling to forestalling and, of most importance here, issues pertaining to waste disposal, drainage and street cleaning. In addition to discussing matters which they felt needed attention, they also responded to petitions from inhabitants and sometimes mediated in disputes between neighbours. Between 1560 and 1599, issues pertaining to sanitation in general were recorded in the burgh council minutes a total of sixty-seven times, ranging from as few as three in the 1570s to as many as thirty-two in the 1580s. This compares to totals of thirty-one and 151 in the first and second half of the seventeenth century, respectively. In the first half of the seventeenth century, they ranged from one discussion in the 1620s to twelve in the 1640s. In the second half of the seventeenth century, they ranged from thirteen in the 1660s to fifty-one in the 1680s. Speaking very broadly, Edinburgh Council devoted a modest amount of time to sanitation issues between 1560 and 1599, substantially less time in the first half of the seventeenth century and a substantially larger amount of time on such issues in the latter half of the seventeenth century.

Between 1560 and 1599, solid waste disposal dominated council discussions within this area of urban management during this period, accounting for 37 per cent of separately recorded discussions relating to this area of city government. This surely resulted from the preponderance of urban agriculture and the consequent production of large amounts of manure, in what was still a relatively sparsely populated city with plentiful open space and backlands. By far the largest sub-category of discussions about solid waste related to the regulation of ubiquitous heaps of manure, known as middings, middens or dunghills, which were stored on wasteland or inhabitants' private forefronts. They peppered Edinburgh's landscape throughout this period, largely as a result of relatively heavy involvement in necessary urban agriculture in backlands. Although at this time the backlands were already starting to become built up, there was more open space on which to raise animals and grow crops between 1560 and 1599 than there would be in the seventeenth century. Within the area of solid waste disposal, the council discussed the transportation of rubbish out of the city and inhabitants' taking their 'ease' or 'easie' in public places. In November 1580, for example, Edinburgh Council prohibited inhabitants from 'doing their ease at the said close heids as is most uncomely to be sene ... under the paine of x li so often as they fail'.[158] A similar statute was passed in April 1586.

> Proclamatioun to be maid dischargeing all persouns of voiding of thair filth and doing thair eases at the close heids as they have done in times past, under the paine of wairding [i.e. imprisoning] thair persouns and punessing [i.e. punishing] of thame that may be tryet or apprehendit at the will of the magestrats and payment of ane unlaw [i.e. fine] be the maisters of the houses whose servants do the same, so often as they fail.[159]

This proclamation makes it clear that a servant's actions were deemed to have been the ultimate responsibility of the master of the house, by which the council effectively delegated each household's environmental regulation to each householder.

Some of the poorest inhabitants who lived in the closes may well have lacked stationary privies and indoor facilities, such as close stools and perhaps even chamber pots.[160] It is impossible to draw firm conclusions, but that these inhabitants went deliberately to the close heads to take their 'easie' does suggest a degree of consideration. They might have considered, for example, that it was easier to collect waste from the close heads with a horse and cart than it was to shovel it into a wheel barrow, wheel it up the steep hill to the close head and then onto a cart at the top of the close. It could also have been a deliberate attempt to deposit waste away from their own dwellings situated further down in the closes. Clearly, however, Edinburgh Council disapproved of the manner in which the waste was being deposited, which was 'uncomely to be sene', as well as to the fact that they were leaving waste in the public street. As far as the council minutes and accounts show, Edinburgh Council only maintained a few public privies in the tolbooth, the college and prison. In 1684, it funded the construction of two new public privies, one near the entrance of the Fleshmarket and another 'at some close foot at the land mercate'.[161] However, neighbours could well have constructed and maintained semi-private privies for the use of several adjacent households, which never entered the written record. It is impossible to say exactly how many private, semi-private and public privies there were in Edinburgh, but it is highly likely that there were many more than the written records suggest.

While solid waste disposal was clearly the most pressing issue in the late sixteenth century, street cleaning was only discussed the second least frequently, receiving less attention than dirty trades, liquid waste disposal and livestock respectively. The second most frequent category of discussion at council meetings, between 1560 and 1599, was that of dirty trades, accounting for 27 per cent of discussions. Indeed, dirty trades seem to have been much more problematic in this early period than they subsequently became in the seventeenth century, when the population of inner Edinburgh increased much more rapidly. The overwhelming majority of Edinburgh Council's discussion of dirty trades during this period was spent regulating the city's fleshers, particularly where they slaughtered their livestock and how they disposed of their malodorous and unsavoury offal waste. Edinburgh Council also spent a significant amount of time regulating the candlemakers, whose production process of melting tallow down to form candles was extremely malodorous and consequently became a perennial source of contention and complaint among the inhabitants.[162] Edinburgh Council also discussed walkers and and lime-slakers in relation to environmental regulation, but very rarely indeed. There is no extant evidence of an effort to regulate tanners, soap-boilers, dyers or any other so-called dirty trades, though several tanners who operated on the shore of the Nor' Loch do appear in the Dean of Guild Court minutes in relation to building nuisances. Perhaps they did not cause any sufficiently significant pollution problems to warrant Edinburgh Council's attention.

The issue of regulating the presence of livestock in public areas did attract Edinburgh Council's attention, but it was by no means a major issue within the context of overall environmental regulation, only having been referred to ten times in total between 1560 and 1700, and only accounting for 10 per cent of total discussion in the period 1560 and 1599. However, seven of the ten discussions across the whole period occurred between 1560 and 1599, suggesting that livestock was a more serious issue in this period than it was throughout the seventeenth century. Sheep, nolt (i.e. cattle) and oxen were supposed to be kept in fields beyond Edinburgh, whereas small numbers of pigs, hens, geese, horses and milk cows were often accommodated in backlands. Inhabitants were required by local statute to keep the latter group of livestock, especially swine, securely bound, which contemporaries termed as being 'in band', on their properties in order to prevent them from causing damage, insanitary nuisances and general havoc on the streets and on neighbours' property. Allowing one's livestock to roam freely in public areas was a serious offence, and potentially problematic in the context of outdoor sanitation, because free roaming swine and other animals could deposit their own waste on the streets, rummage in sewers and charge into market stalls and dunghills, damaging goods and spreading carefully piled manure across the streets. Therefore curtailing free-ranging livestock's presence on urban streets complemented local governors' wider attempts to improve sanitation. The majority of discussions and statutes in this area pertained to swine, which were not only raised by fleshers, but also on a much smaller scale by inhabitants who housed them in small enclosures known as 'cruives' on their backlands. This statute regarding swine was passed in 1592.

> Item for the honestie and clenes [i.e. cleanliness] of this toun it is ordanit auld statute that all maner of persons having swine within this burgh … either tak thame and put thame furth of the toun or els keip thame in festnes or bands so that none be sene upoun the streets or common vennells under the paine of warding of the persouns owners thairof will thay pay ane unlaw of 18 schillings so oft as thay failyie.[163]

The council clearly linked streets devoid of free roaming swine to both cleanliness and 'honestie', by which they were perhaps referring to decency in a more general sense. A burgh statute was passed in 1590 regarding fleshers' cattle having been kept in the churchyard.

> For divers guid causses and consideratiouns it is thocht expedient … that na flesher plaice thair nolt or guids in the kirk feild yaird under the paine of xl d to be taine [i.e. taken] of each heid [i.e. each animal] fund thairunto and ordains the baillies to caus putt the sam to execution and the deikin of the fleshers [i.e. the head of the Butcher's Guild] to adverteis [i.e. advertize] the samin.[164]

It required substantially less labour and effort for a flesher to slaughter his livestock closer to the point of sale and further from the land on which he was grazing it. It is unsurprising that the fleshers took advantage of grazing their cattle in the kirkyard, close to their workshops. Despite its religious connotations, in practical terms the kirkyard was essentially a piece of open land in what was still a pre-modern, heavily agricultural city in the late sixteenth century. Similarly, in Aberdeen, although cows were principally kept on the burgh muir, sometimes contemporaries inexpediently grazed them on pasture within the burgh. For example, in 1579, Aberdonian councillors stipulated 'na cattell sall haff pastuir of gress upoun ... this brught'.[165] Fleshers frequently moved cattle from the burgh muir to workshops to slaughter them, but leaving them in the streets overnight was unacceptable across Scotland. As late as 1664, Glaswegian fleshers were ordered not to 'suffer their kyne to stand on the hie streits in the night time'.[166] Regulation was essential to ensure that fleshers grazed their livestock outside of the burgh and not on key open spaces such as kirkyards.

Liquid waste disposal was discussed infrequently between 1560 and 1599, perhaps because liquid waste drained away relatively quickly, and had less potential to accumulate into long-term, obstructive and malodorous nuisances. Liquid waste disposal systems across early modern urban Britain tended to have been constructed from an eclectic range of available materials, and repaired in a piecemeal manner by successive generations of tenants over time. Like most early modern urban centres, Edinburgh had an intricate web of major and minor ditches or sewers, but the drainage infrastructure was largely uncovered and it was by no means comprehensive. John Harrison claims that in Scotland, sewers were generally known as watergaits or watergangs when they were open ditches and as syvers or syres when they were covered or they ran underneath buildings, but the Dean of Guild minutes refer to many ditches which are clearly open sewers as 'syres', suggesting that there was significant overlap between the use of such terms.[167] Jaw holls or cobills were vertical or diagonally sloping pipes, usually made of lead, which drained liquid waste from inside dwellings into outdoor sewers. Grooves carved into stone paving slabs in yards and in front of buildings, specifically to aid and direct drainage paths, were known as run channels.[168] Edinburgh, being a landlocked burgh, drained its liquid waste from the north side of the city into the Nor' Loch and the liquid waste from closes descending from the south side of the High Street drained into the Cowgate and its sewers.[169]

The Nor' Loch could not have been as appallingly insanitary as one might imagine, however, because Edinburgh Council referred to the swans which inhabited the loch in the 1690s. It recorded that the council had considered a bill from George Wilson and his spouse, Rachel Crawford,

> narating that ther wes ane house built for the swans in the north loch to shelter them in the winter time within ane close pertaining to him at the north loch side and soe craved that the Councill would either grant to him ane yearly rent of twenty pound for all years bygone and twenty four pound yearly in time coming or else to cause remove the said house off his propertie.[170]

While a significant amount of liquid waste from the north side of the city was undoubtedly manually swept and washed with rainwater down into the loch, it was sufficiently large to accommodate that liquid waste without becoming unbearably malodorous. Towards the end of the eighteenth century and throughout the nineteenth century, Edinburgh's increasing volumes of liquid waste began to drain into several burns descending from the city via various routes into the sea. Leith, the New Town and the western and southwestern suburbs drained into the Water of Leith and down to the sea at Leith; the southern suburbs drained to the Jordan or Pow Burn and down to the sea at Portobello; and the Nor'Loch, Cowgate and Meadows of the old town drained into Craigentinny burn, the original Foul Burn. These burns became known as the 'foul burns' of Edinburgh, but they were not known as such before 1700, when liquid waste was far less problematic due to the rarity of wet, flushing privies and the relatively smaller population. Between 1560 and 1700, some of Edinburgh's liquid waste would have inevitably drained from the Nor' Loch, Meadows and Cowgate into the Craigentinny Burn and down to the sea, but there are no references to this burn, or to any 'foul burn', in the manuscript council minutes between 1560 and 1700, which suggests that such drainage did not cause any significant problems, at least at a citywide level.[171]

One particularly contentious issue within the sub-category of drainage was that of jaw holls and cobills (vertical or diagonally sloping drainage pipes). They were a common source of contention between neighbours because they were often shared by two or more properties and frequently fell into disrepair, typically causing them to leak liquid waste into communal areas. Edinburgh Council also discussed the issues of stagnant, insanitary puddles in public areas, resulting from inadequate drainage, and they discussed the issue of inefficient drainage from public wells. Undoubtedly, a minority of inhabitants emptied dirty water down the streets instead of pouring it carefully into sewers without causing any major problems. Yet, that Edinburgh Council discussed liquid drainage far less than the deposition of solid waste suggests that the former proved to be far less problematic than the latter. Water purity was discussed only once in the late sixteenth century, but *ad hoc* payments were made throughout the period for cleaning public wells, suggesting that while liquid waste disposal was not a major priority for Edinburgh Council, they were certainly not indifferent to water purity. In the financial year 1591–1592, for example, city treasurer Jhoun Macmorane paid 13s 4d Scots for 'clenying of St Margarets well' and 15s for clenying of the new well'.[172]

The modest devotion of Edinburgh Council's time towards sanitation and environmental regulation between 1560 and 1599 can perhaps be attributed to relatively steady population growth during this period and the relatively larger area of open space available within the city, though that might well have been responsible for this period's relatively more serious problems in relation to free roaming livestock. In 1560, the population of inner Edinburgh was around 12,500, and while the population increase in this period was not as rapid as it would later become in the seventeenth century, by 1592 it had increased by about 20 per cent to around 15,000.[173] During the late sixteenth century, neighbourhoods in Edinburgh were far more socially cohesive and less transient than they were by the seventeenth century because they contained fewer immigrant residents.[174] There was also significantly more open space in the late sixteenth century, before the influx of immigrants in the seventeenth century drove more intensive infilling of closes than had occurred in the sixteenth century, the erection of even higher, multi-storey tenements and the subdivision of those tenements. Before 1600, at least, there was more open space in which inhabitants could supplement their income through urban agriculture.

1600–1650

Waste disposal and environmental regulation were discussed a total of thirty-one times during this period, fewer than during the preceding four decades, despite its extra decade comparatively, and significantly fewer than the 151 discussions in the second half of the seventeenth century. As in the preceding four decades, solid waste disposal dominated council discussions of this area of city government, accounting for 36 per cent of sanitation discussions.[175] During this period, Edinburgh Council was focusing on removing accumulations of muck and rubbish in public areas around the city, but they were also working towards designing a more permanent, proactive and progressive system, integrated with street cleaning. In the financial year 1649–1650, for example, city treasurer John Liddell paid 26s 8d Scots for two 'new schoulls [i.e. shovels] for clenying & dichting the filth from about St Geills churche' and 40s for 'for 3 new schod schoulls for dichting & cleansing away the filth fra [i.e. from] about the parliament house'.[176] Indeed, the city treasurer's accounts even recorded one payment for removing rubbish from a private garden, that of the Earl of Haddington, who held a prestigious title in the Scots peerage.[177] In the financial year 1626–1627, city treasurer James Rae paid 3 li 4s scots to a man 'that caried away the red [i.e. rubbish] from the earle of hadingtownes bak garden'.[178] Many inhabitants accumulated middings on their own private forefronts and transported the muck away sufficiently frequently to their own arable land or else sold it to local farmers privately. Muck which was deposited in public areas, however, caused problems by impeding the efficient flow of traffic through thoroughfares and also in terms of malodorous nuisances if the muck was left unremoved for lengthy time periods. The council spent a great deal of time and energy removing muck which had been dumped anonymously at public locations, however, they may well have benefited from selling the muck which they collected from such locations to local farmers.

As well as passing statutes to ensure that inhabitants cleaned out their own privies sufficiently regularly, to prevent them from overflowing, leaking or becoming 'noysome', Edinburgh Council also maintained the public privies in the tolbooth, the college and prison. In the financial year 1625–1626, for example, city treasurer George Suittie paid 12s Scots to two workmen for 'redding the previes in the prissone hous'.[179] And, in the financial year 1626–1627, moreover, city treasurer James Rae paid seven pounds Scots 'dichting the latrens in the colledge this yeir' and three pounds scots for '30 laid of sand to the [college] latrine'.[180] In the financial year 1627–1628, furthermore, the city treasurer, James Rae, paid 4 li 16s Scots for '12 laid of lime to the latrine' in the college.[181] Lime and sand were deposited into dry privy pits periodically in an attempt to partially seal the waste in order to reduce the stench emitted from it. The college was effectively the city's university, which was paid for and established by the burgh in 1582 and was referred to in council minutes and accounts as 'the college'.

Street cleaning had become proportionately much more important by this period, receiving the second largest amount of attention within sanitation between 1600 and 1650, compared to the second lowest amount of attention within sanitation discussions during the previous four decades. Street cleaning discussions only accounted for 16 per cent of discussions in this period, but they largely concerned citywide, macro-scale street cleaning, in stark contrast to the micro-scale, reactive and repetitive discussions about the cleaning of particular streets and closes which had characterized discussions about street cleaning in the preceding four decades. This suggests that local governors were taking a distinctly proactive approach to cleaning the entire city rather than merely reactively cleaning particular streets if and when they became intolerably dirty. The issue of appointing a scavenger was also given a significant amount of attention. The traditional, medieval system of street cleaning, whereby householders were expected to clean their own forefronts and the main street beyond them, to the crown of the causeway, was clearly becoming impracticable in such a densely populated city complete with multi-storey tenements and Edinburgh's councillors began to search for a more centralized alternative. 'Cleanse the Causeway' was a popular phrase in Scotland during this period. It literally meant to clean the street, but it was often used metaphorically to describe street riots. For example, it was used in relation to political events in 1520, when the rival Hamiltons and Douglasses were feuding after the arrest of Sir George Douglas, and the friction continued, culminating in the Edinburgh street battle known as 'Cleanse the Causeway' which claimed the lives of seventy-two, including Sir Patrick Hamiltoun.[182]

In the first half of the seventeenth century, Edinburgh's governors really began to embrace the challenge of revolutionizing the city's street cleaning processes and systems. The sanitation ordinance passed at the Selkirk Convention of Burghs on 6 July 1608, referred to in chapter two, may well have inspired an attitudinal change among Edinburgh's councillors, because they did subsequently work towards improving long-term street cleanliness by developing an innovative citywide street cleaning system which took shape over the course of the seventeenth century.[183] Edinburgh's councillors recorded their acknowledgement of the ordinance on 21 October 1608. Some years later, in April 1633, inhabitants were instructed to deposit their waste onto the streets daily before 6am.[184] The councillors then commissioned the Baillies to 'agrie with sum honest man for keeping ane horse and kairt', with which to collect the waste each morning, and they employed others 'to pas with quheill barrowis [i.e. wheel barrows]' to carry dirt to the close heads.[185] In December 1648, Edinburgh's councillors expanded this nascent street cleaning system by exacting 12d from each substantial householder to finance 'carieing away the mucke and keiping the streitt and vennells of this brugh clean'.[186] The street cleaning taxes were used to purchase more horses, carts and employees, known as muckmen, to load the carts. Indeed, there is much evidence of purchases of equipment with which to clean the streets in the treasurer's accounts around this time. In the financial year 1644–1645, for example, city treasurer John Faireholme paid to William Patoun, a smith, three pounds scots for '4 great batts of Iron with 4 great pinns of Iron maid for the corpe cairts that caried the rubbish of the streits'.[187] And in the financial year 1645–1646, city treasurer John Jowssie paid 1 li 12s for 'a carre sadell to a mucke leader' and 16s for 'five cast of flaring nails to naill two cuppe sladds [i.e. sledges] to carrie filth out of the cittie'.[188] Clearly, Edinburgh Council was making significant investments in providing employees with suitable equipment in order to improve the cleanliness of the streets, in the face of an increasing population density.

Dirty trades accounted for only 13 per cent of sanitation discussions between 1600 and 1650. The council made numerous official attempts to move Edinburgh's slaughterhouses away from residential properties. In 1618, as we saw, the Scottish Privy Council intervened to ban the fleshers from depositing 'the blood and filth of slauchtered goodis upoun the streits', ordering them to transplant their slaughter houses to 'remote pairts of the burgh ... whair thair is no houses'.[189] Although noxious trades could not be expelled from the burghs entirely, because they produced vital goods for urban populations, regulating their activities in busy central streets was integral to enhancing the urban environment's olfactory and aesthetic qualities. Edinburgh's, Glasgow's, Stirling's and Aberdeen's burgh councils also restricted fleshers. In 1522, for example, Stirling's fleshers were banned from publicly slaughtering livestock because of its unsightly appearance and unpleasant smell: 'no fleschor ... slay ... any flecht [i.e. flesh] but on the baksyid [i.e. backlands] or in thar bouis [i.e. booths]'.[190] Moreover, in 1670, Aberdonian fleshers faced a similar ban, stipulating that 'no flesher ... kill or slay any of the fleshes upon the streets, or befor ther dores looking thereunto'.[191] Similarly, in 1666, Glaswegian councillors ordered 'none of the fleshours within this burgh ... to tak upon hand to kill, slay or blood any kine, oxen, bull, sheip or lamb ... in view of the hie streit'.[192] That two Glaswegian fleshers, James Jhonstoune and Robert Brume, were apprehended in 1606 for 'slaying of ky [i.e. cattle] in the foirgait, contrary [to] the statutes' suggests that such rules were upheld.[193] Although these statutes were all passed primarily to hide unsightly and noxious slaughters from public view, they may also have aimed, secondarily perhaps, to curtail the deposition of offal and blood into public streets. It is significant that the city's surgeons do not feature in either the council minutes or Dean of Guild Court minutes in relation to inadequate disposal of human blood and other forms of human excreta, produced as a result of the procedures which the surgeons carried out on their patients. Rather than signifying that human blood caused less offence to inhabitants than animal blood and offal, however, it is far more likely that the city's surgeons buried such waste efficiently without ever creating problems sufficiently significant to enter the written council records. Similarly, there are no references to inadequate disposal of human blood or other excreta by the surgeons in York. If the surgeons had deposited large amounts of human blood and other forms of human excreta in the streets, neighbours would surely have complained to the council or approached the Dean of Guild Court to have the nuisance suppressed. It is possible, however, that this occurred but nobody complained and therefore the nuisance continued unregulated.

Between 1600 and 1650, only 7 per cent of discussions related to liquid waste disposal. Most of these discussions pertained to maintaining the efficient flow of the city's web of open and closed sewers which ran down most main streets and down some closes. Indeed, there are many references to payments for work on the city's sewers in the treasurer's accounts. In the financial year 1673–1674, for example, city treasurer James Southerland paid two masons, George Gigo and Hew Stoddart, 20 pounds scots for '22 days work at the syre in and beneath the correction hous and the syre of leith wynd leading therto'.[194] Sewers inevitably sometimes became blocked with solid waste and overflowed into streets, closes and even into subterraneous floors of properties, known as 'laich' or 'laithe' tenements. Sewers might have been uncomplicated, but they were well considered, planned and laid in convenient places. Sometimes, inhabitants impeded the flow of sewers by building bridges over them for the purposes of crossing them when they ran near to their properties, as described in a discussion in September 1655.

> As be severall acts of counsell and proclamations emitted [to] the heretors [i.e. owners] of the lands of the Cowgait were ordained to remove thair brigstains [i.e. bridgestones] from befoir thair laiche houses [i.e. basements] which doeth stop the current of the watter and overflow the streits. Which hitherto hes never beine fullie obeyit notwithstanding of all the certifications therin conteined.[195]

Anyone who failed to remove their bridgestones would find them having been 'broken and removed upoun thair awine chairges beside punishment of thair persone at the will of the magestratts'.[196] Although heretors were expected to maintain the sections of the sewers which flowed past their properties, and they had liberty to construct small-scale edifices to facilitate convenient drainage from and access to their properties, Edinburgh Council could and did intervene to regulate such constructions if and when they became problematic in terms of causing damage to neighbours' properties or preventing efficient drainage of liquid waste both within respective neighbourhoods and across the city.

Exploring Edinburgh Council's attitudes towards the issue of water purity in this period is arguably anachronistic, being a characteristically modern-day concern. But, while contemporaries were yet to understand the link between dirt, germs and disease fully, they certainly understood that allowing dirt and rubbish to pollute the water supply was not conducive to good health or to the commonwealth. The issue was discussed explicitly and unambiguously, albeit only once, in a statute passed in 1649 which forbade inhabitants from placing middings near to wells and from allowing their horses to drink at the public wells, thus suggesting that the councillors were well aware of the potential dangers of allowing muck to come so close to the water supply. Another two discussions regarded cleaning wells, but they are somewhat ambiguous in that the councillors could well have been more concerned about the aesthetic appearance and tidiness of the wells rather than the dirt's potential to contaminate the water supply. It is certainly significant that urban governors at this time devoted civic resources to cleaning wells. In the financial year 1635–1636, for example, city treasurer Charles Hamiltoun paid 10s scots for '2 new bucketts to dicht [i.e. clean] the wells'.[197]

Between 1600 and 1650, the population of inner Edinburgh had increased significantly, by a further 25 per cent, from around 15,000 in 1592 to at least 20,000 by the mid-seventeenth century.[198] Consequently, sanitation was placed under significant strain as increasing amounts of waste were produced in the city. The transplantation of the Scottish court to England in 1603, however, drew a lot of prestigious visitors' and observers' attention away from Edinburgh and towards London, which may well have reduced the pressure to keep the streets clean at least somewhat. Despite the relatively low number of dedicated discussions of sanitation among Edinburgh Council during this period, however, they nevertheless invested significant time and energy into designing and laying the foundations of the centralized street cleaning system which would be rolled out in full in the latter half of the seventeenth century.

1651–1700

In the second half of the seventeenth century, the population of inner Edinburgh increased even further by about a third from around 20,000 in the mid-seventeenth century to approximately 30,000 by 1700.[199] This population increase must be appreciated in the context of the relatively small geographical area of Edinburgh, which put extreme pressure on housing, and forced the subdivision of tenements and the infilling of closes even more rapidly than, but in addition to, the population increases of the previous decades. In the first half of the seventeenth century, Edinburgh lost many of its most prestigious visitors after the royal court moved south to London in 1603. The late seventeenth century saw a reverse trend as many elites flocked from London to Edinburgh following the decision in 1680 by King Charles II to appoint the Duke of York as Lord High Commissioner of Scotland, and James' consequent residence at the Palace of Holyrood House.

Sanitation was discussed a total of 151 times during the latter half of the seventeenth century, which far exceeded the total number of discussions of this area of city government over the previous ninety years. Clearly, after 1650, Edinburgh Council came under unprecedented pressure to improve and centralize the city's waste disposal processes and systems as a result of both the population increase and political pressure from Scotland's national governing institutions.[200] Street cleaning became yet more of a proportionate priority in the second half of the seventeenth century, dominating the council's discussion of sanitation, accounting for 36 per cent of such discussions in this period, and overtaking solid waste disposal as the most prevalent category in the previous two periods. An increasingly progressive attitude towards improving and adapting the processes and systems pertaining to the city's street cleaning became especially pronounced towards the end of the seventeenth century, and particularly in the 1680s, when a third of the total council discussions between 1560 and 1700 took place, almost certainly as a direct response to the Duke of York's residence in 1680 at the Palace of Holyrood House and the consequent relocation of many English courtiers from London to Edinburgh.

As can be seen in Figure 4, there was an unmistakable increase in discussions and statutes pertaining to street cleaning over time, especially towards the end of the seventeenth century. Edinburgh's councillors of the late seventeenth century were making significant efforts to reduce inhabitants' street cleaning responsibilities in order to keep the streets of this increasingly busy city clear and relatively clean. In November 1677, in a desperate attempt to combat insanitary streets, the councillors ordered the 'wholl muckmen to be daylie and hourly imployed to cleange the streits'.[201] By October 1682, a 'constant comittie' had been appointed to oversee the street cleaning team which met each Friday immediately after Edinburgh Council's weekly meeting.[202] By 1684, this committee, headed by a General Scavenger with two overseers working under him, supervised what had become a highly centralized team of thirty muckmen. Each night, the muckmen parked their carts at twenty locations to which inhabitants carried their waste after 10pm, and they emptied their carts each morning at the midding steads (holding dumps) at 7am in the summer and at 8am in the winter. The specific locations at which the muckmen parked their carts each night were well considered, very precise and spread evenly throughout the city; they included

Decade	No. of Street Cleaning Discussions and/or Statutes
1560–1569	1
1570–1579	0
1580–1589	0
1590–1599	0
1600–1609	0
1610–1619	1
1620–1629	1
1630–1639	1
1640–1649	2
1650–1659	13
1660–1669	0
1670–1679	15
1680–1689	21
1690–1699	6
Total	**61**

Figure 4 Edinburgh Council minute entries relating to street cleaning, 1560–1699, (by decade)

the foot of West Bow a little from the fountain, 'Sir James Dicks stair foot' and the eastern end of the Magdalene Chapel.[203] During a transitional period, this service was provided in addition to collecting solid waste which was deposited on the streets. However, from 1687, the muckmen stopped collecting waste from the streets, and instead only removed waste from the twenty locations where they parked their carts each night, but they still raked and cleansed the streets and the closes three times a week, and the Canongate and Cowgate in the winter.

The following contract, between Edinburgh Council and Archibald Home, General Scavenger in 1687, provides a useful insight into exactly how Edinburgh's team of muckmen functioned:

> To keep and maintain twentie close cairts well pitched and tarred with ane cover of an tarr saile over each of them with two horses for each cairt at least which carits they are to be sett in such places of the streets as the magistrates shall appoint for receiveing of the excrements of this cittie ... to provide and maintaine upon their charges and expenses thirtie muck men beside twentie cairts and to cause the muck men thrice in the week raick the high streets of Edinburgh and closes therof and the high streets of the Cannogate and Cowgate in the winter time. And in the summer time when the streets are filthie and when dry either in summer or winter to sweep the same in the winter time befor nine a clock in the morning and in the summer time before seven a clock in the morning.[204]

The tar sails were used to protect the valuable muck against the potentially damaging effects of rainfall and evaporation in hot weather, but they would also have had the effect of reducing the emission of malodours into the air. The street-cleaning system was adapted further in 1692, when the muckmen were given the extra duty of patrolling the streets between 9pm and midnight every Saturday to report anyone pouring waste from windows.[205] This adaptation is hugely significant and could even mark the origins of a city 'police' force. The task of a 'police' force is to enforce polite behaviour, which is essentially what these muckmen were doing.

It is clear that in this period street cleaning taxes began to be exacted from substantial householders. For example, Lady Elphinstone, of Penicuik in Midlothian, had to pay street cleaning taxes because she owned a townhouse in Edinburgh. Three of her partially printed receipts have survived, for the years between 1687 and 1689; the second one states 'received by me from the Lady Elvingston the summe of 38sh Scots Money, and that for their proportion for cleanging the streets, viz. from Candlemass 1687 to Candlemass 1688'.[206] These surviving receipts are in partially printed form and clearly represent a much larger volume of mass-produced receipts which were printed, filled in as administrative forms and exchanged for street cleaning taxes from inhabitants at this time. Mark Jenner highlighted a similar system which was established in London in the late seventeenth century, by which time £3,500 was collected in street cleaning rates from Londoners annually by a centralized team of scavengers who supervised respective teams of rakers actually performing the labour of cleaning the streets.[207] In 1690, the constables of Edinburgh petitioned the Provost, Baillies and Councillors for 'the privilege to be free of paying of any stent or inquitition for cleinseing of the streets for the yeres wherin we serve as Constables'.[208] This they asked for in recognition of their extra work duties, 'through the outstanding of the Castle and troublesome times your petitioners wes put to great trouble pains & expencess both be night & day'.[209] It is unclear whether or not this request was granted because there is no reference to a decision either on the document or in the council minutes, perhaps because the decision was conveyed orally, but the constables' request proves that street cleaning taxes were being collected.

Thus, by the late seventeenth century, Edinburgh Council had successfully created a highly centralized and well-organized street cleaning system – a shining example of what could be done towards resolving early modern urban waste disposal problems. It is lamentable that increasing horse-drawn traffic and population growth absorbed much of the improvement which its development should have earned for the benefit of Edinburgh's inhabitants. Foreigners complained about Edinburgh's insanitary conditions into the eighteenth century, and Edinburgh's councillors admitted, in February 1681, that despite their efforts, Edinburgh was 'still mor dirtie then formerlie'.[210] However, that contemporaries rose to the challenge and confronted Edinburgh's sanitation problems is far more important than their ultimate failure to combat it once and for all.

Dirty trades accounted for 18 per cent of discussions between 1650 and 1700. In 1655, Edinburgh Council ordered the fleshers to move their slaughterhouses to between 'the Muse well and the West port'.[211] In 1662, it banned leasing High Street booths to be used as slaughterhouses outright.[212] Despite such official action, nevertheless, some fleshers continued to conduct their trade near to residential properties. However, as we will learn in chapter four, that only 2 per cent of extant insanitary nuisance cases dealt with by Edinburgh Dean of Guild Court pertain to dirty trades suggests that Edinburgh's fleshers were not causing an intolerable offence to a significantly large proportion of inhabitants. Solid waste disposal accounted for 15 per cent of council discussions in this period, and a lot of those discussions concerned the transportation of muck out of the city. Edinburgh produced substantial amounts of manure which was sold to local farmers who used it to fertilize their arable land. Indeed, a century later, in 1795, a Granton farmer, George Robertson, wrote about Edinburgh's manure trade.

> From Edinburgh and Leith are obtained about 40,000 cartload of street-dung annually, which is commonly expended on the lands within 5 miles of town, though there have been a few instances in which it has been carried by sea to a greater distance. For collecting this manure, arising from the sweepings of the streets, which are for this purpose arranged into districts, the town employs scavengers, and the farmers in the neighbourhood furnish carts to carry it daily to byplaces, without the walls of the city, laying it together in dunghills, from which at their leisure they drive it to their lands. It costs from 1s to 1s 6d a load, of about a cubic yard each. Stable-dung is sometimes sold

at a dearer rate, particularly where it is exchanged for straw (the whole dung for the whole litter) when it may cost perhaps 3s 4d. Thirty or 40 load to an acre is the usual allowance, and which has always the greatest effect when laid on new from the streets, but this, however, is only practicable in small quantities, great part of it being kept a whole year before it can be applied.[213]

Assuming that Robertson's estimate was accurate, and that greater Edinburgh and Leith produced 40,000 cartloads of manure in 1795, with a population of approximately 83,000, then greater Edinburgh and Leith may well have been producing as many as 22,650 cartloads of muck in 1700, with an approximate population of approximately 47,000.[214] It is unsurprising, therefore, that the regulation of dunghills occupied such a large proportion of Edinburgh Council's time and energy. They were clearly a ubiquitous feature of Edinburgh's landscape and muck was integral to pre-modern urban inhabitants' way of life.

The team of muckmen functioned relatively well, and removed inhabitants' muck and rubbish much more efficiently as a result of incremental improvements made to the system over time. Between 1560 and the 1680, workmen were sometimes employed reactively to remove accumulations of muck and rubbish in inappropriate locations on an *ad hoc* basis. In the financial year 1666–1667, for example, city treasurer James Currie paid 20 li 6s Scots to 'the 4 men that caried away the rubish & stones out of the parliament close for the Convention of Estats'.[215] In the financial year 1675–1676, moreover, city treasurer Mungo Woods paid 8 li 13s 4d scots for 'taking away redd from Forresters wynd foott'.[216] And in the financial year 1674–1675, city treasurer James Southerland paid 2 li 8s scots for 'clanying the new well within from all sand and filth'.[217] The treasurer's accounts contain payments for such work until 1680 when such *ad hoc* entries disappear from the accounts entirely. The absence of such *ad hoc* jobs after 1680 surely resulted from the fact that by this time inhabitants were efficiently removing rubbish from the streets to the muckmen's carts which were parked each night at twenty permanent locations across the city.

Though Edinburgh Council's top-down, civic-funded provision is important, there is much evidence to prove that inhabitants did not wait helplessly for such official intervention, but rather that they were proactive in improving and maintaining the sanitary standard of their neighbourhoods from the bottom, upwards. In September 1653, for example, five householders petitioned Edinburgh's council to apply for permission to clean the foot of their close. Edinburgh Council recorded,

> the Counsell taking to consideratioun the supplication presented to them be William Mitchell, James Broun, Williame Hutchiesone, Mr Thomas Rig and Hercules Junken makand mentioun that qr [i.e. where] they have certane tenements and housses … at the fute of forresters wynd att the bak of the which land ther is a close east ward wherin fleshers and others cast in hudge middings of filth and consumes ther houses and mightilie annoyes the inhabitants of the samen that they cannot abid therin … Humblie desiring a

warrand to cleny that part and to keip all clein by bigging up the fute of the close at least putting up a door on the fute and another a little above wher ther is no doors nor passages.[218]

Edinburgh Council granted permission to these petitioners 'to put on a doore at the fute of the closse and another in the midst [i.e. middle] of the closse' to remain closed.[219] These neighbours did not wait passively and helplessly for Edinburgh Council to take action to improve their neighbourhood, but took the initiative proactively to improve their micro-scale environment themselves. Similarly, in October 1664, William Monteith and William Douglas, neighbours in Lies Close, complained to the Dean of Guild Court.

> Ane passage … from lies clos to hearts close and which through the badnes of the times when the English were in Edinburgh were spoilled with middings and red [i.e. rubbish] and hes so continued ever since and seeing that … the said passage aught to be clanyed [i.e. cleaned] and declared to be ane opin passage … in all time comeing and they ordained to clang [i.e. clean] the sam and build ther dyke and yaitt [i.e. gate] thereof.[220]

After inspection, the Dean of Guild and Council declared their decision.

> The place compleaned of is ane wild Jacks [i.e. open toilet] not only prejudiciall to nighbours by the smell bot also dangerous for young ones comeing that way and not decent to be within ane civill burgh and that it lies upon them as dewtie to sie the sam redrest [i.e. to see the same redressed]. Therfor grants judge and warrand to the compleaners to clanye and dight [i.e. clean and tidy] the place above specified mak the sam clean of dirt filth water & excraments and ordaines the sam to be ane opin passag for serveing the nighbours.[221]

In this complaint, the minutes note that such a filthy close was 'not decent to be within ane civill burgh'.[222] Clearly, the councillors were pursuing an aspiration to transform Edinburgh into a civil city. In a remarkably similar vein, the following words introduced a 1650 waste disposal regulation in Edinburgh Council's minutes: 'taking into their consideratioun the filthines of the hie streitts and closes the lik wherof is not to be sein in any civill cittie'.[223] Significantly, they wrote that similarly filthy streets were not to be found in any civil city, rather than in any *other* civil city. Therefore, in their minds, Edinburgh's filthy streets prevented it from taking its place as a civil city; thus, revealing the synonymy of cleanliness with civility in officials' minds. Clearly, contemporaries' desire to fulfil a perceived prerequisite of being termed a civil city motivated them to enhance street cleanliness. The foundations of such attitudes were laid in the late medieval period, when, as Carole Rawcliffe asserts, 'clean streets, salubrious market places and well-maintained hospitals constituted a source of communal pride, projecting a conscious image of success, independence and civic virtue'.[224] Standards of sanitation could be interpreted with powerfully deep meanings; good sanitation was integral to much of what was celebrated about well-governed towns and cities. Street cleanliness was integral to the 'common weal' and crucially underpinned the efficient government of a civil city. The inhabitants who complained to the Dean of Guild Court about Lies Close were clearly passionate about improving the standard of cleanliness in the outdoor environment of their neighbourhood. Undoubtedly, many more bottom-up initiatives were undertaken by neighbours themselves, but negotiated verbally and without recourse to official bodies, which left no trace in the records.

Conclusion

Figure 5 shows the broad categories of issues pertaining to waste disposal and outdoor sanitation which were raised and discussed at meetings of Edinburgh Council throughout the period, including both official statutes and general discussions. Over the course of the entire period under discussion, the categories of street cleanliness and solid waste disposal were discussed most frequently, closely followed by industrial waste disposal and dirty trades. Issues pertaining to liquid waste disposal and livestock demanded substantially less attention from the city's councillors and water purity was discussed very infrequently indeed. These patterns are unsurprising in the context of a densely populated, pre-modern city, in which large amounts of solid waste, especially manure, were generated and where dirty trades, such as candle-making and the flesher craft, were necessarily undertaken on a large scale in order to satisfy the needs of a swelling population and that of its hinterland. It is highly likely that Edinburgh Council discussed the most urgent matters most frequently, those which were causing the largest problems in the city's daily functioning, thus suggesting that the areas of street cleanliness, solid waste disposal and, to a lesser extent dirty trades, were most problematic and were under the most severe pressure whereas the areas of liquid

Categories of issues	Number of recorded discussions	Percentage of recorded discussions
Street cleanliness	61	24.5
Solid waste disposal	59	23.7
Combination of two or more categories	51	20.5
Industrial waste disposal and dirty trades	49	19.7
Liquid waste disposal	16	6.4
Livestock	10	4.0
Water purity	3	1.2
Total	**249**	**100**

Figure 5 Categories of sanitation issues recorded by Edinburgh City Council, 1560–1699

waste disposal, livestock and water purity were either functioning relatively well or were not important priorities within large-scale, citywide government.

If, however, the categorized council minutes, both official statutes and general discussions, are split into respective decades, more complex and precise patterns become apparent. Between 1560 and 1700, there was significant variation in the frequency with which Edinburgh Council discussed issues pertaining to environmental regulation, ranging from as little as one single discussion in the entire decade of the 1620s to as many as fifty-one discussions in the 1680s. It is impossible to say with any certainty whether this implies that all areas of environmental regulation and waste disposal were functioning so well in the 1620s that they required hardly any discussion at all by Edinburgh Council or rather that this decade in particular was one of marked indifference to issues pertaining to outdoor sanitation. Similarly, were these areas of city government failing so badly in the 1680s that they commanded Edinburgh Council's frequent attention? Or, alternatively, was this simply a period of time during which the city's governors were especially conscientious about sanitation and therefore were making a special effort to try to improve sanitation systems and processes even though they were functioning relatively well? Richard Rodger noticed a qualitative change in Edinburgh's council minutes between 1677 and 1682, noting that the use of the future tense in the minutes 'indicates a contemporary perception and degree of town planning in the field of environmental welfare'.[225] That in 1680 King Charles II appointed the Duke of York as Lord High Commissioner of Scotland, and that James' residence at the Palace of Holyrood House in Edinburgh prompted many English elites to flock to the city may well have increased Edinburgh Council's motivation to upgrade street cleanliness in the presence of so many prestigious visitors. Perhaps Edinburgh Council was politically motivated to impress powerful and prestigious elites by presenting them with a salubrious urban landscape and environment, but such motivations were not incompatible with simultaneous motivations to improve sanitary conditions for the inhabitants' health and wellbeing. The 1680s might well have been a time during which the city governors were especially conscientious about the cleanliness of the streets rather than a time during which the city was producing significantly more waste or inhabitants were disposing of waste in a more problematic manner. One of the peaks in the discussion of and the passing of orders to regulate and improve sanitation, in the 1580s, coincides with a decade of particularly severe plague epidemics. And the peak in the 1650s may well have been a subsequent reaction to the similarly severe plague epidemics Edinburgh suffered in the 1640s, which would still have loomed large in governors' and inhabitants' recent memories in the 1650s.

Contemporaries responded to malodorous nuisances with a special sense of urgency, due to their belief in miasmatic transmission of plague and the potentially unwholesome properties of malodour in general. Therefore, one would expect to see a greater level of concern leading up to and during the warmer months of the year, when malodours were especially strong and intolerable, than during the colder months, when malodorous nuisances were more tolerable. However, data suggests that the opposite was true, with 64 per cent of sanitation discussions between 1560 and 1700 taking place between October and March, and only 36 per cent taking place between April and September. In fact, issues pertaining to sanitation were discussed most frequently in the month of October (19 per cent) and in the following month of November (14 per cent), which is consistent with practical issues of administration because the feast of Michaelmas in October marked the end of one administrative and financial year and the beginning of another for Edinburgh Council. As the next year's Provost, Baillies, Treasurer, Councillors and other burgh officials took their oaths and the burgh's accounts were audited and the next year's begun, October, and to a lesser extent November, was a natural time at which to renew old statutes or to promulgate new ones pertaining not only to environmental regulation and sanitation, but to all areas of city government. The relatively longer hours worked by many urban inhabitants during the months of extended sunlight, however, may also explain the lesser extent of concern, as reflected in the less frequent council discussions of such matters throughout the summer months.

Temperature, however, might explain the relatively high numbers of discussions and statutes pertaining to outdoor sanitation in March and April, which together account for 21 per cent of all sanitation discussions throughout the period. Perhaps, with previous hot summers and the unpleasant experience of consequent malodorous nuisances in mind, Edinburgh Council took steps, proactively, as the warmer weather approached, to try to prevent malodours from escalating out of control in the forthcoming warm weather. This may also represent a catch-up after the winter months, during which less attention may well have been paid to this area of urban management and also during which short daylight hours could have encouraged increased deposition of waste material under the cover of darkness. This statute, passed by Edinburgh Council in April 1585, to regulate inhabitants' privies, seems to have been passed with imminent hot weather in mind.

> For avoiding of all filth and evill savour wherby any inconvenience may arise in this somer seasoun that na maner of persouns suffer thair swine to pas in the hie streits, commoun clossis or vinells … in any oppin places fra this day furth under the paine of slauchter of the swine and payment of … [40s] and the owner to be putt in the thevs hoill or tolbuith until the unlaw be payet. Siclike that none suffer thair priveis to gorge, brek and run out in the streits, bot that thay caus the sam be clenyeit in dew times nor to haif any filth or middings lyand on the said streits above thre hours at anes under the paine of … [40s] and punishment of thair persouns at the will of the magestrats.[226]

Perhaps badly maintained privies had proven particularly noxious in previous hot summers. The timing of this order is revealing. That it was passed purposely in preparation for 'this sommer season' suggests that the malodours emanating from such leaking privies, which were much more severe in warmer than in colder weather, concerned officials far more than the mere physical presence of privy waste and middings on the streets, which would have been as problematic in winter as in summer. When Edinburgh's councillors prohibited stable owners from piling middings near to wells, in April 1649, they stressed their carelessness 'espeaciallie now in the sommer time'.[227] Dirt's smell was stronger during hotter months, between April and September, than it was during colder months, between October and March, whereas its appearance was equally unsavoury throughout the year.

Mark Jenner maintains that official documents such as council minutes and bylaws should be regarded as 'formulaic rather than describing an empirically observed state of affairs'.[228] But statutes and bylaws were clear and direct responses to councillors' and civic employees' empirical observations and inhabitants' complaints. Admittedly, sections from previous statutes were sometimes reiterated verbatim to remind inhabitants to conform to previous stipulations. Indeed, councillors forbade loose swine within Aberdeen in 1696 using an almost identical copy of a former statute passed in 1654.[229] Although most urban records were written in a formal style, they are not entirely 'formulaic'. Indeed, a significant few are highly opinionated. Statutes and council minutes do permit valuable insights into urban officials' perceptions of dirt. For example, that Glaswegian councillors thought, in 1638, that it was 'cumlie ... decent ... and credible ... to have the calsayes frie of middings', suggests that, conversely, they found streets filled with middings indecent and unworthy of credit.[230] Far from having been written in a mechanical and 'formulaic' style, this statute is loaded with the councillors' attitudes and values. Rather than merely writing the regulation into the council register, they explained why they felt it was necessary. These councillors had a specific standard of sanitation below which they perceived Glasgow's streets to have fallen, and this statute conveys vividly both their desire to improve street cleanliness and their negative perception of dirt.

The frequency with which environmental regulation was discussed at meetings of Edinburgh Council is important, as are the categories of the environmental issues discussed. Top-down provision of facilities, services and regulation formed the foundation of environmental regulation in this period, despite the relatively high level of responsibility which inhabitants held over how they disposed of their waste and the manner in which they were expected to engage in noxious trades and crafts. It is fair to say that Edinburgh Council's response to environmental problems was more reactive at the beginning of the period, in the late sixteenth century, and that it became increasingly proactive towards the end of the period, especially in the late seventeenth century. However, it is important not to discount the important efforts made by inhabitants themselves to improve and maintain sanitary standards in their own neighbourhoods. Environmental regulation in Edinburgh was by no means exclusively top-down. There was significant harmony between bottom-up initiatives and top-down regulation and management.

Conclusion

This chapter has outlined in detail how street cleaning, waste disposal and drainage was undertaken and managed by English town councils and corporations and by

Scottish burgh councils. It has also analysed in depth how street cleaning and waste disposal was organized and managed by York Corporation and Edinburgh Burgh Council during the same period. It has explained where the line lay between the urban governors' and inhabitants' responsibilities and how and why these systems were modified between 1560 and 1700 in many different towns across Britain. In each town, householders understood which services were provided for them and which duties they were expected to carry out themselves. While not all neighbours came out willingly to sweep their forefronts in a harmonious and idyllic fashion, and a significant minority of inhabitants had to be coerced into maintaining the cleanliness of their forefronts and obeying sanitation bylaws, the majority carried out their duties without complaint. No British town or city in this period was equipped with a comprehensive and completely publicly funded sanitation infrastructure, even by 1700. Most of the systems and processes which were put in place to manage waste disposal and street cleaning originated with the local governors and were provided top-down for the benefit of urban inhabitants at large, but it would be grossly inaccurate to conclude that the improvements made to sanitation processes, systems and infrastructure were by any means forced on unwilling populations who did not value the widespread potential benefits of such improvements. In both York and Edinburgh, and in many other towns and burghs, inhabitants displayed a genuine and unmistakable willingness to meet their urban governors at least half way and to fulfil their civic duties as householders. Under the pressure of intense population increases, by 1700, Edinburgh Council had made significantly more acute changes to its street cleaning systems and waste disposal processes than York Corporation had made to their system. However, the local governors of all towns and cities were passionate about presenting the urban environment in the best possible condition of which they and the inhabitants under their governance were capable in the context of necessary urban agriculture, limited fiscal resources and relatively rudimentary technology.[231] By the turn of the eighteenth century, Edinburgh's systems and processes were far more centralized than those of York. But Edinburgh's governors were largely reacting to the pragmatic waste-disposal needs of an expanding population in order to maintain a basic level of sanitation on the streets, rather than proactively adapting processes and systems to improve conditions, whereas York's local governors were under relatively minimal pressure to improve the long-established processes and systems which were already in place and which were functioning well. However, York Corporation's comparatively less discernible improving spirit does not confirm that its members were disinclined to improve conditions. Rather, it should be understood in the context of a city which was disposing of its waste and cleaning its streets with relatively few problems. York's and Edinburgh's local governors were operating and governing their respective cities in very different circumstances.

Notes

1 E. Pickles, 'Interview', *BBC Breakfast News* (BBC1, 30/09/11, 8.00am).
2 Sheffield Archives, ACM/S/116: A Book of Pains and Amerciaments, 1578 (03/04/1578).
3 *The Portmote or Court Leet Records of the Borough or Town and Royal Manor of Salford from the Year 1597 to the Year 1669 Inclusive*, 2 vols, ed. J. Mandley (Manchester: Chetham Society, 1902), vol. 2, p. 32.
4 For more detailed information on the development of the legal definition of thoroughfares, see Webb and Webb, *The Story of the King's Highway*, p. 14–26.
5 Bristol Record Office, JQS/Pr/1: Presentments to the Grand Jury to the Bristol Leet, 1628–1666 (21/04/1635).
6 BRO, C1/1–3: Berwick Bailiffs' Court Book, 1568–1601. All civic employees in Berwick were paid in ewes' grass on which they could rear ewes in order to supplement their diet and income.
7 CRO, Ca4/3: Carlisle Chamberlains' Accounts.
8 CRO, Ca4/3: Carlisle Chamberlains' Accounts; Ca4/139: Audit of Carlisle Chamberlains' Accounts.
9 CRO, Ca4/3: Carlisle Chamberlains' Accounts; Ca4/139: Audit of Carlisle Chamberlains' Accounts.
10 *Records of the Burgery of Sheffield*, p. 113.
11 Bristol Record Office, JQS/Pr/1: Presentments to the Grand Jury to the Bristol Leet, 1628–1666 (21/10/1628).
12 Bristol Record Office, JQS/Pr/1: Presentments to the Grand Jury to the Bristol Leet, 1628–1666 (27/10/1635).
13 Bristol Record Office, JQS/Pr/1: Presentments to the Grand Jury to the Bristol Leet, 1628–1666 (27/10/1635).
14 Jenner, '"Cleanliness" and "dirt"', p. 134.
15 BRO, C1/1–3: Berwick Bailiffs' Court Book, 1568–1601.
16 Jorgensen, 'Sanitation and civic government', pp. 302, 311.
17 BRO, C1/1–3: Berwick Bailiffs' Court Book, 1568–1601.
18 *Records of Dunfermline*, p. 160 (01/09/1628).
19 Reed, 'The urban landscape', p. 306.
20 D. Hey, *A History of Sheffield* (Lancaster: Carnegie, 1998), p. 57.
21 *Records of the Burgery of Sheffield*, p. 27.
22 *Records of the Burgery of Sheffield*, p. 136.
23 Hey, *History of Sheffield*, p. 57.
24 Stirling Archives, B66/20/2: Council Record, 1597–1609.
25 See Oram, 'Waste management', pp. 11–16 for further information regarding the legal context of dung trading.
26 Oram, 'Waste management', pp. 11–16.
27 *Ayr Burgh Accounts, 1534–1624*, ed. G. Pryde (Edinburgh: Scottish Historical Society, 3rd Series, 1937).
28 *Records of the Convention of Burghs*, vol. 2, p. 254 (06/07/1608).
29 BRO, H2/1: Berwick Annual Account Book, 1603–1611 (financial year 1605–1606).
30 Morer, *Short Account*, p. 285.
31 P&KA, B59/16/2: Acts of Town Council, 1618–1635.
32 *Records of the Burgery of Sheffield*, pp. 219, 242.
33 NYCRO, DC/SCB/II/1/: Scarborough Corporation Minute and Order Book, 1621–1649 (03/10/1640).
34 Stirling Archives, B66/20/5: Council Record, 1659–1680 (04/11/1671).
35 Stirling Archives, B66/20/5: Council Record, 1659–1680 (04/11/1671). For more details on Stirling's topography and function, see R. Fox, 'Stirling 1550–1700: the morphology and functions of a pre-industrial Scottish burgh', in G. Gordon, and

B. Dicks (eds), *Scottish Urban History* (Aberdeen: Aberdeen University Press, 1983), pp. 52–70.

36 Skelton, 'Beadles, dunghills and noisome excrements'.

37 H. Summerson, *Medieval Carlisle: The City and the Borders from the Late Eleventh to the Mid-sixteenth Century*, 2 vols (Kendal: *Transactions of the Cumberland and Westmoreland Antiquarian and Archaeological Society*, extra series, 1993), vol. 1, p. 162.

38 Summerson, *Medieval Carlisle*, p. 162. For discussion of other early sanitation systems developed by monastic communities, see R. Magnusson, *Water Technology in the Middle Ages: Cities, Monasteries and Waterworks after the Roman Empire* (Baltimore: John Hopkins University Press, 2001), pp. 155–162.

39 Hutchinson, *History of Cumberland*, p. 659.

40 CRO, Ca3/2/8: Carlisle Court Leet Rolls.

41 BRO, C1/1–3: Berwick Bailiffs' Court Book, 1568–1601.

42 Durham University Heritage Collection, MS 8/I: Subsidiary Manorial Court Records, Stockton Division, Box 7, Bundle 1, Item 5.

43 *Records of the Burgery of Sheffield*, p. 315.

44 TNA, SC 2/315/11: Court Leet of the Borough of Macclesfield (43 Elizabeth I, i.e. 1601).

45 TNA, SC 2/315/11: Court Leet of the Borough of Macclesfield (3 James I, i.e. 1606).

46 NYCRO, DC/SCB/II/1/: Corporation Minute and Order Book, 1621–1649 (14/10/1623).

47 BRO, C1/1–3: Berwick Bailiffs' Court Booke, 1568–1601. [Exact date unknown.]

48 *Records of Glasgow*, vol. 2, p. 313 (05/05/1655).

49 CRO, D/Lons/W8/17/1: Manor of St. Bees Court Book, 1666–1689 (23/04/1667).

50 CRO, D/Lons/W8/17/1: Manor of St. Bees Court Book, 1666–1689 (21/10/1668).

51 CRO, D/Lons/W8/17/1: Manor of St. Bees Court Book, 1666–1689 (21/10/1668).

52 A. Duncan, 'Bideford under the Restored Monarchy', *Transactions of the Devon Association*, 47 (1915), pp. 312–315, on p. 313.

53 BRO, C1/1–3: Berwick Bailiffs' Court Book, 1568–1601.

54 *Council Register of Aberdeen, 1625–1747*, vol. 1, p. 191 (20/11/1639).

55 Sheffield Archives, ACM/S/116: A Book of Pains and Amerciaments, Sheffield Court Leet, 1578 (03/04/1578).

56 P&KA, B59/16/1: Acts of Town Council, 1601–1618 (09/06/1612).

57 *Charters and Documents relating to the Burgh of Peebles, with Extracts from the Records of the Burgh, AD 1165–1710*, ed. W. Chambers (Edinburgh: Scottish Burgh Record Society, 1872), p. 232 (14/10/1556); *Records of Glasgow*, vol. 1, p. 69 (03/06/1578).

58 *Records of Lanark*, p. 96 (13/01/1590).

59 Highland Council Archives, BI/1/1/5: Inverness Town Council Minutes, 1662–80 (09/07/1677).

60 T. Cooper, 'The medieval highways, streets, open ditches, and sanitary conditions of the city of York', *Yorkshire Archaeological Journal*, 22 (1913), pp. 270–286, on p. 271.

61 Palliser, *Tudor York*, pp. 26–7. See also D. Palliser, 'Civic mentality and the environment in Tudor York', *Northern History Journal*, 18, (1982), pp. 78–115, which contains similarly negative conclusions in relation to York's public hygiene provision in the Tudor period.

62 Rawcliffe, *Urban Bodies*, p. 14.

63 Rawcliffe, *Urban Bodies*, p. 25.

64 P. Hartshorne, 'The street and the perception of public space in York, 1476–1586', (unpublished PhD thesis, University of York, 2004), pp. 145, 232–233.

65 Jorgensen, 'Co-operative sanitation', pp. 547, 561.

66 Jorgensen, 'Co-operative sanitation', pp. 561, 564, 566.

67 YCA, B23: York Corporation House Book, 1560–1565 (14/06/1564).
68 YCA, B27: York Corporation House Book, 1577–1580 (13/04/1580).
69 YCA, B27: York Corporation House Book, 1577–1580 (21/10/1580).
70 YCA, B27: York Corporation House Book, 1577–1580 (21/10/1580).
71 YCA, B28: York Corporation House Book, 1580–1585 (10/05/1583).
72 YCA, B28: York Corporation House Book, 1580–1585 (10/05/1583).
73 YCA, B32: York Corporation House Book, 1598–1605 (09/01/1601).
74 YCA, B38: York Corporation House Book, 1663–1688 (01/06/1664).
75 W. Hoskins, *Two Thousand Years in Exeter: An Illustrated Social History of the Mother-City of South-Western England* (Exeter: James Townsend and Sons Ltd, 1960), p. 61.
76 YCA, B30: York Corporation House Book, 1587–1592 (28/02/1587).
77 YCA, CB6: Chamberlains' Books of Account, (1585–1586).
78 YCA, B30: York Corporation House Book, 1587–1592 (15/02/1589/90 and 04/12/1590); YCA, B31: York Corporation House Book, 1592–1598 (16/02/1593).
79 YCA, B30: York Corporation House Book, 1587–1592 (29/07/1590). Out of my data set of the extant records of 1,152 fines for insanitary nuisance received by the Chamberlain as a result of presentments made by various city courts, between 1559 and 1687, ten of the 156 (6%) which detailed the specific location of the nuisance occurred in Hungate, the third most frequently cited location after Toft Green and Without Micklegate Bar.
80 YCA, B30: York Corporation House Book, 1587–1592 (24/11/1590).
81 YCA, B31: York Corporation House Book, 1592–1598 (13/09/1594).
82 YCA, B30: York Corporation House Book, 1587–1592 (18/12/1590).
83 YCA, B31: York Corporation House Book, 1592–1598 (13/06/1593).
84 YCA, B31: York Corporation House Book, 1592–1598 (13/09/1594).
85 YCA, B31: York Corporation House Book, 1592–1598 (24/07/1598).
86 YCA, B24: York Corporation House Book, 1565–1572 (13/07/1565). A similar ordinance was passed in April 1570, see YCA, B24: York Corporation House Book, 1565–1572 (03/04/1570).
87 YCA, B26: York Corporation House Book, 1574–1577 (09/12/1575).
88 YCA, B26: York Corporation House Book, 1574–1577 (09/12/1575).
89 YCA, B30: York Corporation House Book, 1587–1592 (13/06/1589).
90 YCA, B31: York Corporation House Book, 1592–1598 (04/10/1598 and 11/10/1598).
91 YCA, B28: York Corporation House Book, 1580–1585 (31/01/1584).
92 YCA, B29: York Corporation House Book, 1585–1587 (09/08/1585).
93 For in-depth discussion of disease in York in the Tudor period, see D. Palliser, 'Epidemics in Tudor York', *Northern History*, 8 (1973), pp. 45–63.
94 YCA, B32: York Corporation House Book, 1598–1605 (19/03/1600).
95 YCA, B32: York Corporation House Book, 1598–1605 (19/03/1600).
96 YCA, B32: York Corporation House Book, 1598–1605 (19/03/1600).
97 YCA, B32: York Corporation House Book, 1598–1605 (23/04/1600).
98 YCA, B32: York Corporation House Book, 1598–1605 (23/04/1600).
99 YCA, B32: York Corporation House Book, 1598–1605 (23/04/1600).
100 YCA, B32: York Corporation House Book, 1598–1605 (29/03/1603).
101 YCA, B32: York Corporation House Book, 1598–1605 (11/05/1604).
102 YCA, B33: York Corporation House Book, 1605–1613 (18/02/1608).
103 Indeed, out of out of my data set of 1,152 fines for insanitary nuisance received by the Chamberlain as a result of presentments made by various city courts, between 1559 and 1687, nine out of the 156 (6%) which detailed the specific location of the nuisance occurred at the Staith, the fourth most frequently cited location after Toft Green, Without Micklegate Bar and Hungate.
104 YCA, B33: York Corporation House Book, 1605–1613 (05/10/1610).
105 YCA, B33: York Corporation House Book, 1605–1613 (05/10/1610).

106 YCA, B33: York Corporation House Book, 1605–1613 (05/10/1610).
107 YCA, B35: York Corporation House Book, 16251637 (21/09/1627).
108 Northumberland Record Office, PHU/C2: Hexham Dunghill Deed (20/10/1649).
109 YCA, B35: York Corporation House Book, 1625–1637 (24/09/1630).
110 YCA, B35: York Corporation House Book, 1625–1637 (27/09/1632).
111 YCA, B36: York Corporation House Book, 1637–1650 (11/12/1644).
112 YCA, B35: York Corporation House Book, 1625–1637 (05/08/1633).
113 YCA, B35: York Corporation House Book, 1625–1637 (05/08/1633).
114 YCA, B36: York Corporation House Book, 1637–1650 (24/09/1638).
115 YCA, B36: York Corporation House Book, 1637–1650 (15/01/1640).
116 YCA, B36: York Corporation House Book, 1637–1650 (25/02/1644).
117 YCA, B36: York Corporation House Book, 1637–1650 (14/03/1644 and 20/03/1644).
118 YCA, B36: York Corporation House Book, 1637–1650 (11/06/1646).
119 YCA, B36: York Corporation House Book, 1637–1650 (17/05/1645).
120 Borthwick Institute, University of York Library, PR/Y/MS/5: St Michael's Churchwarden Account Book, 1626–1710.
121 Borthwick Institute, University of York Library, PR/YHTG/15: York Holy Trinity Goodramgate Constables' Accounts, 1636–1735, ff. 63–64.
122 *Rare Tracts and Imprints of the Northern Counties*, pp. 14–18.
123 Tyne and Wear Archives, BC.RV/1/2: River Tyne Court Book, 1647–1650 (20/02/1647).
124 Bristol Record Office, JQS/Pr/1: Presentments to the Grand Jury to the Bristol Leet, 1628–1666 (28/04/1629).
125 Bristol Record Office, JQS/Pr/1: Presentments to the Grand Jury to the Bristol Leet, 1628–1666 (28/04/1629).
126 YCA, B34: York Corporation House Book, 1613–1625 (20/03/1614).
127 YCA, B34: York Corporation House Book, 1613–1625 (20/03/1614).
128 YCA, B34: York Corporation House Book, 1613–1625 (28/03/1616).
129 YCA, B35: York Corporation House Book, 1625–1637 (13/05/1633).
130 YCA, B35: York Corporation House Book, 1625–1637 (21/09/1627).
131 YCA, B35: York Corporation House Book, 1625–1637 (05/09/1631).
132 YCA, B37: York Corporation House Book, 1650–1663 (03/02/1652).
133 YCA, B37: York Corporation House Book, 1650–1663 (05/03/1655).
134 YCA, B37: York Corporation House Book, 1650–1663 (05/12/0660).
135 The reports themselves have not survived in the extant archives of York Corporation.
136 YCA, B37: York Corporation House Book, 1650–1663 (27/09/1654).
137 YCA, B38: York Corporation House Book, 1663–1688 (10/11/1664).
138 YCA, B38: York Corporation House Book, 1663–1688 (26/02/1667).
139 YCA, B38: York Corporation House Book, 1663–1688 (12/05/1675).
140 YCA, B38: York Corporation House Book, 1663–1688 (02/03/1682).
141 YCA, B39: York Corporation House Book, 1688–1700 (09/12/1691).
142 YCA, B37: York Corporation House Book, 1650–1663 (05/03/1655).
143 YCA, B38: York Corporation House Book, 1663–1688 (07/05/1673).
144 YCA, B38: York Corporation House Book, 1663–1688 (12/05/1675).
145 YCA, B39: York Corporation House Book, 1688–1700 (25/02/1696).
146 YCA, B38: York Corporation House Book, 1663–1688 (24/07/1674).
147 YCA, B38: York Corporation House Book, 1663–1688 (26/01/1674).
148 YCA, B38: York Corporation House Book, 1663–1688 (03/02/1673).
149 YCA, B38: York Corporation House Book, 1663–1688 (03/11/1675).
150 YCA, B39: York Corporation House Book, 1688–1700 (28/08/1689).
151 Borsay, *Urban Renaissance*, p. vii. For comparison with the eighteenth century, see P. Borsay, 'Politeness and elegance: the cultural re-fashioning of eighteenth-century York', in M. Hallet and J. Rendall (eds), *Eighteenth-Century York: Culture, Space and Society* (York: Borthwick Publications, 2003), pp. 1–12.

152 Borsay, *Urban Renaissance*, pp. 17, 37, 41.
153 Borsay, *Urban Renaissance*, p. 69.
154 Borsay, *Urban Renaissance*, p. viii.
155 Wood, 'The neighbourhood book', pp. 89–90.
156 R. Houston, 'Fire and filth: Edinburgh's environment, 1660–1760', *The Book of the Old Edinburgh Club, New Series*, 3 (1994), pp. 25–36, on p. 28.
157 R. Toolis and D. Sproat, 'The transformation of an early post-medieval town into a major modern city: excavation and survey of the Waverley Vaults, New Street, Edinburgh, Scotland', *Post Medieval Archaeology*, 41:1 (2007), pp. 155–79, on p. 172. See also S. Carter, 'A reassessment of the origins of the St Andrews "garden soil"', *Tayside and Fife Archaeological Journal*, 7 (2001), pp. 87–92; and J. McKenzie, 'Manuring practices in Scotland: deep anthropogenic soils and the historical record', in B. Ballin Smith, S. Taylor and G. Williams (eds), *West Over Sea: Studies in Scandinavian Sea-Borne Expansion and Settlement before 1300* (Leiden: Brill, 2007), pp. 401–17.
158 ECA, SL1/1/6: Edinburgh Town Council Minutes, 1579–1583.
159 ECA, SL1/1/8: Edinburgh Town Council Minutes, 1585–1589.
160 For further discussion of the ownership of waste-disposal receptacles in East Anglia and North East England, see Green, 'Heartless and unhomely?' pp. 69–101.
161 ECA, SL1/1/31: Edinburgh Town Council Minutes, 1684–1686.
162 See, for example, the petition against the candlemakers, submitted to Edinburgh City Council in 1592/1593: ECA, SL1/1/9: Edinburgh Town Council Minutes, 1589–1594.
163 ECA, SL1/1/9: Edinburgh Town Council Minutes, 1589–1594.
164 ECA, SL1/1/9: Edinburgh Town Council Minutes, 1589–1594.
165 *Extracts from the Council Register of the Burgh of Aberdeen 1398–1625*, 2 vols, ed. J. Stuart (Aberdeen: Spalding Club, 1844–1848), vol. 1, p. 33 (24/07/1579).
166 *Records of Glasgow*, vol. 3, p. 43 (15/10/1664).
167 Harrison, 'Public hygiene', p. 69.
168 M. Sanderson, *A Kindly Place?* p. 75; Harrison, 'Public hygiene', p. 69.
169 Makey, 'Edinburgh', p. 201.
170 ECA, SL1/1/33: Edinburgh Town Council Minutes, 1689–1691.
171 P. Smith, 'The foul burns of Edinburgh: public health attitudes and environmental change', *Scottish Geographical Magazine*, 91:1 (1975), pp. 25–36.
172 ECA, uncatalogued (removed from the Silver Safe): Treasurer's Accounts, 1581–1596.
173 Dingwall, *Late Seventeenth-Century Edinburgh*, pp. 13–16.
174 Dingwall, *Late Seventeenth-Century Edinburgh*, pp. 13–16.
175 ECA, SL1/1/10–17: Edinburgh Town Council Minutes, 1600–1653.
176 ECA, uncatalogued (removed from the Silver Safe): Treasurer's Accounts, 1636–1650.
177 J. Balfour-Paul (ed.), *The Scots Peerage*, 9 vols (Edinburgh, 1904–1914).
178 ECA, uncatalogued (removed from the Silver Safe): Treasurer's Accounts, 1623–1636.
179 ECA, uncatalogued (removed from the Silver Safe): Treasurer's Accounts, 1623–1636.
180 ECA, uncatalogued (removed from the Silver Safe): Treasurer's Accounts, 1623–1636.
181 ECA, uncatalogued (removed from the Silver Safe): Treasurer's Accounts, 1623–1636.
182 G. Donaldson, *Edinburgh History of Scotland vol. 3: Scotland James V–James VII* (Edinburgh: Oliver & Boyd, 1976), p. 35.
183 *Records of the Convention of Burghs*, vol. 2, p. 254 (06/07/1608).
184 ECA, SL1/1/14: Edinburgh Town Council Minutes, 1626–1636.
185 ECA, SL1/1/14: Edinburgh Town Council Minutes, 1626–1636.
186 ECA, SL1/1/17: Edinburgh Town Council Minutes, 1648–1653.
187 ECA, uncatalogued (removed from the Silver Safe): Treasurer's Accounts, 1636–1650.
188 ECA, uncatalogued (removed from the Silver Safe): Treasurer's Accounts, 1636–1650.
189 *Register of the Privy Council of Scotland*, vol. 11, p. 311.
190 *Records of Stirling*, vol. 1, p. 17 (27/10/1522).
191 *Council Register of Aberdeen, 1625–1747*, vol. 2, p. 270 (27/10/1670).

192 *Records of Glasgow*, vol. 3, pp. 84–85 (20/09/1666).
193 *Records of Glasgow*, vol. 1, p. 253 (09/09/1606).
194 ECA, uncatalogued (removed from the Silver Safe): Treasurer's Accounts, 1666–1690.
195 ECA, SL1/1/18: Edinburgh Town Council Minutes, 1653–1655.
196 ECA, SL1/1/18: Edinburgh Town Council Minutes, 1653–1655.
197 ECA, uncatalogued (removed from the Silver Safe): Treasurer's Accounts, 1623–1636.
198 Dingwall, *Late Seventeenth-Century Edinburgh*, pp. 13–16.
199 Dingwall, *Late Seventeenth-Century Edinburgh*, pp. 13–16.
200 *Register of the Privy Council of Scotland*, vol. 11, pp. 530–531 (04/03/1619).
201 ECA, SL1/1/29: Edinburgh Town Council Minutes, 1677–1680.
202 ECA, SL1/1/30: Edinburgh Town Council Minutes, 1681–1684.
203 ECA, SL1/1/32: Edinburgh Town Council Minutes, 1686–1689.
204 ECA, SL1/1/32: Edinburgh Town Council Minutes, 1686–1689.
205 ECA, SL1/1/34: Edinburgh Town Council Minutes, 1692–1694.
206 National Archives of Scotland, GD/18/1914: Papers of Clerk Family on Penicuik, Midlothian, 1373–1966 – Receipts to the Lady Elphinstone for annuity tax and proportion for street cleaning, 1687–1689.
207 Jenner, '"Cleanliness" and "dirt"', p. 64.
208 National Archives of Scotland, RH9/14/66: Petition of the Constables of Edinburgh, 1690.
209 National Archives of Scotland, RH9/14/66: Petition of the Constables of Edinburgh, 1690.
210 ECA, SL1/1/30: Edinburgh Town Council Minutes, 1681–1684.
211 ECA, SL1/1/18: Edinburgh Town Council Minutes, 1653–1655.
212 ECA, SL1/1/21: Edinburgh Town Council Minutes, 1661–1662.
213 G. Robertson, *General View of the Agriculture of the County of Mid-Lothian: with Observations on the means of its Improvement* (Edinburgh, 1795), pp. 141–142.
214 M. Flinn, et al. (eds), *Scottish Population History: from the seventeenth century to the 1930s* (Cambridge: Cambridge University Press, 1977), pp. 198–199.
215 ECA, uncatalogued (removed from the Silver Safe): Treasurer's Accounts, 1666–1690.
216 ECA, uncatalogued (removed from the Silver Safe): Treasurer's Accounts, 1666–1690.
217 ECA, uncatalogued (removed from the Silver Safe): Treasurer's Accounts, 1666–1690.
218 ECA, SL1/1/18: Edinburgh Town Council Minutes, 1653–1655.
219 ECA, SL1/1/18: Edinburgh Town Council Minutes, 1653–1655.
220 ECA, Sl144/1/6: Edinburgh Dean of Guild Court Minutes, 1656–1667.
221 ECA, SL144/1/6: Edinburgh Dean of Guild Court Minutes, 1656–1667.
222 ECA, SL144/1/6: Edinburgh Dean of Guild Court Minutes, 1656–1667.
223 ECA, SL1/1/17: Edinburgh Town Council Minutes, 1648–1653.
224 Rawcliffe, *Urban Bodies*, p. 3. See also the discussion of civility in early modern England by J. Barry, 'Civility and civic culture in early modern England: the meanings of urban freedom', in P. Burke et al. (eds), *Civil Histories: Essays Presented to Sir Keith Thomas* (Oxford: Oxford University Press, 2000), pp. 181–97; and K. Thomas, 'Cleanliness and godliness in early modern England', in A. Fletcher and P. Roberts (eds), *Religion, Culture and Society in Early Modern Britain: Essays in Honour of Patrick Collinson* (Cambridge: Cambridge University Press, 1994), pp. 56–83.
225 Rodger, 'Evolution of Scottish Town Planning', p. 79.
226 ECA, SL1/1/7: Edinburgh Town Council Minutes, 1583–1585.
227 *Records of Edinburgh, 1589–1718*, vol. 8, p. 197 (18/04/1649).
228 Jenner, '"Cleanliness and "dirt"', p. 144.
229 *Council Register of Aberdeen, 1625–1747*, vol. 2, pp. 143, 319–320 (09/08/1654 and 30–09/1696).
230 *Records of Glasgow*, vol. 1, p. 396 (22/12/1638).
231 E. Jones and M. Falkus, 'Urban improvement and the English economy in the seventeenth and eighteenth centuries', *Research in Economic History*, 4 (1979), pp. 193–233.

4   Regulating insanitary nuisances

Introduction

The majority of urban dwellers valued a clean environment in the outdoor public spaces where they lived and worked. Contemporaries went to considerable lengths to protect their collective neighbourhood standards of outdoor cleanliness against the minority of neighbours whose inconsiderate waste disposal arrangements and noxious activities threatened to undermine those standards. In the urban neighbourhoods of sixteenth- and seventeenth-century Britain, the overwhelming majority of neighbours lived in streets and vennels which hosted a necessary, but problematic, combination of human activities. The confluence of noxious, unsavoury waste materials emanating from the workshops of butchers, dyers, tanners, soap-boilers, skinners and tallow-chandlers, as well as those from both agricultural backlands and dwellings, was potentially overwhelming, especially during periods of hot weather. Such conditions were not conducive to harmonious neighbourly relations. Keith Wrightson noted in his important essay, 'The "Decline of Neighbourliness" Revisited', that 'the evidence surviving for the ... early seventeenth century abundantly demonstrates the vitality of the concept of neighbourliness as both a centrally important social relationship and a primary social ideal'.[1] While neighbourliness was, indeed, a central social ideal, this chapter argues that the daily business of living together, in often very densely populated urban streets, vennels and closes, strained neighbourly relations. Insanitary nuisance was a perennial problem, which quite often caused conflict between more and less fastidious neighbours. For example, in October 1635, the Bristol Court Leet Jurors presented Robert Evans and fined him 10s 'for throwing downe fish water in St Mary Porte Streete being very noisome to the passers by as also to the neighbours and beinge by them reproved ... answered contemptuously he would doe it againe in spite'.[2] This chapter explores the bottom-up, micropolitics which surrounded insanitary nuisances in the urban neighbourhoods of several English towns before focusing on the case studies of Edinburgh and York. It explains inhabitants' positive reactions to suffering insanitary nuisances as such experiences encouraged them to develop their attitudes towards sanitation and to use their local courts proactively not only to suppress nuisances but also to prevent their recurrence in the long term. It highlights the large extent to which inhabitants could and did engage with, and thereby supported, environmental regulation from above by initiating complaints at their courts, petitioning their urban councils to request more stringent regulation and complying with bylaws pertaining to waste disposal and noxious trades themselves. Neighbours in the Low Countries also worked together to force urban governors to improve the environment. On 30 October 1633, neighbours living in the Hoogstraat, the Poel and the Drabstraat in Ghent complained to their local governors about the erection of a salt refinery.[3] The Ghent governors supported the neighbours, discontinuing the refinery's activities and henceforth buildings which produced noxious fumes could not be erected until the entrepreneur had obtained the written permission of their neighbours. As Harald Deceulaer notes, formal neighbourhood organizations were absent in the Low Countries in the middle ages, and therefore this neighbourhood institution marks an important discontinuity in the early modern period, highlighting that Ghent's neighbours played no formal institutional role in the administration of justice or in the policing of the town until after 1584.[4]

By asking local courts and urban officials to punish such neighbours, urban dwellers demonstrated their willingness to participate in micro-scale, environmental regulation out of both self-interest and in the interests of their neighbourhood as a unit, rather than in response to top-down coercion by urban governors. Christopher Hamlin highlights 'it would be naïve to think that these legal means' in relation to the suppression of insanitary nuisances 'lessened conflict, protected health or represented an ideal civil society in any sense'.[5] While such legal facilities for the suppression of insanitary nuisances do not represent an 'ideal civic society' through modern-day eyes, sixteenth- and seventeenth-century urban courts presented, warned and fined a significant minority of inhabitants for creating insanitary nuisances which reduced their neighbours' life quality and without their environmental regulation, urban insanitary nuisances would certainly have been more prolific. While many such court presentments resulted from official ward inspections, undertaken by civic employees such as beadles, constables, wardens or baillies, not a few insanitary nuisance cases resulted from neighbours having complained directly to court jurors or civic employees. Some complained as individuals; others complained in groups. While this chapter necessarily focuses on the minority of inhabitants who disobeyed sanitation bylaws, it is important to remain mindful that the majority of householders did not create insanitary nuisances. In early modern British towns, careless disregard was the exception and careful maintenance of both economically valuable waste products and the various facilities to which households had access was the norm. Evidence of rules forbidding insanitary nuisances merely underlines the importance of careful waste disposal in early modern urban society. The exceptions, in the form of the minority of inhabitants who were presented for contravening sanitation bylaws, very much proved those rules.

English towns

Urban courts passed a plethora of bylaws to suppress and prevent perennial public nuisances committed by a small minority of inhabitants, from leaving dunghills in the streets for longer than was permitted, allowing livestock to roam freely, throwing human waste out of windows, sullying wells and rivers and blocking open sewers with solid waste. In 1652, for example, Liverpool's portmoot court forbade inhabitants to 'allow any dung to lie in the street for more than three days', or else to pay a penalty of 5s, 'this being a public nuisance'.[6] And, in 1637, Barnard Castle's Manorial Court ordered that nobody should 'conveye anye myre dunge, earth or other noisome excrements to his neighbours front' under the threat of 12d.[7] Local bylaws applied exclusively to particular manors' or urban corporations' jurisdictions, but many towns passed similar versions of the same regulations against nuisances. Urban authorities often took great care to ensure that the population heard and understood new proclamations and bylaws by paying civic officials to read them aloud in publicly prominent locations in order to ensure their maximum efficacy. To prevent the public nuisances of pigs and other free-ranging animals disrupting middens, obstructing highways and polluting streets and wells with their waste, Maidstone's Burghmote Court passed a bylaw in 1645, stipulating that 'proclamacion be made by the cryer ... upon the two next market dayes' that nobody allow 'theire hogg' to roam freely in the streets upon pain of 4d for every hog.[8] In 1654, the Newcastle upon Tyne Borough Court ordered the Bellman to read aloud a bylaw stating that 'inhabitants ... shall every Saturday night make cleane theire fronts', elaborating that 'offendeinge partyes' would pay 'severall rates'.[9] In 1633, the Carlisle Court Leet Jurors ordered 'that the booke of the orders and constitutions of this city shalbe seene and read openly in the common hall by the clarke at some freehold court yearly' and that every person who required 'a copy thereof shall have the same granted unto them'.[10] Although preventative bylaws' efficacy was potentially low, most inhabitants understood their own town's bylaws because local courts ordered town criers and bellmen to read new bylaws aloud repeatedly to ensure that they prevented, rather than merely punished, nuisances. Indeed, Mark Jenner found that London's environmental regulation was designed 'to obtain compliance rather than to exact retribution'.[11]

As public servants, constables and wardens were both formally obliged and actively encouraged to report nuisances within their view and to present contraveners of insanitary nuisance bylaws to local courts. In Carlisle, contraveners of hygiene bylaws and orders were presented and fined at Court Leets. Extant accounts record 1s payments to the beadles before each Court Leet for their 'note' or 'callender' of bylaw contraveners.[12] Carlisle's beadles, therefore, were potentially powerful representatives and tools of local law enforcement, comparable to constables elsewhere.[13] Depositing waste at town halls and churches was especially problematic and inevitably attracted constables' attention. In 1641, Barnard Castle's manorial court ordered John Wrightson, George Thompson and Richard Alderson to 'carry away there dunghills ... and other rubbish and excrements, at the side of the Toole Boothe staires' under the pain of 3s 4d.[14] And Richard Urland, of Coventry, was presented in 1674 'for making a dunghill against the chappell wall'.[15] Constables also noticed waste deposits which obstructed streets. Liverpool's portmoot court fined John Chandler 2s in 1650, for example, for 'letting muck lie in the street'.[16]

Constables presented people for not scouring their ditches and sewers. In 1685, Stockton Manorial Court fined Thomas Thomson and Elizabeth Kitching 3s 4d for 'not scouring theire guter'.[17] Similarly, in 1674, the Warwick Quarter Session presented Richard Gibbs for 'not scouring the ditch leading from his own house ... being a great annoyance to the highway'.[18] And, in 1693, Darlington Manorial Court presented 'Ralph Bainbridge ... for not suffitiently scoureing his gutter ... opening [into] the water suer adjoining the highway'.[19] Noxious trades were integral to urban economies, but when they became intolerable, constables eagerly presented businesses for creating a public nuisance. In 1616, Southampton Court Leet fined Mr Philipp Delamote, a dyer, 12d because his servants cast 'dyenge water out of the dye howse ... which ... causeth unsavorie smells to the people passinge bye, and therefore [is] not sufferable'.[20] It also fined another dyer, Mistress Judith de Lamotte, a widow, 12d in 1624 for 'casting out into the street dirty water from her dye-house'.[21] In 1688, Nottingham's Mickleton Jury fined widow Hazard 5s for her 'bleache howse'.[22] And James Heames, a Coventry feltmaker, was presented in 1682, 'for a nusance by throweing downe hatters water stale and soapsuds to the annoyance of his neighbours'.[23] All of these presentments resulted from constables' inspections or those of other representatives of local law enforcement, and without these men, appointed by urban governments across England, a great number of insanitary nuisances might well have continued unsuppressed.

Many urban court presentments refer to, and sometimes detail the extent of, neighbours' annoyance, thus suggesting that they resulted from neighbours having reported insanitary nuisances directly to constables and wardens themselves, or at least suggesting some discussion between constables and those offended by the nuisance. Dressed in their council liveries, these representatives of urban government were clearly visible and accessible to urban inhabitants who might have been less likely to have approached a formal court in person. Carlisle's beadles wore liveries made from 'tawny brown broadcloth'.[24] Neighbours could approach constables in unison to complain about a public nuisance. In 1681, Barnard Castle's manorial court ordered inhabitants to cease polluting a sewer with dung because 'great damage hath been to several neighbours'.[25] In 1626, Nottingham Borough Court fined Rodger Ryley 3s 4d for 'anoying the street withe fillthie stinkinge dreane watter ... to the great anoyance of neybors'.[26] And it presented Maister Nicholas Masten in 1630 for 'sufferinge his dreane water to be kepte in a well, and then beinge heald thear so longe, that the stinke and odious smell of it is verie noisome, to the great hurte of neighbors'.[27] Some presentments clearly resulted from an individual neighbour's complaint. In 1688, the constables of St Saviour's, Southwark, presented Burton Woolwich and Robert Thomas because dirty water from their privy leaked through Thomas Storey's cellar wall.[28]

Obviously, Storey complained because cellars are beyond constables' view and would not have been noticed during the course of an inspection.

Many presentments resulted from noxious dunghills being stored in public areas or close to neighbours' properties for lengthy time periods. In 1626, Nottingham's Mickleton Jury fined Thomas Stevensonne 3s 4d for 'anoyinge Hallifaxe lane withe a verie great muckehill, [which was] very noisome to his neybors'.[29] And, in 1651, Liverpool's Portmoot Court fined Edward Moore 1s for 'letting dung lie in Castle street to [the] annoyance of neighbours'.[30] In 1677, George Newcome, of Coventry, was presented for 'a nusance in laying a muckhill against William Bent's wall'.[31] In Berwick, for example, in 1592, 'the neighbours of the windemill hole' were presented to the Bailiffs' Court because they made 'a dunghill at John Saintes howse whiche is verye noisome and hurtfull to him'.[32] In 1625, moreover, Elizabeth Shepperd, of Scarborough, was presented at the Sheriff's Tourn 'for her full [i.e. rubbish] & dirt lying against William Headleys wall att her back doore to his great annoyance'.[33] In 1667, Liverpool's portmoot court ordered James Heyes, under pain of 10s, to remove muck from his backland 'which annoys Widow Formeby, and ... to prevent the water from annoying her'.[34] And, in 1616, Robert Mayor, of Southampton, built a 'new skeelinge' on his backland, which blocked the 'auntient light' into John Sparrow's kitchen; Southhampton Court Leet ordered Mayor to restore Sparrow's light under pain of 5s.[35] Though pre-litigation mediation is irretrievable, most of these neighbours had probably attempted in the first place to resolve nuisances privately and had been unsuccessful. As Janet Loengard observes, 'self-help has the virtues of speed, simplicity and cheapness'.[36] For example, an Elizabethan Chancery case mentions a four-year period preceding it during which Edmund Nicholson and Thomas Yates suffered from a nuisance created by Godfrey Bradshaw. Living above Nicholson and Yates's shop in which they sold woollen goods in the London parish of St Augustine, near Paul's Gate in the ward of Bread Street, Bradshaw allowed 'noisome waters and licors' to fall down 'in exceeding great aboundance into the said shop and entrie upon the said wares, their shewboards, themselves [and] their servants' from 'time to time by the space of these fower yeres last past'.[37] Before resorting to Chancery, Nicholson and Yates had,

> In gentle and friendly manner often times desired and repaired the said Bradshawe to repaire and amend the said flower [i.e. floor] joists and beames of his said kitchin for according of soe unneighbourly and unconscionable annoyance ... he the said Godfrie Bradshaw hath and doth utterly refuse.[38]

This case demonstrates the pre-litigation negotiations and conflict which could precede an insanitary nuisance court case between neighbours.

Local courts sometimes failed to protect inhabitants against nuisances. It took Southampton Court Leet three attempts, between 1602 and 1604, to compel William Parmett to amend 'that filthie noisome gutter runinge out of ... [his] howse into John Graunts ditche ... [which] lyeth most filthie & unseemly'.[39] John Graunt's frustration surely increased as this nuisance case lasted for three years.

Nevertheless, in most cases local courts resolved nuisances satisfactorily. Local rather than national central courts heard the overwhelming majority of insanitary nuisance cases. Indeed, Chris Brooks was right to deny Sir William Holdsworth's assumption that 'local justice was either inactive or unimportant'.[40] And Marjorie McIntosh rightly emphasizes local courts' 'key roles' in regulating contemporaries' lives.[41] Christopher Harrison, moreover, found that manorial courts were 'central to the governance of Tudor England', and that their records are 'evidence of a greater skill and sophistication in the general populace than educational historians have allowed'.[42] Keith Wrightson's research into the micropolitics of rural constables' presentments revealed a 'reluctance to prosecute', which he attributes to constables having been both their fellow villagers' friends or kin and officers of the law.[43] But densely populated towns' nuisances were prosecuted rigorously by urban constables who operated in quite different circumstances from those of their rural counterparts. Urban centres' significantly larger populations reduced urban constables' likelihood of presenting inhabitants at court with whom they were acquainted personally. Urban constables were also under significantly more pressure than their rural counterparts were to present offenders.

Urban court presentments for insanitary nuisances were far from merely ceremonious routines effectively selling permission to maintain nuisances. Local court presentments offered real solutions to real and urgent problems which were impacting negatively on people's daily lives. Even a prestigious social status did not excuse one's creation of an insanitary nuisance at the expense of one's neighbours having jeopardized the life quality of one's neighbours in local jurors' eyes. Nottingham Mickleton Jury was prepared to humiliate Maister Robert Sherwine, one of Nottingham's very own aldermen, because he had erected a 'swinecote in Pepper Street, to the annoyance of people goeing to Church'.[44] Across Britain, urban courts and constables made significant efforts to protect inhabitants' life quality against public and private insanitary nuisances. They were not unwilling to regulate insanitary nuisances rigorously.

York

In York, where four separate courts held simultaneous and overlapping jurisdiction over environmental regulation, the overwhelming majority of fines for insanitary nuisances in the period 1559 to 1689, charged by all four courts and detailed in all sixty-one extant annual lists of fines received by the Chamberlain between these years, were charged for the offence of permitting one's livestock to roam freely through public areas (see Figure 6). This reflects and explains the frequency of bylaws and corporation meeting discussions relating to this particular issue, discussed in chapter three (representing 15 per cent of York Corporation's discussions and bylaws pertaining to sanitation between 1560 and 1700). It was not necessarily the most problematic nuisance on the streets and it was not necessarily regulated so stringently specifically because this nuisance was adversely affecting inhabitants' life quality more so than other nuisances. It may simply have been, rather, the most frequently committed nuisance, and therefore the easiest one to fine, thereby raising more funds for the corporation. However, it is true that free roaming livestock did cause serious problems by depositing their own waste in public areas and by blocking strategic thoroughfares which needed to remain passable for the purposes of trade. The second most frequently presented sanitation offence which resulted in a fine over the whole period was street cleanliness, perhaps a relatively easy offence to fine because dirty forefronts which contravened the city bylaws would have been very obvious to civic officials when they performed street inspections. With almost as many fines as street cleanliness, the third most frequently fined sanitation offence was solid waste disposal, which would also have been very easily spotted during a street inspection. Liquid waste disposal and drainage offences were fined far less over the course of the whole period, in fourth place, followed with even fewer fines as a result of offences associated with dirty trades. While liquid waste and drainage nuisances could cause significant problems within the micro-scale environment of a neighbourhood, they had a far less serious capacity to block thoroughfares or to cause other significant citywide problems. Inadequate drainage and disposal of liquid wastes also tended to cause comparatively less serious consequences which often drained away, causing only short-term problems. That offences relating to dirty trades generated the fewest fines over the whole period is surprising, and suggests that these crafts and trades might well have been regulated in house at the guild level. It is also possible that those working in dirty trades managed their production processes and waste materials relatively diligently in order to avoid complaints, intervention by civic officials and fines. That there was only a relatively small pool of inhabitants who could potentially have created insanitary nuisances associated with dirty trades, compared to the numbers of householders who could dump solid waste in public areas or neglect to clean their forefronts, for example, might also explain the relatively low numbers of fines for offences in this category.

In the period 1559 to 1599, the most frequent category of sanitation offences which resulted in a fine was free roaming livestock which reflects the highest category of fines for insanitary nuisances over the whole period. The second most frequent category of offence was solid waste disposal, the offence which was most frequently discussed in council meetings during this period. This suggests

Category	Number of fines
Livestock	432
Street cleanliness	319
Solid waste disposal	301
Liquid waste disposal and drainage	88
Dirty trades	12
Total	**1,152**

Figure 6 Categories of insanitary nuisance fines exacted by various courts in the city of York, 1559–1689

that there was a rough degree of symmetry in relation to one issue which was being both quite heavily regulated in the city and discussed in depth by the corporation. However, whereas street cleaning was discussed very frequently by the corporation throughout this period, there was only one fine for this offence during these years. This suggests that inhabitants were largely fulfilling their obligations in relation to street cleaning while the corporation were, perhaps, more concerned about the issue than was necessary. Nuisances pertaining to dirty trades and liquid waste disposal failed to bring in any fines at all during this period, which is surprising as these are exactly the sorts of nuisances which caused significant problems in the micro-scale environment of particular neighbourhoods.

In the first half of the seventeenth century, as in the late sixteenth century, livestock was the most frequently presented insanitary nuisance, followed by street cleanliness. Clearly, free roaming livestock was a common nuisance, but the extent to which inhabitants were fined for this nuisance does seem excessive and it is impossible to discern from the fines alone to what extent this nuisance actually annoyed inhabitants or contributed to poor outdoor sanitation. What is most striking in the statistics is that nuisances pertaining to street cleanliness increased from one fine in the last four decades of the sixteenth century to the second most frequently fined offence in the first half of the seventeenth century. This significant increase perhaps reflects the corporation's concern over street cleanliness in response to the threat of plague during this period in particular as York suffered plague epidemics in 1604, 1631 and 1645. Efforts to rid the streets of foul-smelling waste products which were perceived by contemporaries as potential sources of infectious miasma clouds would have been at least partly facilitated and achieved by heavy regulation of street cleanliness by all four of the city's courts which had jurisdiction in this area of urban life. Solid waste disposal nuisances were the third most common fine for insanitary nuisance during this period, which was perhaps an integral part of the civic officials' urgent campaign to rid the streets of malodorous matter in order to reduce the potential sources of miasma. Nuisances relating to liquid waste disposal and drainage were the fourth most frequently fined category and nuisances pertaining to dirty trades were the least frequently fined offences, only generating twelve fines over the period.

Between 1650 and 1689, in sharp discontinuity from the preceding ninety years, insanitary nuisances pertaining to street cleanliness, and to a slightly lesser extent solid waste disposal, dominated fines for insanitary nuisances. Although the threat of plague had passed, the corporation of the late seventeenth century might have been more fastidious about street cleanliness and therefore less tolerant of badly kept forefronts and malodorous and unsightly waste in the streets. In the context of Peter Borsay's provincial 'urban renaissance', which gathered speed after 1660, such attitudinal changes in relation to dirt and waste would have been highly likely. Fines for nuisances pertaining to livestock became a significantly less serious issue, or at least a less heavily regulated issue, during this period and no fines at all were received for nuisances relating to dirty trades. Only a few fines were received for nuisances concerning liquid waste disposal and drainage. The statistics are not necessarily the result of changes in the prevalence of the different categories of nuisances on the streets, but rather they could well reflect the changing priorities within the corporation which could have been passed on in turn to the court jurors, wardens and constables who instigated such presentments.

That the offenders' forenames were recorded alongside 98 per cent of the fines in the Chamberlains' account books means that they can be split according to the gender of the offender. Unsurprisingly, as shown in Figure 7, it is clear that the overwhelming majority of offenders (90 per cent) was male, suggesting that very often men took responsibility as heads of household for nuisances caused by those within their families, including their servants who were often responsible for waste disposal and cleaning forefronts. Only a small minority (8 per cent) was female. Out of this small minority of female offenders, however, interesting patterns emerge, such as that livestock nuisances, most of which involved the inadequate housing of swine, and nuisances pertaining to the disposal of solid waste accounted for 66 per cent of female offences. Women managed household food purchases and familial food consumption, and were consequently responsible for administering residual food waste to swine. They were also responsible for the disposal of solid waste, especially of manure produced by pigs and other animals housed on backlands. It is unfortunate that we cannot ascertain how many of these female offenders lived without a husband as widows or single women, and were therefore the default offenders in relation to a nuisance committed by someone living in a family of which they were the head, and how many lived with a husband. Some nuisances might have been perceived as having been more closely related to a woman's than a man's domain. Unsurprisingly, the only category of offences committed exclusively by men was that of dirty trades, which were overwhelmingly male dominated. A similar pattern was discerned from Carlisle's seventeenth-century court leet records. Only one insanitary nuisance offence was committed by more women than men: obstructing the streets with swine troughs. Moreover, in Carlisle, three insanitary nuisance offences were committed exclusively by men: leaving raw materials and rubbish in the streets, drying noxious skins in public areas and leaving animals unburied. The first two were associated with primarily male crafts and trades which required bulky raw

	Male		Female		Both		Unspecified		Total	
	No.	%	No.	%	No.	%	No.	%	No.	%
Livestock	391	91	30	7	–	–	11	3	432	38
Street cleanliness	296	93	21	7	–	–	2	1	319	28
Solid waste disposal	264	88	29	10	1	(0.3)	7	2	301	26
Liquid waste disposal and drainage	78	89	9	10	1	1	–	–	88	8
Dirty trades	11	92	–	–	–	–	1	8	12	1
Totals	1040	90	89	8	2	(0.2)	21	2	1,152	100

Figure 7 Categories of insanitary nuisances fined in York City by gender, 1559–1689

materials and which produced large amounts of rubbish; the third might have resulted from women's disinclination, or indeed inability, to move and dispose of heavy animal corpses.[45]

The ward in which the insanitary nuisance offence was committed was not recorded in the overwhelming majority (77 per cent) of cases in the Chamberlains' accounts (see Figure 8). Within the minority of nuisance fines for which the ward was recorded, however, there was a striking degree of symmetry across the wards, a difference of only eighteen between the ward with the most insanitary nuisances, Monk Ward, and that with the fewest, Micklegate Ward. Considering that Walmegate and Micklegate Ward had most open space, one would expect to see most nuisances in Bootham and Monk Ward and fewest in Micklegate and Walmegate Ward, which is indeed the case, according to these statistics, but only by a minimal degree. Nevertheless, this does suggest that more open space perhaps led to fewer insanitary nuisances. Phil Withington undertook some detailed research into York's social composition and local government, highlighting a 'civic neighbourhood' which extended westwards along Micklegate and eastwards through Ousegate, and finding that Micklegate and Walmgate wards housed the fewest non-citizens (only 1 per cent of its rate-paying householders), whereas Bootham and Monk wards housed a population of which a much more substantial 9 per cent of its rate-paying householders were non-citizens, suggesting that it was less affluent.[46] This suggests that the higher socio-economic status of Micklegate and Walmegate wards' inhabitants, compared to that of the inhabitants of Bootham and Monk wards, might have contributed to fewer insanitary nuisance presentments in addition to the fact that they featured more open space than Bootham and Monk wards.

Even fewer insanitary nuisance fines specified a more precise location than a ward (14 per cent), but the statistics are still potentially meaningful. The locations with only one recorded nuisance were obviously less problematic hotspots than those associated with seventeen and thirteen throughout the period. Toft Green was the location in the city most frequently associated with an insanitary nuisance, accounting for 11 per cent of those nuisances which detailed a specific location. This was an open area on which inhabitants could graze their livestock, but it became a popular and convenient hotspot on which many inhabitants chose to

Ward	No. of fines	Percentage of fines
Monk Ward	74	6
Bootham Ward	68	6
Walmgate Ward	63	6
Micklegate Ward	56	5
Unspecified	891	77
Total	1152	100

Figure 8 Insanitary nuisance fines exacted in York City by ward, 1559–1689

leave their rubbish and manure. The second most common location noted in the chamberlains' accounts was Without Micklegate Bar, accounting for 8 per cent of nuisances with a specific location, which suggests that although inhabitants were dumping rubbish in a public place which had not been specifically set aside for waste disposal, they did at least take the time and make the effort to remove it into a suburb beyond the city walls. That the minority of inhabitants who dumped rubbish in inappropriate public places did so in places which were relatively less problematic than those in central thoroughfares suggests that insanitary nuisance offenders might not have been completely indifferent to disposing of waste carefully. Even those who broke sanitation bylaws might still have respected their cityscape to some extent. The third most common location was Hungate, accounting for 6 per cent of nuisances with a specified location, which was an unusually straight street descending down to the River Foss, which provided an excellent location for the watering of cattle because it was relatively easy to drive cattle down the street. Moreover, it was also the site at which muck was loaded onto boats to be transported to Tang Hall down the River Foss. The street attracted waste from driven cattle as well as muck dumped by inhabitants. While the insanitary nuisance fines in York are not very detailed and they were recorded in list form, they still reveal much about the regulation of insanitary nuisances in the city. While they might have been extracted by a fiscally motivated corporation, that they were even described as offences confirms that such behaviour was unambiguously unacceptable and by the very existence of fines, this sort of behaviour was discouraged.

Sometimes, York Corporation took focused action to regulate a particular insanitary nuisance. In September 1613, the malodorous nuisance of crab-apple mills was causing concern.

> Ther is Complaint made by divers of the most sufficientest Inhabitantes in Spurriergate and Jubbergaite against those that kepe Crabb [i.e. apple] milnes in Jubbergate beinge in the middest of this Cittie alledgeinge by ther peticon the infectious smells which cometh & groweth by the kepeinge of that which remaineth after they be grund and likewise much compleined of by straingers and gentlemen who lodge in ther Innes nere unto the same mills of the evill smells that growe of them and a great disquietinge of them by reason they often work all or the most parte of the night. It is therfore thought mete and so ordred by this court that such as now have or use any crab milnes in the aforesaide strete or that hereafter shall have and occupie any in the same strete shall once everie daie at the least clense and take awaye all that which remaineth of the crabes so grund and caried forth of the strete and kepe ther milnes clean & sweete so as the same maie not be any annoyance to their neighboures or straingers. And that they shall not grinde any crabes in ther milnes after nine of the clock at night upon paine of ... such fine as at the discretion of the Lord Maior.[47]

Clearly, the smell of the ground crab-apples, rather than the unsavoury appearance of such material, caused annoyance, indeed alarm, and motivated York Corporation to suppress the nuisance. The malodours produced by the mill are referred to as 'evil' and 'infectious' and the desired result of clearing away the remains of the ground apples at least 'once everie day' was to maintain a 'clean & sweete' mill which would no longer annoy the neighbours or visitors. In the context of contemporary understandings of miasmatic contagion, permeable skin and humoralism, malodorous nuisances tended to be perceived as dangerous, potentially fatal, health risks rather than merely as annoying inconveniences and these understandings clearly fuelled efforts to remove insanitary sources of noxious vapours.[48] In this sense, describing 'evil smells' might have been no exaggeration. The 'great disquieting of them by reason they often work all or most parte of the night' was also a motivating factor for the suppression of this nuisance in what was clearly a civil area of the city in which strangers and gentlemen slept.

Insanitary nuisances in York were understood as unambiguously unacceptable by civic offials and inhabitants across the city. Neither civic officials nor those governed by them ignored malodours released from industrial production processes, the dumping of noxious or unsightly waste materials in inappropriate public areas, a neighbour's failure to clean their forefront, livestock being permitted to roam freely or neighbours neglecting their communal or individual obligations to maintain liquid drainage infrastructure. While the regulatory systems which functioned to enforce sanitation bylaws in the city were neither comprehensive nor robust, they represent the consistent efforts of local governors to maintain a clean, functioning and salubrious cityscape for the benefit of inhabitants, visitors and themselves.

Edinburgh

In Edinburgh, the majority of insanitary nuisances were suppressed by the city's Dean of Guild Court. Edinburgh Dean of Guild Court had jurisdiction over a relatively wide area beyond Edinburgh itself: the old royalty of the burgh, encompassing Canongate, West Port, Potterrow, Pleasance and Leith.[49] Even by the end of the sixteenth century, Edinburgh Dean of Guild Court's jurisdiction of cases of neighbourhood was still relatively new, only having been delegated officially from Edinburgh City Council by the Decree Arbitral in March 1584, the council's direct response to the growing number of neighbourhood disputes with which it had to deal. The largest category of insanitary nuisance presented at the Dean of Guild Court between 1566 and 1607 was problematic waste disposal into jaw holls and sewers, accounting for 36 per cent of extant insanitary nuisances presented to the court during these years. The waste which was disposed of into jaw holls and sewers was overwhelmingly liquid, consisting mainly of dirty water from cooking and cleaning, urine and blood. Solid waste tended to be added to dunghills outside of properties. However, even liquid waste could still be malodorous and it still had the potential to reduce neighbours' life quality. In December 1580, for example, James Fowlis, who lived on the east side of Forrester's Wynd, a close descending steeply from the High Street, complained to the Dean of Guild Court that John Mosman, the owner of a building directly to the south of his tenement, 'had laitlie at his own hand ... sett ane jaw holl upoun the eist side of his land' where there never was one before and made the 'water gait ... of the said jaw holl directlie to fall upoun the entrie and door of ane hous lyand at the nether end' of the close of the complainer's lodging.[50] The Dean of Guild and his Council inspected the properties and found

> the said Jhone Mosman to have done wrang in striking furth of the said jaw holl in maner foresaid and thairfore ordains him to remove and tak the same away and to big and close up his wall with stone and lime as the same was before the striking furth thairof without prejudice always.[51]

In this case, James Fowlis was intolerant of the nuisance of his neighbour's liquid waste exiting the jaw holl so near to the entrance of his home. He approached the court to request that his neighbour remove the jaw holl and repair the wall to its previous condition. Submitting an official complaint to the Dean of Guild Court may well have been his last resort, after one or more verbal attempts to rectify the situation. Alternatively, he might have approached the court in the first place. Either way, James clearly believed in the court's ability to suppress the nuisance and he was sufficiently intolerant of this nuisance to potentially jeopardize relations with a nearby neighbour. It is impossible to say how long this jaw holl had been offending James before he approached the court, but that it was a new construction suggests that it had been there for a relatively short period of time, perhaps a few months.

The high proportion of nuisances pertaining to liquid waste disposal and drainage in this period contrasts markedly with the lack of discussion of such matters in meetings of Edinburgh Council during roughly the same time period. This suggests a certain amount of asymmetry between top-down efforts to prevent the creation of such nuisances in the first place by enforcing ordinances across the city and the aspects of environmental regulation which were causing most problems for inhabitants themselves in their neighbourhoods, as represented by their complaints to the Dean of Guild Court. It is possible that after the decree of 1584, by which exclusive jurisdiction of neighbourhood cases was handed over from Edinburgh Council to the Dean of Guild and his court, there was far less communication between the two institutions and therefore Edinburgh Council was unaware of the issues about which neighbours were complaining most vociferously. It is impossible to draw any firm conclusions here. If there there was minimal communication between the two institutions, inhabitants' complaints might not have been used to influence and shape discussions about sanitation at council meetings, and thereby the top-down regulations which were issued by Edinburgh Council and enforced across the city. If this were the case, it would have to be assumed that the only way in which inhabitants were able to directly influence top-down, citywide regulation by Edinburgh Council was in the form of a direct petition. What is much more likely, however, is that liquid waste disposal and drainage nuisances did not cause significant problems in the context of macro-scale city government, even if this type of nuisance caused relatively serious problems for small numbers of inhabitants living in particular neighbourhoods. While liquid waste nuisances were often unpleasant for those living very close to them, especially if the waste was malodorous, ineffective drainage did not have a huge potential to cause severe problems across the city in terms of blocking thoroughfares and adversely affecting trade, industry and economic growth.

Problematic solid waste disposal, however, accounted for 31 per cent of nuisances between 1566 and 1607 as well as 37 per cent of council discussions in roughly the same period, thus suggesting that both Edinburgh's governors and inhabitants were keen to prevent and suppress this type of nuisance, whether or not there was significant communication between the two institutions of Edinburgh Council and the Dean of Guild Court. Unlike liquid waste, solid waste not only caused potentially long-term malodorous nuisances and obstructed closes and entrances in the micro-scale environment of individual neighbourhoods, but it also tended to block strategic thoroughfares which Edinburgh Council had to ensure remained passable for the purposes of trade and the city's political functions as Scotland's capital. In September 1578, for example, James Spottiswood, who lived at the foot of Libbertoun's Wynd, complained to the Dean of Guild Court because David Dickinson had caused the wall of James' tenement to become so 'rottin and consumed by certan muck middings gathered and heaped be the said David' on a 'piece of waste land of his adjacent to the said James'.[52] The court ordered David to 'remove and take away the muck and filth gatherit in the said waste with all diligence possible'.[53] Solid waste had a much greater potential to accumulate over a long period and create severe long-term problems whereas liquid waste posed a comparatively temporary problem until it drained away. Both the Dean of Guild Court and Edinburgh Council regulated the problematic disposal of solid waste relatively rigorously.

The nuisances of leaking and noxious privies and throwing waste directly from doors were relatively uncommon in this period, accounting for 13 per cent and 9 per cent of presented nuisances, respectively. In the absence of heavy population pressure, while inhabitants were still living in relatively long-established neighbourhoods with more open space, only a tiny proportion of Edinburgh's population was presented for throwing chamber pots out of windows, an offence which either increased in real terms or was presented by the Dean of Guild much more rigorously in the seventeenth century. The nuisances of obstructing a neighbour's sewer or jaw holl and the failure to scour one's own sewer or jaw holl accounted for only 7 per cent and 5 per cent of nuisances presented during these years, respectively. While these nuisances posed serious problems for individual neighbours, and it is important that those neighbours refused to tolerate them, they perhaps did not cause citywide problems.

Between 1613 and 1646, improper disposal of human waste out of windows and doors directly onto neighbours' roofs, backlands and streets and closes was the proportionately largest category of insanitary nuisance presented to and suppressed by Edinburgh Dean of Guild Court. It accounted for 45 per cent of insanitary nuisances during that period, a substantial proportional increase when compared to the mere 9 per cent of insanitary nuisances of this category between

1566 and 1607. This nuisance clearly contravened contemporaries' standard of what constituted good neighbourhood. It may well reflect the significant increase in population density and the consequent subdivision and heightening of tenements, which meant that significantly more domestic waste was being produced within the same geographical area. In March 1624, for example, William Bruce and his spouse, Rachel Johnston, who lived in Wilsons Close, complained that their next door neighbours, Mr Johne Sanderlands, Laurence Cockbrane and John Pringel,

> cast out at the windows ... all maner of filth and vile excraments and thaire watter potts and casts out wesche [i.e. stale urine] furth thairof upone the ruiff of one tenement and dailie falls down ... in the said clos whereby no man or person may cum up or doun [i.e. down] the said clos unfiled with all sort of dirt and filth. Which will mak the said complainers land altogether unproffitabill that none are abill to dwell or remaine therin be the grait and filthie taist and savor arising be the casting out of the said filth and excrements.[54]

This was a time when contemporaries believed that inhaled malodours could damage their permeable bodies in the same way as ingested rotten food could, which explains why in this case, nobody was 'abill to dwell or remaine therin be the grait and filthie taist and savor arising'.[55] The minutes were written by scribes, but the details of this case originated with the inhabitants who lived with this nuisance on a daily basis and they clearly meant this in a literal sense. No tenant would reside in the property unless the nuisance was suppressed. Indeed, an insanitary nuisance's malodour was often what motivated complainants, first and foremost, to approach the Dean of Guild Court to have it suppressed. Ensuring that the air they inhaled was wholesome, rather than unwholesome, was a hugely important aspect of environmental regulation in contemporaries' minds. Neighbours could and did threaten to leave their rented property if insanitary nuisances continued. By threatening to withdraw their rent, they forced their landlord to respect their perceived need, and possibly even their perceived 'right', to live in a clean and sweet-smelling environment. William Bruce was able as a tenant to engage quite powerfully in the environmental regulation of his neighbourhood to protect his and his spouse's life quality.

Inappropriately situated middings and rubbish heaps were also a frequent source of conflict in Edinburgh's densely populated neighbourhoods, accounting for 19 per cent of presented nuisances between 1613 and 1646. Middings, or dunghills, were inevitable by-products of necessary urban agriculture and horse-drawn transportation, but they caused a nuisance in the city when they blocked passages, impeded drainage or were left unremoved near to dwellings for long periods of time. In May 1619, John Eistum, a maltman, complained that Beatrix Hode's tenants,

> Has cast onto ane filthie midding all kind of filth and fulyie [i.e. muck or rubbish] to the bak sidwall of his foir tenement of land lyand adjacent to the

bak land perteining to the said Beatrix in lifrent lyand under the castle wall on the north side of the kinges hie stret which condemms the gutters and easing dropps of the saids lands and causes the same to run in throw the sidwall of his said tenement and it hes consumed his said sidwall that the same is likely to fall.[56]

The Dean of Guild and his Council ordered

Beatrix to remove the midding and filth cassin [i.e. thrown] to the said persewars [i.e. complainant's] bak wall and to keip the said wall frie of her filth and middings in time cuming and that thair may be frie passige for the persewars easing drop.[57]

Notably, it was not the presence of the midding itself which caused annoyance, but rather the obstruction which it caused to drainage and the consequent damage which inefficient drainage caused to John's sidwall. In February 1641, similarly, William Dalgleish, a baxter, and his spouse, Margaret Hall, complained that their neighbour, James Scott, 'casts in muck and fulyie and … and maks ane midding stead … whereby they rott and consum the syidwall' of William Dalgleish's land 'and causis the watter to stand and gorge and rune in throw his said walls and fill the same full of underwatter'.[58] The court ordered James Scott to have the dunghill conveyed away and to make no more there in the future. Most dunghills were stored on private property, they were integral to pre-modern, urban life and inhabitants surely accepted their ubiquity in the urban landscape. But dunghills had to be situated and maintained in such a way that they did not adversely affect neighbours' properties and life quality. If they caused problems to neighbours or to horse-drawn traffic and trade, these valuable accumulations could be and were confiscated without compensation.

Inadequately maintained, leaking or noxious wet and dry privies were less contentious, accounting for only 9 per cent of nuisances in this period, possibly due to the fact that wet and dry stationary privies were not universally available in Edinburgh at this time. In March 1614, for example, Elizabeth Thomson, who lived at the head of Millers Wynd, complained that her neighbour, Alexander McMath, kept 'ane wett privie which runs doun to ane other privie so full of excraments that the same breks out and passis in ane laithe [i.e. low] sellar of the said complainers tenement'.[59] After the usual court inspection, which involved a site visit by the Dean of Guild and several members of his council to inspect the nuisance on the ground, Alexander McMath was ordered to 'clenye his said privie and to keip the said complener & her said tenement of land harmles and skaithles' henceforth.[60] Similarly, in April 1620, Alexander Dick complained that all of the neighbours of a tenement in Master Mushe Close, owned by Mr Adixsunne, 'has two wett privies within his land which summe times hes brokin furth in the said close and is presentlie brokin up and entering within ane sewir … so that no persone may enter therin'.[61] Mr Adixsunne was ordered to 'cleny the two wett privys'.[62] Notably, wet privies tended to be far more problematic than dry privies. Dry privies were simply deep pits in the ground beneath a seat which, providing sand and lime was applied periodically and they were emptied sufficiently frequently so that they did not become noxious, were relatively unproblematic. Wet privies required much more maintenance in terms of ensuring that they remained watertight and drained efficiently into their designated sewers without leakage, usually through a rudimentary system of several connected pipes.

In Edinburgh, as in all pre-modern urban settlements, animals were raised and slaughtered near to residential properties. Significantly, only 2 per cent of insanitary nuisances across the whole period 1560–1700 concerned butchery waste, and only 3 per cent of insanitary nuisances between 1613 and 1646. For a significant few unfortunate neighbours, however, the sensory experience of living next to an inconsiderate flesher's booth proved unbearable. In October 1615, Michael Lynner complained that his neighbour, Alexander Johnson, a flesher, and his servants,

> casts doun the soill filth and excraments of thair bestiall of sheip and nolt [i.e. cattle] slane be thame beneth the hinging stair [i.e. outdoor staircase] of the said complainers dwelling hous lyand on the eist side of stevin laws close and ... the fleshe and blood of thair bestiall [comes] throw the wall of the dwelling hous.[63]

Alexander was ordered to dispose of his waste more efficiently, ensuring that it did not come through the wall of Michael's house any more under the pain of five pounds Scots.

In the context of citywide insanitary nuisance, clearly, throwing waste directly out of doors and windows was by far the most pressing problem in the first half of the seventeenth century. Balancing the needs of individuals against the needs of the whole city is a perennial problem for any governing body, regardless of the time period. The Dean of Guild Court was given sole jurisdiction of neighbourhood cases so that it could deal with the needs of individuals in order to allow Edinburgh Council to concentrate fully on citywide problems.

The most frequently presented nuisance in the period 1656 to 1700 was, again, that of throwing waste directly from doors and windows, which accounted for 34 per cent of extant insanitary nuisances. In January 1687, John Trotter, the owner of a tenement in Trotters Close, opposite to Blackfriar Wynd, complained that the neighbours who lived adjacent to the west and north parts of the backclose, James Graham, William Gilchrist and James Sibbalds and their servants, 'doe daily throw filth and dirt out at their windowes so it proved very noysome to his tennents & could have noe access to their cellars there'.[64] The defenders were ordered 'to have put closs glass or tirles and stanchells [i.e. glass, tiles and stanchions or bars] upon their opening windowes that nothing be casten furth [i.e. out] therat'.[65] It is significant that the court ordered the offenders to take action to prevent this nuisance's recurrence, in a proactive manner, rather than merely fining them for the nuisance. The court, therefore, prioritized suppressing the nuisance in the long term above the benefits of short-term fiscal gain. The insanitary nuisance of throwing human waste directly out of windows and doors into streets and other public areas was the most commonly presented nuisance in the extant minutes of Edinburgh Dean of Guild Court throughout the whole seventeenth century. It clearly occurred to a limited extent, but disposing of one's waste in this way was by no means a 'normal' waste disposal method. Indeed, the very fact that this nuisance offended neighbours to the extent that they went to the effort of presenting it to the Dean of Guild and his Council confirms that throwing human waste out of windows and doors was unambiguously unacceptable. Clearly, it fell below the collectively upheld standard of what both inhabitants themselves and the Dean of Guild Court called 'guid nichtborheid'.[66]

Edinburgh Council tried in earnest to prevent the nuisance of casting waste out of windows and doors. It even funded the construction of two new privies, as described by this extract from August 1684,

> the Counsell appoints two jaques [i.e. toilets] to be made the one at the foot of the close bewest Thomas Wilsones new howse neir to the entrie of the flesh mercate and ane other at some close foot at the land mercate and that a board be pute up at the saids closs heads for directing them that are to ease themselves to find the saids Jaques and that the same be convoyed by ane syre [i.e. sewer] to the northe loch.[67]

Given the lack of universal literacy in Edinburgh at this time, it would be useful to know how the toilets were symbolized on this board. Perhaps it was a picture or symbol of some kind rather than the word privy or jaques. Despite the existence of some privies, however, the majority of inhabitants used simpler receptacles such as close stools, chamber pots and even simple buckets and pails, which were sometimes emptied directly into public areas. Edinburgh Council passed several orders to regulate this method of waste disposal, seemingly with minimal success, given that the largest category of insanitary nuisance reported to Edinburgh Dean of Guild Court was the practice of casting human waste directly out of windows and doors into public areas below. Edinburgh's multi-storey tenements had forestairs, running down exterior walls in the street rather than inside of the building, which often fell into a poor state of repair and became unsafe. The forestairs described in this Dean of Guild building nuisance case, submitted in 1687, for example, were very dangerous indeed,

> Ane petitione given in be George Mastertoune writer [i.e. lawyer] & James Peacock barbour mentioning that where they had property pertaining to them severall stories of ane foretenement of land lying upon the north side of the high street of Edinburgh opposite to the court of guard the forestone stair of which tenement belonged whollie to them but by reasone of the shortnes of the steps of the said stair persones repairing up & doun the same were in great hazard of breaking their legs & many times have actuallie fallen doun & hurt themselves neither can one person pass by another

upon the stair the passage being soe very narrow ... and therfor they granted warrand to the supplicants to take down the steps of the said stone stairs & put up new steps in stead.[68]

Casting waste out of windows and doors was clearly unacceptable, which is why neighbours complained to the court about the practice and Edinburgh Council regulated it. It is highly likely that this offence was committed only by a small minority of inhabitants and not in an entirely thoughtless and inconsiderate manner. The motivation for throwing waste out of windows might well have resulted at least partly from the fact that many inhabitants were living in high, multi-storey buildings with outdoor forestairs, which made carrying heavy chamber pots a dangerous task posing an unacceptable risk for some. The practice of 'casting over' was nowhere near as common in the late sixteenth century, when population density was lower, there were not as many high buildings and many tenements had not yet been subdivided, than it subsequently became in the seventeenth century.

Insanitary nuisances relating to liquid waste disposal were a similarly common occurrence between 1656 and 1700, accounting for 20 per cent of extant insanitary nuisances. Problematic waste disposal into jaw holls or sewers and blocking or interfering with a neighbour's syre or jaw holl were also common nuisances in this period, accounting for 13 per cent and 11 per cent, respectively. Drainage spouts or shoots in walls or floors, known as jaw holls or easing drops, drained liquid waste directly into the network of covered and open ditches, running down the centre or sides of closes and streets, known as syres or watergangs. Most drainage-related insanitary nuisances pertained to neighbours' failure to scour their own sections of these rudimentary drainage systems regularly, inhabitants having situated them inconsiderately so that they emptied onto neighbouring land or neighbours having negligently blocked them with solid waste. In April 1657, for example, Robert Weir, a baker who lived on the north side of the Canongate 'a little beneath the flesh stocks', complained that his neighbours, James White, a Cutler, and his spouse, Elizabeth Baillie,

> cast furth ... of ane holl or watter spoutt in the foirstaire all thair filth and wild excraments in such great abundance as no neighbour can gett entred [to] the close unspoilled [and] likwayes they cast furth of ane jaw holl or watter passadge in the back of thair said tenement all [of] thair filth which abuises the Complainers closs so that no persone is abill to abid the smell thairof which is liklie to cast his dwelling houss waist to his heavie prejudice and contrairie to good neighbourheid.[69]

After inspection of the close, the Dean of Guild and his council ordered,

> James White and Elizabeth Baillie his spous to close up the said jaw holl or watter spoutt in the foirstaire of thair said tenement and to mak ane timber spoutt in the backsid thairof for conveying away thair watter and to putt ane

graitter of iron at the heid therof [so] that nothing be cast furth of the samen butt watter in all time coming.[70]

Fitting a 'graitter of iron' at the head of the jaw holl was a proactive measure taken to ensure that this nuisance did not recur in the long-term future. That 'no persone' was 'abill to abyd the smell' caused by this drainage nuisance was included in the official court minutes, thus emphasizing the large extent to which contemporaries were concerned about the olfactory quality of their outdoor environment.

The nuisance of flesher waste only accounted for 2 per cent of extant nuisances in the latter half of the seventeenth century. In December 1656, for example, William Gibstowne complained to the Dean of Guild Court that his neighbour, George Suittie, a flesher,

> haveing ane slaughter booth occupied and possest be him … lyand at the castill wynd foote … out of which booth … [he] daylie cast furth his muck and blood upon the gavell [i.e. the end wall of a building or the gable] of the said Complainers tenement the wall thairof being liklie to be consumed.[71]

The Dean of Guild and his council visited the slaughter house and ordered George Suittie to 'clainy [i.e.clean] the said boundis and to keip it cleine in all time coming' under the pain of twenty pounds Scots.[72] Similarly, in December 1657, Alexander Haithie, a wright and burgess, complained that his neighbour, John Forester, a bookbinder,

> hes maid a greatt syre holl in his wall adjacent to his bounds throw which he and his tennentts (who killes bestial wher thair wes never anie killed before) castis furth all filth both of living and dead beasts in and upon the Complainers bounds so that thair is not a tennent abill to duell in anie of his housses for the wild smell of the corrupt blood and … excraments.[73]

That there were 'never anie killed before' in this area underpinned the complainant's argument because a precedent had not yet been established; this was a new insanitary activity which had been inflicted on the neighbours only recently. After inspection of the property, John Forrester was ordered to 'close up the said syer holl with stone and lime' and he was to 'keep no slaughter hous ther heirefter so that the Complainer and his tennentts and bounds may be frie of filth in time coming … under the penaltie of twentie pounds'.[74] In Edinburgh, as in all pre-modern urban settlements, animals were raised and slaughtered near to residential properties, but the majority of Edinburgh's fleshers seem to have disposed of their waste sufficiently considerably to avoid large numbers of complaints about the waste they produced having been submitted to the Dean of Guild Court. Nevertheless, some inhabitants' daily lives were adversely affected by living near to a flesher producing excessively malodorous waste.

The detailed and hugely informative minute books of Edinburgh's Dean of Guild Court, sometimes referred to as the 'Neighbourhood Book', are key to understanding how Edinburgh's inhabitants interacted with and sensed their own environment, how important the sanitary condition of outdoor spaces was to them and how well the legal mechanism of the Dean of Guild Court protected neighbours against insanitary nuisances in their outdoor environment. Street cleanliness, efficient drainage and what contemporaries called 'sweet and clean' or 'wholesome' air was hugely important to Edinburgh's inhabitants, who could and did use the legal facility of the Dean of Guild Court to self-regulate the micro-scale environment of their neighbourhoods, either directly in person or indirectly through their landlords in the case of tenants who rented their dwellings. As Figure 9 shows, by far the largest category of complaint regarding insanitary nuisance over the entire period, accounting for 35 per cent of such complaints submitted between 1566 and 1700, was improper disposal of human waste out of windows and doors directly onto neighbours' roofs, backlands and streets and closes below. Although this statistic overshadows the fact that 'casting over' was not the most significant insanitary nuisance before 1607, the practice clearly contravened contemporaries' standard of what constituted good neighbourhood throughout the whole period. Inappropriately situated middings and rubbish heaps accounted for a not inconsiderable 21 per cent of such complaints and, unsurprisingly, were a frequent source of conflict in Edinburgh's densely populated neighbourhoods. Problematic waste disposal into jaw holls or sewers accounted for 17 per cent of insanitary nuisances and blocking or interfering with a neighbour's sewer or jaw holl accounted for 7 per cent of such nuisances. Inadequately maintained, leaking or noxious wet and dry privies were a less contentious issue, accounting for only 6 per cent of complaints pertaining to insanitary nuisances, possibly due to the fact that wet and dry stationary privies were not universal in Edinburgh at this time. Dirty trades were discussed frequently by Edinburgh Council, and removing them from the city centre to the urban periphery was clearly a major priority in the context of citywide sanitation, accounting for 20 per cent of Edinburgh Council's discussions and orders in relation to sanitation between 1560 and 1700. However, the production processes of, and noxious waste materials produced by, dirty trades were clearly far less significant issues in the micro-scale environments of individual closes and streets, only accounting for only 2 per cent of insanitary nuisances presented to the Dean of Guild Coourt over the course of the whole period 1560 to 1700. Conversely, throughout the course of the whole period 1560 to 1700, issues relating to liquid waste disposal were not discussed frequently at meetings of Edinburgh Council, accounting for only 6 per cent of council discussions and orders pertaining to outdoor sanitation, whereas 23 per cent of insanitary nuisances submitted to the Dean of Guild Court related to liquid waste disposal and drainage. This seems to have been an area of outdoor sanitation which caused significant controversy between particular neighbours in the micro-scale environment of individual streets and closes, whereas it was an area which Edinburgh Council did not deem a sufficiently important priority in the context of citywide consideration and management to warrant extensive discussion.

Categories of insanitary nuisance cases	Number of cases	Percentage of cases
Throwing waste directly from doors and/or windows	106	35.2
Midding and/or rubbish left unremoved	63	21.0
Problematic waste disposal into jaw holls and/or sewers	52	17.3
Obstructing the flow of a neighbour's syre and/or jaw holl	20	6.6
Leaking and/or noxious privy	19	6.3
Air pollution	11	3.7
Area used as common jake	11	3.7
Flesher waste	7	2.3
Failure to scour syre and/or jaw holl	6	2.0
Industrial nuisance	2	0.7
Livestock	2	0.7
Dirty house	1	0.3
Dirty well	1	0.3
Total	**301**	**100**

Figure 9 Categorized insanitary nuisance cases submitted to Edinburgh Dean of Guild Court, 1566–1700

While the categories of insanitary nuisance about which inhabitants complained are important, so are the numbers of insanitary nuisance cases submitted over time and in relation to other types of case handled by the court. While the extant minutes are neither complete nor continuous, and there are some lengthy gaps of a year or more between the records of courts convened, the numbers of extant cases can still indicate important patterns over time. Assessing the proportion of insanitary nuisance cases, within the total of all cases including mercantile disputes or building nuisances, takes into account the variables of how active the court was and how litigious inhabitants were at particular points in time. However, the large gaps in the minutes' survival, notably those between 1646–1656 and 1667–1687, preclude in-depth, conclusive statistical analysis of change over time. As can be seen in Figure 10, the proportion of insanitary nuisance cases rises steadily until the lengthy gap between 1667 and 1687, after which the proportion drops significantly in relation to other categories of complaints. It is highly likely that the proportion of insanitary nuisance cases began to drop substantially just as the citywide street cleaning system reached its full potential towards the end of the 1680s, following the especially large amount of time devoted to the discussion of street cleaning by Edinburgh Council throughout the 1680s (see Figure 4). Clearly, alleviating the pressure of inhabitants' waste disposal responsibilities throughout the 1680s reduced insanitary nuisances experienced by individual neighbours in the micro-scale environment of their own streets and closes.

Fortunately, around 70 per cent of extant insanitary nuisance cases submitted to Edinburgh Dean of Guild Court between 1566 and 1700 detail the geographical

Minute book	Total cases	Insanitary nuisance cases	Proportion (%)
1566–1607	294	45	15.3
1613–1623	469	65	13.9
1624–1646	400	63	15.8
1656–1667	285	61	21.4
1687–1695	503	35	7.0
1695–1698	329	26	7.9
1699–1700	151	6	4.0
Total	**2,431**	**301**	**12.4** *(mean)*

Figure 10 Proportion of insanitary nuisance cases submitted to Edinburgh Dean of Guild Court, 1566–1700 (by extant minute book periods)

location of the insanitary nuisance. A substantial 20.6 per cent of those which refer to a particular location occurred in one of only six locations: Forrester's Wynd, High Street, Cowgate, Canongate, Libbertoun's Wynd and West Bow. Significantly, West Bow, Libbertoun's Wynd and Forrester's Wynd are situated in very close proximity, thus suggesting that this was an area of Edinburgh which was especially prone to the development of insanitary nuisances.[75] If the cases which occurred in closes running down from the High Street are split according to whether they descended from the north or the south side of the High Street ridge, an overwhelming majority of 72 per cent of the 105 cases which occurred in such closes developed in those descending from the south side of Edinburgh's High Street. This can perhaps be explained by the fact that the North Loch, which lay at the foot of the closes descending from the north side of the High Street, was a beneficial natural receptacle for the drainage of liquid waste and perhaps some solid waste too. Closes running down from the south side of the High Street, however, drained far less efficiently into the Cowgate. In relation to the Cowgate, Margaret Wood suggested that 'nothing but torrential rain could have washed that street clean'.[76]

If the geographical location data is split broadly by time period and the proportionate occurrences of cases in particular locations is compared over time, much more subtle patterns emerge. The most frequently cited location in the late sixteenth century was the High Street, closely followed by the Cowgate. The former is unsurprising because the High Street hosted activites which produced a potentially chaotic mixture of residential, business and agricultural waste. The Cowgate, however, is more surprising because in the sixteenth century it was a largely residential area which housed relatively high status inhabitants. Perhaps the Cowgate did not feature the highest numbers of insanitary nuisances, but rather it housed higher status inhabitants who were more likely to use the Dean of Guild Court to suppress the nuisances which did occur. In the first half of the seventeenth century, however, Forrester's Wynd hosted the highest number of prosecuted insanitary nuisances in the city, followed by Steven Law's Close, and to a lesser extent, followed by the High Street, the Cowgate, Mary King's Close, the Netherbow, Jackson's Close and Bell's Wynd. Clearly, as the closes descending from the High Street became more densely populated into the seventeenth century, far higher numbers of insanitary nuisances occurring in them were reported to the Dean of Guild Court. The Cowgate, which declined in terms of the social status of its inhabitants into the early seventeenth century, hosted a markedly smaller proportion of the city's prosecuted insanitary nuisances compared to the previous period, perhaps as it lost increasingly more of its wealthier inhabitants who were less tolerant of poor sanitation. As the Cowgate became increasingly densely populated and it housed even lower status inhabitants in the latter half of the seventeenth century, however, the Cowgate became the most frequently cited location, followed by West Bow, the Canongait and the High Street and, to a lesser extent, followed by Libbertoun's Wynd and Gray's Close. During this period, there would have been increasingly less space available in the Cowgate within which to store and dispose of waste considerately, efficiently and carefully. It is also likely that the Cowgate's lower status inhabitants would have been engaging in industrial and agricultural activities, to a greater extent than their social superiors who inhabited the area in the late sixteenth century, which would have been much more likely to create offending malodours and unsavoury waste materials.

The legal mechanism of Edinburgh's Dean of Guild Court is a shining example of an early modern legal facility designed to protect urban inhabitants against insanitary nuisances in their outdoor environment as their neighbourhoods became increasingly densely populated. That so many complainants approached this court to have insanitary nuisances suppressed, and indeed that so many tenants clearly pressured their landlords to approach the court on their behalves, often by threatening to leave their rented tenement if the nuisance continued, suggests that the sanitary condition of outdoor spaces in the environment was highly important to Edinburgh's inhabitants. While landlords arguably complained to protect their rental income, rather than their tenants' life quality, first and foremost, what is important is that their tenants were intolerant of insanitary conditions. When neighbours' waste disposal arrangements reduced inhabitants' life quality, crossing the line in contemporaries' minds between acceptable and unacceptable, acceptable having been labelled collectively as 'guid nichtborheid', inhabitants could and did use the facility of Edinburgh's Dean of Guild Court to reclaim an acceptable standard of outdoor cleanliness. While the minutes of this court were written by scribes, in admittedly rather formulaic language, the details of the complaints originated with the inhabitants themselves, whether they owned or rented the properties concerned, and these minutes are testimony to their efforts to maintain an acceptable standard of sanitation in the outdoor micro-scale environment of their neighbourhoods. Indeed, Margaret Wood agrees that these cases demonstrate that the 'inhabitants had the will, if not the means, to be cleanly'.[77]

Conclusion

One aspect of the whole, overarching and seamless system of early modern urban government has been artificially isolated and called environmental regulation for the purposes of analysis. But contemporaries themselves had neither a name nor an administrative department for this area of urban management precisely because it was not conceptualized separately. This chapter has explained, nevertheless, that the regulation of insanitary nuisances was certainly not an exclusively top-down attempt to force and regulate passive and unwilling inhabitants to keep their outdoor environment clean. Many inhabitants participated willingly in their urban governors' regulation of insanitary nuisances. Maintaining an acceptable standard of outdoor cleanliness, in the context of necessary urban agriculture, horse-drawn traffic and relatively uncomplicated sanitation processes and systems, was far more deeply integrated into and less alienated from daily life, far more hands-on and far more beholden to the compliance and efforts of householders than it is today.[78] Its effective functioning relied on inhabitants' support, compliance and self-regulation at the level of respective neighbourhoods in order for the systems to function efficiently. Many of the examples which have been quoted resulted unambiguously from intolerant neighbours' complaints, whether individually or in groups, and neighbourhood concern over insanitary nuisances in the urban landscape seems to have been strong, at least among the majority of urban dwellers. Indeed, the nuisance cases submitted officially to beadles, local courts and burgh councils are, by definition, the ones which neighbours had failed to resolve informally, privately and verbally, and many more insanitary nuisances than ever entered the documentary record were resolved quickly and efficiently within private conversations between neighbours. Concern over the sanitary condition of the urban landscape was high.

The evidence presented in this chapter strongly suggests that, throughout the period, the overwhelming majority of urban dwellers acted as an informal, but remarkably coherent and effective, institution in their collective and individual efforts to regulate their micro-scale environment by suppressing their less fastidious neighbours' insanitary nuisances. Such a communal sense of responsibility for sanitation continued intact from the fifteenth century, when Carole Rawcliffe found that residents of London and other English towns 'regarded dirty streets and polluted watercourses as a source of collective shame', when local governors exhibited a 'widespread reliance upon the salutary effects of peer pressure and public shame', which she claims suggests 'a sense of communal responsibility, or active membership of the urban body'.[79] In the case of environmental self-regulation, self-interest and community interest were not mutually exclusive. Rather, individuals' complaints contributed to and checked the salubriousness of the whole neighbourhood and demonstrate how unacceptable it was for one to allow their waste disposal arrangements or the sanitary condition of their property to fall below the collectively upheld neighbourhood standard of outdoor cleanliness, termed by contemporaries simply as 'keeping neighbourhood'. Clearly, urban governors and the majority of urban inhabitants were far from indifferent to the sanitary condition of outdoor public spaces and contemporaries certainly valued having a relatively clean outdoor environment. The people who inhabited the urban neighbourhoods of Edinburgh and York between 1560 and 1700 necessarily had a vested interest in upholding a tolerable standard of cleanliness and olfactory sensation in the urban landscape which framed their daily lives.

In York, as in Edinburgh, the city governors had less than full control over environmental regulation and worked with rather than against the urban populations they were managing. The sanitation systems and processes in operation throughout the period could not have functioned without significant effort and compliance from most householders. That these systems functioned at all is testimony to the majority of inhabitants' efforts to keep their outdoor environment clean. The behaviour of the minority of people who created insanitary nuisances and neglected their communal street cleaning duties was perceived by their peers as unambiguously unacceptable. Such compatibility between top-down governance and bottom-up concern, and the generally positive attitude towards waste disposal and street cleanliness, continued at least up to the turn of the eighteenth century, by which point a plethora of substantial, if not comprehensive, sanitation infrastructures and regulatory systems had emerged across urban Britain.

Notes

1 K. Wrightson, 'The "Decline of Neighbourliness" revisited' in N. Jones and D. Woolf (eds), *Local Identities in Late Medieval and Early Modern England* (Basingstoke: Palgrave MacMillan, 2007), pp. 19–49, on p. 22.

2 Bristol Record Office, JQS/Pr/1: Presentments to the Grand Jury to the Bristol Leet, 1628–1666 (27/10/1635).

3 Deceulaer, 'Implications of the street', pp. 197, 205.

4 Deceulaer, 'Implications of the street', pp. 197, 205.

5 C. Hamlin, 'Public sphere to public health: the transformation of "nuisance"', in S. Sturdy (ed.), *Medicine, Health and the Public Sphere in Britain, 1600–2000* (London: Routledge, 2002), pp. 189–204.

6 *Liverpool Town Books, 1649–1671*, ed. M. Power (Liverpool: The Record Society of Lancashire and Cheshire, 136, 1998), p. 36.

7 Durham County Record Office, MS D/HH/11/142: Barnard Castle Courts, 1621–1788, f. 29.

8 *Records of Maidstone: Being Selections from Documents in the Possession of the Corporation*, ed. K. Martin (Maidstone: Maidstone Borough Council, 1926), p. 117.

9 *Extracts from the Newcastle-Upon-Tyne Council Minute Book, 1639–1656*, ed. M. Hope Dodds (Newcastle upon Tyne: Publications of the Newcastle upon Tyne Record Society, 1920), pp.182–184.

10 CRO, Ca3/2/10: Carlisle Court Leet Rolls.

11 Jenner, '"Cleanliness and "dirt"', p. 188.

12 CRO, Ca4: Chamberlains' Accounts, 1602–1694.

13 For a detailed analysis of seventeenth-century Carlisle's sanitation processes and systems, see Skelton, 'Beadles, dunghills and noisome excrements', pp. 21–38. See also L. Skelton, 'Environmental regulation in Edinburgh and York, c.1560–c.1700: with reference to several smaller Scottish burghs and northern English towns' (unpublished PhD dissertation, Durham University, 2012).

14 DCRO, MS D/HH/11/142: Barnard Castle Courts, 1621–1788, f. 40.
15 *Coventry Constables' Presentments, 1629–1742*, ed. L. Fox (Stratford upon Avon: Dugdale Society, 1986), p. 19.
16 *Liverpool Town Books*, p. 79.
17 Durham University Heritage Collection, MS 8/I: Subsidiary Manorial Court Records, Stockton Division, Box 7, Bundle 1, Item 5.
18 *Quarter Sessions Records [of Warwick], Easter 1674 to Easter 1682*, ed. S. Ratcliff and H. Johnson (Warwick: L. Edgar Stephens, 1946), vol. 7, p. 11.
19 Durham University Heritage Collection, MS 8/I: Subsidiary Manorial Court Records, Darlington Division, Box 3, Bundle 1, Item 9.
20 Hearnshaw (ed.), *Court Leet Records*, p. 503.
21 Hearnshaw (ed.), *Court Leet Records*, p. 599.
22 *Records of the Borough of Nottingham, being a Series of Extracts from the Archives of the Corporation of Nottingham,* 7 vols, ed. Nottingham Borough Council (Nottingham: Forman, 1882–1947), vol. 5, p. 353.
23 *Coventry Constables' Presentments*, p. 40.
24 CRO, Ca4/1.
25 Durham County Record Office, MS D/HH/11/142: Barnard Castle Courts, 1621–1788, f. 54.
26 *Records of the Borough of Nottingham, being a Series of Extracts from the Archives of the Corporation of Nottingham,* 7 vols, ed. Nottingham Borough Council (Nottingham: Forman, 1882–1947), vol. 5, p. 110.
27 *Records of the Borough of Nottingham*, vol. 5, p. 139.
28 Central London Record Office, Southwark Sessions Papers, Box 17, St Saviour's for 1688, quoted in Jenner, '"Cleanliness" and "dirt"', pp. 192–193.
29 *Records of the Borough of Nottingham*, vol. 5, pp. 111–1§12.
30 *Liverpool Town Books*, p. 22.
31 *Coventry Constables' Presentments*, p. 30.
32 BRO, C1/1–3: Bailiffs' Court Book, 1568–1603 (Michaelmas, 1592).
33 North Yorkshire County Record Office, DC/SCB/II/1/: Corporation Minute and Order Book, 1621–1649 (25/05/1625).
34 *Liverpool Town Books*, p. 213.
35 *Court Leet Records*, p. 507 [of Southampton].
36 Loengard, 'The Assize of Nuisance', p. 144.
37 TNA, C 2/Eliz/N2/36: Court of Chancery: Edmund Nicholson and Thomas Yates v Godfrey Bradshawe (1558–1603, exact date unknown).
38 TNA, C 2/Eliz/N2/36: Court of Chancery: Edmund Nicholson and Thomas Yates v Godfrey Bradshawe (1558–1603, exact date unknown).
39 *Court Leet Records*, pp. 376, 398 [of Southampton].
40 Brooks, *Pettyfoggers and Vipers*, p. 34.
41 M. McIntosh, *Controlling Misbehaviour in England, 1370–1600* (Oxford: Oxbow Books, 1998), p. 34.
42 Harrison, 'Manor courts and governance', p. 45.
43 K. Wrightson, 'Two concepts of order: justices, constables and jurymen in seventeenth-century England', in J. Brewer and J. Styles (eds), *An Ungovernable People? The English and their Law in the Seventeenth and Eighteenth Centuries* (London: Hutchinson, 1980), pp. 21–46, on p. 31.
44 *Records of the Borough of Nottingham*, vol. 5, p. 178.
45 Skelton, 'Beadles, dunghills and noisome excrements', pp. 56–57.
46 Withington, 'Views from the bridge', p. 132.
47 YCA, B34: York Corporation House or Minute Books, 1613–1625.
48 P. Slack, *The Impact of Plague in Tudor and Stuart England* (London: Routledge and Kegan Paul, 1985), pp. 69–74.

49 J. Campbell-Irons, *Manual of the Law and Practice of the Dean of Guild Court: With Synopsis of the Law, relating to Building Restrictions, Servitudes, etc* (Edinburgh: Green & Sons, 1895), pp. 33–54.
50 ECA, SL144/1/2: Edinburgh Dean of Guild Court Minutes, 1566–1607.
51 ECA, SL144/1/2: Edinburgh Dean of Guild Court Minutes, 1566–1607.
52 ECA, SL144/1/2: Edinburgh Dean of Guild Court Minutes, 1566–1607.
53 ECA, SL144/1/2: Edinburgh Dean of Guild Court Minutes, 1566–1607.
54 ECA, SL144/1/5: Edinburgh Dean of Guild Court Minutes, 1624–1646.
55 ECA, SL144/1/5: Edinburgh Dean of Guild Court Minutes, 1624–1646.
56 ECA, SL144/1/4: Edinburgh Dean of Guild Court Minutes, 1613–1623.
57 ECA, SL144/1/4: Edinburgh Dean of Guild Court Minutes, 1613–1623.
58 ECA, SL144/1/5: Edinburgh Dean of Guild Court Minutes, 1624–1646.
59 ECA, SL144/1/4: Edinburgh Dean of Guild Court Minutes, 1613–1623.
60 ECA, SL144/1/4: Edinburgh Dean of Guild Court Minutes, 1613–1623.
61 ECA, SL144/1/4: Edinburgh Dean of Guild Court Minutes, 1613–1623.
62 ECA, SL144/1/4: Edinburgh Dean of Guild Court Minutes, 1613–1623.
63 ECA, SL144/1/4: Edinburgh Dean of Guild Court Minutes, 1613–1623.
64 ECA, SL144/1/7: Edinburgh Dean of Guild Court Minutes, 1687–1695.
65 ECA, SL144/1/7: Edinburgh Dean of Guild Court Minutes, 1687–1695.
66 This term was used in a large proportion of insanitary nuisance cases throughout the period. See ECA, SL144/1/2–9: Edinburgh Dean of Guild Court Minutes, 1566–1702.
67 ECA, SL1/1/31: Edinburgh Town Council Minutes, 1684–1686.
68 ECA, SL144/1/7: Edinburgh Dean of Guild Court Minute Book, 1687–1695.
69 ECA, SL144/1/6: Edinburgh Dean of Guild Court Minutes, 1656–1667.
70 ECA, SL144/1/6: Edinburgh Dean of Guild Court Minutes, 1656–1667.
71 ECA, SL144/1/6: Edinburgh Dean of Guild Court Minutes, 1656–1667.
72 ECA, SL144/1/6: Edinburgh Dean of Guild Court Minutes, 1656–1667.
73 ECA, SL144/1/6: Edinburgh Dean of Guild Court Minutes, 1656–1667.
74 ECA, SL144/1/6: Edinburgh Dean of Guild Court Minutes, 1656–1667.
75 ECA, SL144/1/2–9: Edinburgh Dean of Guild Court Minutes, 1566–1702.
76 Wood, 'The neighbourhood book', p. 96.
77 Wood, 'The neighbourhood book', pp. 89–90.
78 For a more general discussion of the relationship between man and the environment in the sixteenth and seventeenth centuries, see Thomas, *Man and the Natural World*, pp. 243–254.
79 Rawcliffe, *Urban Bodies*, pp. 11, 118.

Conclusion

Establishing the cultural attitudes and values of late-sixteenth- and seventeenth-century English and Scottish urban dwellers towards the cleanliness of outdoor, public spaces has been this book's key task. It has explored how local and national governors, civic employees and urban inhabitants, living in Edinburgh, York and many other towns and cities across Scotland and England, managed the disposal of waste and limited the creation of insanitary nuisances in the urban landscape. Regardless of their ultimate failure to achieve the pristine streets towards which they passionately aspired, and to eliminate insanitary nuisances completely, they were highly and consistently motivated to invest significant amounts of their time, money and effort into improving sanitation. Urban governors and the majority of those under their governance certainly wanted to curtail malodours and unpleasant and problematic waste within collectively tolerable parameters for the benefit of inhabitants and visitors alike. They valued living, and perhaps more importantly breathing, in a clean environment, in their streets and in other outdoor public spaces, and they aspired towards a clearly defined and collectively imagined standard of cleanliness in the urban landscape. It is indisputable that early modern urban dwellers and their governors appreciated inhabiting an environment which was devoid of foul smells and unpleasant waste materials, and they certainly made a distinction between what they labelled unambiguously as a 'nasty', 'filthy' or 'noisome' street and, conversely, what they labelled as a 'sweet' and 'clean' street. In short, contemporaries drew a line between what they considered acceptable and unacceptable and they endeavoured to maintain that standard, as individuals, as neighbours, as wards and parishes, and as inhabitants of the respective towns and cities of which they were clearly so very proud. How clean the environment actually was matters far less than contemporaries' changing perceptions of it and their variable efforts to improve it and to uphold or to attempt to uphold their own standards of cleanliness.

Human experiences and perceptions of the outdoor environment have been analysed in depth at the expense of making an attempt to reconstruct the physical condition of the environment itself. But an appreciation of the wider social, political, economic and cultural context of this important element of daily life takes us to the heart of the issues involved. It is by analysing available technologies, the necessity of urban agriculture and the nature of urban governance that we gain real insights into the driving forces behind improvements in sanitation provision. Within such a context, we can discover the options which real people had available to them. The real story of how and why people endeavoured to improve the cleanliness of their outdoor urban environment is far more complicated than the entertaining story told by derisory descriptions of filthy streets and of slothful inhabitants haplessly pouring waste out of doors and windows. The extant archival manuscript volumes, containing financial accounts and the minutes of council meetings and court cases, are the vaults in which the real history of sanitation lies, or at least the best possible pathway towards understanding it. Many urban inhabitants were uncomfortable, and some even feared for their lives, when they were near to malodorous nuisances and large volumes of unpleasant waste. Not a few could and did take action to develop their own, or to shape their governors', environmental regulations in order to improve the quality of their own, their families' and their neighbours' daily lives. We cannot imagine the circumstances in which they faced their immense sanitation challenges, but we can stop deriding and looking down on their relationship with dirt and we can stop laughing at their dunghills and open sewers from the lofty heights of our own very fortunate, and effortlessly indirect, sanitary arrangements. Sixteenth- and seventeenth-century urban dwellers battled against sanitation in a very different set of cirumstances from those faced by urban inhabitants and their town councils today, so markedly different in fact that any comparisons at all between our sanitation and theirs are meaningless except in their enormous capacity to feed our own reassuring self-gratification. The condescending modern-day images of early modern towns in which chamber pots are routinely tipped over window sills and townspeople slip and slide along streets filled with a plethora of filthy materials are an injustice to the complexity of early modern British sanitation, the strong desire for and the widespread efforts to improve sanitary standards, at least before 1700.

Macro-scale action to improve urban sanitation, in the form of council regulations, citywide street-cleaning initiatives and the provision of courts to suppress insanitary nuisances in the first place, are important. But equally important are the micro-scale actions taken by inhabitants themselves to improve the neighbourhoods which they called home, such as petitions to councils and complaints made to either their landlords or directly to the courts. Throughout the period, in the course of their daily lives, the majority of urban neighbours acted as an informal, but remarkably coherent and effective, institution in their collective and individual efforts to regulate their micro-scale environment by suppressing their less fastidious neighbours' insanitary nuisances.

York's waste disposal systems and processes became increasingly centralized between 1560 and 1700, albeit not as dramatically as those in Edinburgh were transformed in the same time period. While York's householders' waste disposal responsibilities decreased somewhat, after the introduction of the scavenger system in 1580 – the most significant change in this area of city government over the course of fourteen decades – inhabitants still retained many of their traditional responsibilities due to the survival of the medieval forefront system alongside the scavenger system. Civic scavengers were paid to remove as much waste as a man put out at his door and to clean the main thoroughfares thrice weekly. But, in reality, householders were still responsible for cleaning their forefronts, scouring their gutters and removing a large proportion of their own waste, or at least moving it to a designated disposal point in their ward or parish. From these communal disposal points, muck was transported by boat along the River Fosse to Tang Hall pastures near Heworth where they were used to fertilize crops. While there was a distinctly and unmistakably more serious tone as well as a numerical increase in the council discussions and bylaws pertaining to this area of city government in the first half of the seventeenth century, and York Corporation clearly made a significant effort to improve street cleanliness in order to combat plague during that period, for the most part before and after this surge of focused attention, the corporation reacted to problems on an *ad hoc* basis. Apart from establishing the scavenger system in 1580, and several minor innovations throughout the seventeenth century in terms of allocating specific locations at which to bury offal, managing the movement of livestock and regulating the sale of urban muck to local rural farmers, waste disposal processes and systems remained relatively stagnant. Indeed, the medieval forefront system survived intact right up to the turn of the seventeenth century, at least, and although inhabitants had to be reminded to keep their forefronts clean, it seems to have functioned quite well.

In Edinburgh, the majority of inhabitants, the city governors who were responsible for Edinburgh's environmental regulation and the national governors who interfered in it intermittently were far from indifferent to the sanitary condition of outdoor public spaces in the city. The people who inhabited Edinburgh necessarily had a vested interest in upholding a tolerable standard of cleanliness and olfactory sensation in the outdoor public spaces which framed their daily existence. Edinburgh's inhabitants and governors designed, improved and maintained far more sophisticated systems with which to drain and clean the cityscape of which they were so proud than historians have tended to appreciate. Their respective efforts to improve sanitation complemented and reflected one another to a remarkable extent. It is clear that inhabitants' responsibilities declined increasingly over time as the council took on a greater role in disposing of inhabitants' waste and cleaning the streets on their behalves. These services were provided in return for the street cleaning taxes extracted from 'substantial' householders and the proceeds of the muck which they sold as fertilizer to local farmers. This marked change took place within the context of significant population density increase, a wider intensification of local and national government from the late sixteenth into the early seventeenth century and in conjunction with increasing desires to portray the urban landscape as a 'civil' environment.[1] Contemporaries surely understood exactly where the line between theirs and the burgh authorities' responsibilities lay, and the majority of inhabitants fulfilled their obligations without complaint. The minority who did not could find themselves, or their landlords on their behalves, facing the Dean of Guild Court. It was unambiguously unacceptable for one to allow their waste disposal arrangements or the sanitary condition of their property to fall below collectively upheld neighbourhood standards of outdoor cleanliness, which contemporaries termed 'keeping good neighbourhood'. It is lamentable that Edinburgh's population density increase in the seventeenth century cancelled out much of the improvement which would otherwise have ensued from the developments in street cleaning and waste disposal if the population of the city remained relatively stable. Edinburgh's streets were almost certainly dirtier in 1700 than they had been in 1560, but the proactive and enthusiastic manner in which the city's governors responded to the sanitation challenge and their progressive cultural attitudes and values in relation to dirt and cleanliness, are far more significant than their ultimate failure to improve conditions.

Environmental regulation in both Edinburgh and York generally functioned in a necessarily, but by no means exclusively, top-down manner. Orders originated from Edinburgh Council, to the baillies and then to the inhabitants through the medium of verbal announcements accompanied by the 'sound of drum'. From York Corporation, sanitation orders were passed to the officers of the wards, then to the constables and then down to the inhabitants either by oral announcement in the streets or through the medium of their parish churches. But environmental regulation was not a one-way process. Inhabitants could petition their governors to complain about insanitary nuisances which were reducing their life quality or to request liberty to implement solutions to insanitary nuisances themselves, such as hanging a locked door or building a gate across a vennel to prevent inhabitants from dumping rubbish on private land. They could also organize their own informal waste disposal methods and facilities within their own neighbourhoods, such as communal dunghills. Inhabitants could flout bylaws and dump their rubbish where they saw fit, taking care to remove it beyond the city walls, even though such behaviour was officially forbidden. On the surface, the formulaic, official records give a misleading impression that Edinburgh Council and York Corporation were trying to forcefully control the inhabitants by limiting their dirty, unthoughtful and chaotic waste disposal arrangements and techniques in a one way manner, but in reality both cities' governing bodies encountered a great deal of bottom-up resistance and inhabitants in both cities made significant efforts to shape waste disposal themselves. Even flouting bylaws and dumping rubbish illegally was action from the bottom-up, and such behaviour sometimes forced local governors, eventually, to sanction requests in the form of petitions to modify and improve dumping grounds in Edinburgh and to make informal waste disposal locations official in York. There does seem to have been significantly more bottom-up resistance and more negotiation and compromise between York Corporation and its inhabitants than between Edinburgh Council and the people of Edinburgh. Perhaps ultimately in the absence of acute population density increases, there was far less pressure and therefore more spare capacity within York's governmental systems than there was in Edinburgh's to accommodate such compromises and negotiations between the inhabitants and their governors. The members of York Corporation did not have to find effective solutions as quickly and urgently as did their counterparts in

Edinburgh, who had to act swiftly to meet the ever-increasing needs of a growing population and its augmented waste.

The fact that bylaws and reminders of previous bylaws were repeated several times throughout the period in both Edinburgh and York does not infer that the systems were failing. In terms of the lengthy period of fourteen decades, it is an achievement that such bylaws only needed to be promulgated every few years, sometimes only once a decade. The inhabitants of sixteenth- and seventeenth-century Edinburgh and York were far from indifferent to the need to regulate their environment and to keep their streets clean and they respected their respective cityscapes immensely. In 1700, inhabitants living in York and in Edinburgh, respectively, may well have had fewer sanitation responsibilities than their mid-sixteenth-century counterparts. But throughout the whole period, the majority of inhabitants expressed a strong sense of concern over the cleanliness of the outdoor environment and they disposed of their waste carefully and considerately, not least because most of their 'waste' was not waste at all; it was a potentially saleable asset.

Contemporaries living in smaller towns, too, across Scotland and England, Borsay's 'bedrock of the urban system', benefited from sophisticated and useful, albeit not comprehensive, sanitation infrastructure and facilities.[2] In these smaller towns too, there was a high degree of symmetry between the efforts of inhabitants and governors to improve and maintain sanitary standards in the urban landscape. Smaller towns generally attracted fewer visitors and were under far less pressure from national institutions to present a clean and orderly townscape. But the governors and inhabitants of smaller towns still invested huge energy and effort into disposing of their waste efficiently and they still had a vested interest in keeping streets passable and other open public spaces clean. Far from having had to coerce unwilling and 'dirty' urban populations to clean their micro-scale outdoor environment, inhabitants were using their own initiative to pursue and then to maintain an acceptable standard of salubrity. As we have seen, a relatively large area combined with relatively few inhabitants tended to feature far less serious waste disposal problems and insanitary nuisances. But there was no simple formula relating population density to sanitary standards. While a low population density undoubtedly created less pressure on sanitation systems in terms of domestic waste, more open space tended to facilitate and encourage more inhabitants to engage in urban agriculture, which produced large amounts of waste in the form of manure and more potentially unpleasant agricultural insanitary nuisances such as noxious pig sties. Despite York's low population density, its problems associated with free roaming livestock were actually worse than those experienced in relation to livestock in more densely populated Edinburgh. The latter's severe gradients coupled with the density of its housing precluded large-scale animal rearing within the city whereas York was flat, boasting much more open space, which facilitiated and encouraged animal rearing together with its associated problems within the city walls.

The walls around settlements such as Edinburgh, York and Carlisle failed to act as barriers to either further housebuilding or population growth. As walled towns and cities expanded throughout the seventeenth century, they did so through the growth of poorer suburbs which tended to feature infrastructure of a lesser quality than that installed within the walls, in the case of Carlisle and York, or by encouraging the development of higher, multi-storey buildings within the walls, as was the case in Edinburgh. Nevertheless, demographic density was the most influential variable factor impacting on urban governors' ability to manage sanitation effectively. The populations of towns including York, Carlisle, Ayr, Sheffield, Kendal, Berwick and Glasgow were relatively small and stable, which meant that their sanitation infrastructure was not placed under immense strain by the deposition of a rapidly expanding population's domestic waste, as occurred in contemporary London and Edinburgh, whose governors faced the most serious sanitation challenges before 1700. It was also demography, first and foremost, which drove the expansion of urban facilities and public services in the early modern Low Countries. Manon van der Heijden attributes the 'long-term transitions from private to public' in this area of urban management and government between 1400 and 1800 to population growth and urbanization, but he highlights that 'such alterations were always firmly rooted in traditional conceptions of how common interest should best be served'.[3]

It is not surprising that the 'chamber pot in the window' myth has entered the current, popular, historical imagination in relation to the early modern period. After all, in many eighteenth- and nineteenth-century British towns and cities, mass urbanization and increased housing density caused in part by the subdivision of dwellings combined to create very serious sanitation problems. The practicalities of disposing of the augmented domestic and industrial waste which was produced in relatively small areas proved to overwhelm the governors of many towns and cities from 1700 onwards. But around a century before this nationwide development, in the seventeenth century, London and to a lesser extent Edinburgh underwent the demographic changes which did not reach most of the smaller, provincial towns until well into the eighteenth century. Consequently, Edinburgh and London experienced serious sanitation challenges a whole century before other towns and cities such as York, Ayr, Carlisle, Glasgow, Kendal, Stirling and Sheffield, whose populations remained relatively stable throughout the seventeenth century. With the exception of London and Edinburgh, then, Britain's urban sanitation problems were of a distinctly different character in the seventeenth and the eighteenth centuries, respectively. By the eighteenth century, increasing industrialization and urbanization together with a marked decline in the strength and presence of local government was increasing the pressure and scale of sanitation problems, pushing them into an almost completely different context. This perhaps explains the extremely negative depictions of urban streets presented by Emily Cockayne, in *Hubbub*, which conflated the period 1600 to 1770 – a period which in relation to sanitation, at least, should not be presented as one epoch of continuity within one thematic book.

As we have seen, Edinburgh Council responded to the augmented waste and worsening insanitary nuisances in the city in a proactive manner by centralizing and expanding the scale of its street cleaning provision, by removing slaughterhouses to the edge of the city and by delegating neighbourhood nuisance cases exclusively to the Dean of Guild Court. But even these improvements were insufficient to keep pace with the worsening conditions. There is much evidence to suggest that despite the actions of its council, Edinburgh's streets and closes became dirtier over the course of the seventeenth century and the offence of throwing the contents of chamber pots directly out of windows and doors into the streets below did become a more serious problem than had been the case in the sixteenth century before rapid population expansion. A report written in 1735 claimed that in 1687 'dung ... was ... lying on the streets [of Edinburgh] ... like mountains, and roads were cut through them to the closes or shops'.[4] However, this sensationalistic account described Edinburgh at the end of the period under discussion, in a city which was experiencing acute augmentation of waste due to population increase and in which its inhabitants and governors were making enormous efforts to improve conditions. The application of the 'chamber pot in the window' stereotype is not justifiable either in relation to Edinburgh, London or large numbers of other early modern British towns and cities whose populations remained relatively stable and which did not experience serious sanitation challenges, at least before 1700. Even though Edinburgh's and London's exploding populations did pose serious challenges to their sanitation infrastructure before 1700, the administrative and legal records which their governors left behind are a testament to consistent efforts, and the genuine desire and intention, to combat sanitation problems and improve salubrity. Sixteenth- and seventeenth-century urban governors were far from aquiescent when insanitary conditions worsened.

While not as influential a factor as population density, a town's geographical location, topography and proximity to rivers also had a significant impact on environmental regulation. All towns benefited from rural hinterlands complete with convenient markets of local farmers who were necessarily interested in purchasing urban dung to use as fertilizer in the cultivation of their crops, but a hinterland which was primarily arable, such as Edinburgh's, Berwick's and York's, provided a potentially larger market for the sale of urban dung than one which was primary pastoral, such as that of Kendal or Carlisle. Moreover, Scarborough, Ayr, Berwick, Bideford, Whitehaven and Aberdeen were situated on the coast, which provided very convenient drainage of liquid waste into the natural receptacle of the sea. The proximity of one or more rivers was often the main reason for the original placement of a town; most of the towns which have been discussed had access to at least one river. Edinburgh's inhabitants lacked access to a river whereas York's inhabitants had access to the River Ouse and the River Fosse. In practical terms, this made York's drainage of liquid waste significantly less challenging than that of Edinburgh. Carlisle was situated strategically close to three rivers: the River Eden to the north; the River Caldew to the west; and the River Petteril to the east, into which the city's sewerage network drained.[5] Berwick's inhabitants enjoyed convenient access to the River Tweed as well as to the sea, those living in Sheffield could access the River Don and those who inhabited Inverness enjoyed access to the River Ness. All of these rivers were used as natural receptacles for liquid waste. Edinburgh's liquid waste drained into the Nor' Loch, which was of a sufficiently large scale to absorb the waste without becoming seriously insanitary.[6]

York's topography was reasonably flat and prone to flooding whereas Edinburgh featured extremely steep gradients, which in times of heavy rainfall facilitated excellent natural drainage and relatively easy manual sweeping of the streets. Sheffield was situated on a ridge, and benefited from the wind and very steep gradients down to the natural receptacle of the River Don for its drainage, whereas Whitehaven and Carlisle were relatively flat, thus making drainage more challenging.[7] Lots of very narrow and steep closes ran down from both sides of Edinburgh's High Street, which limited the practicalities of street cleaning, eventually forcing Edinburgh Council in the seventeenth century to employ men with wheel barrows to bring the waste to the close heads because it was impossible for a horse and cart to move down them. It is also important to remember that inhabitants who lived in a town or city featuring steep gradients had to invest significantly more time and effort into reaching rivers and wells for the purposes of washing and bearing water, which was an integral part of keeping the urban environment clean. Perhaps this is why Sir William Brereton noticed, in 1635, that the inhabitants of Edinburgh 'fetch not fresh water every day: but onely every other day: which makes their water much worse (espetially to drinke) which, when itt is att best, is bad enough'.[8] Once an urban settlement had become established, the advantages and disadvantages of a town or city's geographical location, topography and proximity to rivers were immoveable parameters which necessarily limited inhabitants' ability to maintain a clean environment. As they endeavoured to improve and maintain the sanitary standard of their town and cityscapes, governors and inhabitants had to work around their natural characteristics and the situation of the settlement, which shaped the way in which waste was produced, disposed of and regulated to a large extent.

In this period, most towns were incorporated, but some were not. Carlisle was an incorporated city governed by a corporation which consisted of a mayor, several senior officials, eleven aldermen and twenty-four capital citizens; Carlisle's mayor was elected annually, at Michaelmas, from twelve men; the residual eleven then served as aldermen. The senior officials were the chamberlain, the sword-bearer, two bailiffs, a coroner, a clerk, two sergeants and an attorney.[9] Berwick and Scarborough were also governed in this way, but Sheffield was unincorporated, governed by a town trust of twelve Church Burgesses. Edinburgh and York and other towns north and south of the border, respectively, were governed under nationally different administrative, legal and governmental structures which had evolved separately over centuries. Scottish burghs were not only answerable to the Scottish Parliament, but they were also under the jurisdiction of the Convention of Burghs whereas England lacked an exclusively urban, representative, national governmental body which held authority over its towns. In Scotland, moreover, there were administrative and economic differences between burghs of barony and royal burghs. Royal burghs had a monopoly on national and foreign trade, leaving burghs of barony merely as local market centres which were relatively limited in terms of potential growth. Hawick and Old Aberdeen were burghs of barony, for example. However, there were differences between burghs of barony too; whereas Hawick lacked sewers and paving until well into the eighteenth century, Old Aberdeen had a relatively sophisticated drainage system and some paving by the beginning of the seventeenth century.[10] There were some cultural differences between Scottish and English towns, as we have seen in relation to activities such as clothes-washing, but in terms of the practicalities of the daily processing of waste, attitudes towards outdoor sanitation and efforts to improve sanitary standards in the urban landscape, Scotland and England were remarkably similar, not only to each other but also in comparison to many other European towns, especially in Scandinavia, the Low Countries and Italy.[11] In short, nationality was by no means a significant factor in shaping the management of waste in the urban landscape. There were marked and important differences between the administrative and practical management of sanitation from one town to another within the two respective kingdoms of England and Scotland and the majority of urban inhabitants were careful with waste and valued a clean environment above and below the Anglo-Scottish border. A town's particular sanitation needs, management and regulation over time can be best, and perhaps only, understood in its own unique context analysing in detail and paying significant attention to demography, governmental and administrative systems, geographic location and topography and functions.[12]

Edinburgh was the seat of national government whereas York was not. Consequently, far more time and effort was ploughed into regulating Edinburgh's environment than that of York. Scotland's national governors interfered in the issue of Edinburgh's street cleanliness because they were keen to present a clean and orderly capital city to the swathes of prestigious visitors who frequented its streets. The issue of York's street cleanliness did not receive anywhere near as much attention from England's national governors, but this could be explained partially by the fact that the city's governors were not experiencing similarly severe sanitation problems as those faced in Edinburgh. Carlisle was a walled city which had a castle and a cathedral, and it functioned as Cumberland's market, ecclesiastical, legal and military centre. Scarborough and Whitehaven functioned as ports, and Berwick functioned as both a garrison and as a port. A town or city's function affected the number of visitors it attracted; hosting the Scottish Circuit Courts or the English Assizes, or hosting royalty in either country, generated significantly more motivation to present a clean urban landscape, especially in main thoroughfares and central, public open spaces such as marketplaces. Court Days were prestigious occasions for towns. Glaswegian councillors ordered the burgh's streets to be cleaned in 1656, for example, because 'the judges is to be heir at the Sircueit Court'; this clean was in those judges' exclusive honour.[13] Similarly, Mark Jenner observes that in sixteenth- and seventeenth-century London, there were specially extensive clean ups for coronations, processions of new city mayors and the annual Spittle Sermons at Easter, which were a major tourist attraction.[14] In May 1633, moreover, York Corporation passed a bylaw stipulating that the Constables of each parish give notice to the inhabitants that they were not to 'suffer any of their kine swine or mastive dogs to come within the streetes of this citty' during the time of 'his Ma[jes]ties abode in this citty' under the pain of 40s.[15] Clearly, this move to clear the streets of livestock was not for inhabitants' benefit, but in King Charles I's honour. Civic pride motivated urban governors to present their towns in optimum condition for important occasions, but in this respect their concern was not for the inhabitants' collective health; it was for their towns' praiseworthiness through social elites' eyes. The more prestigious the function of a town, the higher was the motivation to present the streets in a clean condition. A town's or city's function had a significant impact on waste management and the regulation of insanitary nuisances.

While the topography, geographical location and proximity of a town to rivers were immoveable characteristics, the style, design and building materials of the houses and infrastructure which were installed into the urban landscape could be altered to aid drainage and street cleaning, providing that sufficient resources were available or could be raised. Edinburgh had significantly higher residential buildings than York, which made the disposal of domestic waste more challenging in the former than in the latter. Some towns had sewers running down the centre of thoroughfares and some built them into each side of the street. While most towns had sewers, some, such as Hawick and Kendal, did not acquire them until well into the eighteenth century.[16] This inadequacy can be attributed not only to early modern governors, but also to their medieval predecessors. Some sewers were covered, and ran underneath buildings whereas others were totally open. Access to water also had a significant impact on urban inhabitants' ability to maintain clean forefronts, especially during dry periods of weather, as did paving. Even in towns where the main thoroughfares were paved, lanes and vennels were often merely bare earth, which became muddy and absorbed debris, detritus and waste liquids, making them very difficult to keep clean. The built infrastructure of a town shaped the manner in which liquid waste drained away and solid waste was removed and it also affected the efficacy of that waste removal, in some cases making it easier and some cases making it even more challenging.

Comparing the major case studies of Edinburgh and York to several other urban settlements across England and Scotland only highlighted national patterns in terms of administrative, governmental and legal systems of environmental management and regulation. Beneath these organizational national frameworks, which had evolved separately in the two kingdoms over centuries, attitudes and values in relation to this area of daily life were remarkably similar above and below the Anglo-Scottish border. This research has highlighted that characteristics other than nationality exerted a far larger influence over a town's environmental regulation, characteristics such as: size of settlement and demographic density; geographical location, topography and proximity to rivers; administrative and governmental structures; function; and building tradition and infrastructure. Each urban settlement boasted a necessarily unique combination of such characteristics, which collectively shaped the management and regulation of waste disposal, street cleaning and insanitary nuisances. Some towns' environmental regulations were shaped more by one characteristic than by others, but by and large, population density was the most salient influencing factor in the scale, structure, composition and ultimately the efficacy of most urban settlements' environmental regulation.

Regardless of the many variable differences between urban settlements, none of the urban governors was indifferent to the sanitary condition of outdoor public spaces. Rather, they understood that sanitation was integral to the efficient government of a town or city, that it contributed to the 'commonweal' and that it was crucial to maintaining a good image in the eyes of prestigious visitors and wider society. When discussing early modern towns, one must be extremely careful to distinguish between those which were still functioning very much in their medieval forms, and which were largely untouched by mass urbanization, increased housing density and serious sanitation challenges, and those such as Edinburgh and London which were already embracing those challenges in the seventeenth century. But even in the context of such severe sanitation problems as those faced in Edinburgh and London, governors and inhabitants still valued cleanliness and their efforts to embrace the problems provide testimony to their desire to live in an environment which did not cause intolerable offence to their senses. Whatever they labelled this area of urban management, urban dwellers certainly cared about what we now call public hygiene and they were far from indifferent to controlling, or at least trying to control, how much and what types of waste entered and remained in particular areas of their outdoor environment. At a time when understandings of the link between dirt and disease, notably plague, were still only implicit, civic pride was a key driving force behind improvements to outdoor cleanliness, but the desire to breathe sweet and clean air and to live in an environment which was perceived as conducive to wellbeing were also significant motivating factors in an age before explicit conceptions of public health. In late-sixteenth- and seventeenth-century towns, breathing what was termed sweet and clean air was hugely important to contemporaries because they believed that it enhanced their health and wellbeing; whereas they believed that evil-smelling air, conversely, would adversely affect their health at best and potentially endanger their lives at worst. It is important to remain mindful that it was contemporaries' perceived need to breathe sweet and clean air in order to preserve their health, wellbeing, and sometimes even their lives, rather than aesthetic considerations, which fuelled their efforts to improve public hygiene first and foremost. For this reason, sixteenth- and seventeenth-century urban dwellers might well have engaged with the issue of outdoor sanitation far more passionately than their twenty-first-century descendants do today.

As a result of the improvements made in municipal street cleaning and waste disposal systems in sixteenth- and seventeenth-century towns and cities, not only in Scotland and England, but across Europe, and through the implementation of better and more rigorously enforced sanitation bylaws, many early modern towns and cities became cleaner and more pleasant olfactory environments in which to live and work, or at least cleaner than they would have been in the absence of efforts towards improvement. The settlements which did not become cleaner in real terms, due to population and housing density increase – of which Edinburgh and London are examples – nevertheless developed better, more centralized systems for coping with waste. Edinburgh and London were certainly less dirty by 1700 than they might well have been in the context of dramatic population increase without having made substantial large-scale improvements to their sanitation systems. The stereotypical image of the majority of a town's inhabitants pouring effluent out of their windows and of a general disinclination to improve street cleanliness and to dispose of waste efficiently is a gross misrepresentation, at least before 1700. The people who inhabited urban neighbourhoods necessarily had a vested interest in upholding a tolerable standard of cleanliness, olfactory sensation and arguably olfactory safety too in the urban landscape which framed their daily lives. Only when findings such as those presented above are communicated to scholars and to the wider public will the deeply entrenched misconception, that early modern urban dwellers were disinclined to pursue and uphold sanitary standards, be corrected. The topic is in its infancy, and much about it is still unknown, though several significant contributions have been made. This hugely important aspect of daily life is in need of much deeper and wider research, in the form of both respective case studies and comparisons of different settlements, if this area of early modern history is to be understood more fully. There has been little progress in relation to sanitation in early modern Welsh towns, and it would be useful to use the focused lens of sanitation in order to test Harold Carter's conclusion that the sixteenth and seventeenth centuries represent a period of 'urban decay' and 'a hiatus between the well developed, restrictive burghal society of the medieval town and the equally well developed, mercantile bourgeoisie of the latter eighteenth and early nineteenth centuries'.[17] Further studies of the use of urban dung as fertilizer in towns' rural hinterlands by agricultural and environmental historians would also inform this topic, as would studies of the regulation of insanitary nuisances in rural settlements. In particular, how do we account for the absence of references to flies in documents which describe, often explicitly, nuisances involving putrefying organic material? How firm were the distinctions made between human and animal excrement in terms of acceptable and unacceptable storage, reuse and disposal? And how was sanitation and waste disposal organized in the temporary military encampments of the British Civil Wars or in relatively large-scale refugee camps such as the one established in Lincoln's Inn Fields following the Great Fire of London?

Sanitation always has been, and always will be, an aspect of daily life for human beings living together in settlements, especially densely populated settlements. Just as the built environment shaped inhabitants' daily life experiences, so too did the built environment's sanitary condition. Improving the sanitary condition of the urban landscape occupied far more of urban inhabitants' and their local governors' time, thoughts, resources and efforts than historians have tended to appreciate so far. So, the next time you see cartoon images or dramatizations in flims or on television depicting maidservants throwing the contents of chamber pots out of a sixteenth- or seventeenth-century windows, do spare a thought for some of the fascinating people we have met above: Elleanor Harris, a widow of Whitehaven, who refused to accept her physical debarment from being able to scour her sewer; the indefatigable Edinburgh Council and its employment of a very well-organized army of muckmen who hauled thousands of tonnes of manure out of their city; Mr Blanshard of Coney Street in York who approached his city corporation for permission to keep his street free of manure by means of a lock and a key; the workman paid by Carlisle Corporation to transform a simple herring barrel into a close stool; and the thousands of urban dwellers represented by these people. The progressive, imaginative and positive attitudes towards sanitation, expressed by the majority of sixteenth- and seventeenth-century urban dwellers, surely are of more significance than the non-compliance and inconsiderate actions of the minority, a contingent which emerges and always will emerge as part of every new generation – a contingent which is certainly alive and well in modern-day Britain's towns and cities.

Notes

1 Slack, *Reformation to Improvement*, pp. 53–76; Borsay, *Urban Renaissance*, p. 68.
2 Borsay, *Urban Renaissance*, p. 4.
3 Van der Heijden, 'New perspectives', pp. 271–272.
4 Manuscript proposals referring to previous Taxation Acts of 1687, (1735), quoted in D. Laing, 'Proposals for cleaning and lighting the city of Edinburgh in the year 1735: with explanatory remarks', *Proceedings of the Society of Antiquaries of Scotland*, 3 (1859), pp. 171–180, on p. 174.
5 Skelton, 'Beadles, dunghills and noisome excrements', p. 22.
6 Smith, 'Foul burns of Edinburgh', pp. 25–36.
7 Hey, *History of Sheffield*, p. 57.
8 Brereton, 'Journal', p. 31.
9 CRO, Ca2/17: *The Dormont Book*; T. Denton, *A Perambulation of Cumberland* (1687–88), ed. A. Winchester and M. Wane (Durham: Surtees Society, 207, 2003), p. 264.
10 Scottish Borders Archive, TDS/1/2: Hawick Town Court Book, 1640–1681; W. Robson, *The Story of Hawick: An Introduction to the History of the Town*, 2nd edn (Hawick: R. Deans & Co., 1937), p. 63; Dennison, Ditchburn and Lynch (eds), *Aberdeen Before 1800*.
11 Jorgensen, 'Co-operative sanitation', pp. 547, 561, 564, 566. Deceulaer, 'Implications of the street'; Van Bavel and Gelderblom, 'Origins of cleanliness'; Van der Heijden, 'New perspectives'; Schama, *Embarrassment of Riches*; Wheeler, 'Stench in sixteenth-century Venice'; Henderson, 'Public health'.
12 See Skelton, 'Beadles, dunghills and noisome excrements' for a very detailed discussion of sanitation in seventeenth-century Carlisle.
13 *Records of Glasgow*, vol. 2, p. 332 (19/04/1656).
14 Jenner, '"Cleanliness" and "dirt"', pp. 129–131.
15 YCA, B35: Corporation House Book, 1625–1637 (13/05/1633).
16 Scottish Borders Archive, TDS/1/2: Hawick Town Court Book, 1640–1681; Robson, *The Story of Hawick*, p. 63; *The Boke of Recorde of the Burgh of Kirkby Kendal*, ed. R. Ferguson (Carlisle, 1892). There are no references to sewers in either of these towns' records.
17 Carter, *The Towns of Wales*, p. 32.

Works cited

Archival and manuscript sources

Berwick on Tweed Record Office, Berwick on Tweed

C1/1–3: Berwick Bailiffs' Court Book, 1568–1601.
H2/1: Berwick Annual Account Book, 1603–1611.

Borthwick Institute, University of York Library, Heslington, York

PR/Y/MS/5: St Michael's Churchwarden Account Book, 1626–1710.
PR/YHTG/15: York Holy Trinity Goodramgate Constables' Accounts, 1636–1735.

Bristol Record Office, Bristol

JQS/Pr/1: Presentments to the Grand Jury to the Bristol Leet, 1628–1666 [catalogued with the Quarter Sessions as they were stored with them originally, but they are the records of presentments to the Court Leet on the lawday].
28048/D1: Lease of a Sope Workhouse, Grotelane, Bristol, between James Birkin and Abraham Barnes (21/05/1636).
37941/1: Lease of the Ridlings between John Bubb, esq., and Thomas Child (25/03/1698).

Carlisle Record Office, Carlisle

Ca4/1–3: Carlisle Chamberlains' Accounts, 1602–1694.
Carlisle City Probate Wills and Inventories, 1596, 1601–1611, 1661–1671.
Ca2/2/1: Corporation of Carlisle Order Book, 1639–1654 [including an earlier insert of bylaws dated 1568].
Ca3/2/1–26: Carlisle Court Leet Rolls, 1597–1698.
Ca4/139: Audit of Carlisle Chamberlains' Accounts, 1597–1682.
Ca2/17: *The Dormont Book*, 1561.
D/Lons/W8/17/1: Manor of St. Bees Court Book, 1666–1689.
D/MH/10/7/1: Carlisle Chamberlains' Accounts, 1597–1598.

Durham County Record Office, Durham

Da/DM/5/2: Darlington Borough Book, 1612–1633.
MS D/HH/11/142: Barnard Castle Courts, 1621–1788.

Durham University Heritage Collection, Durham

MS 8/I: Subsidiary Manorial Court Records, Stockton Division, Box 7, Bundle 1, Item 5.
MS 8/I: Subsidiary Manorial Court Records, Darlington Division, Box 3, Bundle 1, Item 9.

Edinburgh City Archives, Edinburgh

SL144/1–9: Edinburgh Dean of Guild Court Minute Books, 1529–1702.
SL144/4/1–4: Edinburgh Dean of Guild Accounts, 1552–1720.
SL1/1/3–36: Edinburgh Town Council Minutes, 1558–1701.
Uncatalogued (in silver safe): Edinburgh Town Treasurer's Accounts, 1581–1690.

Highland Council Archives, Inverness

BI/1/1/5: Inverness Town Council Minutes, 1662–1680.

Huntingdon Library, San Marino, California

HM MS 70160: Diary of Sir John Archer, 1663.

Kendal Record Office, Kendal

Uncatalogued: Sundry Court Leet Papers, sixteenth and seventeenth centuries.

National Archives of Scotland, Edinburgh

GD/18/1914: Papers of Clerk Family on Penicuik, Midlothian, 1373–1966 – Receipts to the Lady Elphinstone for annuity tax and proportion for street cleaning, 1687–1689.
PA3/2/3: 'Supplicatioune of the heretours of the landwart parrosche of Perth', Charles II Scottish Parliament held at Stirling on 23/05/1651, additional sources 28/05/1651 [filed in error with May 1650].
PA2/32: 'Act for cleansing the streats of Edinburgh', at Scottish Parliament in Edinburgh on 29/04/1686 (Legislation 08/06/1686).
RH9/14/66: Petition of the Constables of Edinburgh, 1690.
RH0/14/68: 'Edinburgh and Leith Papers, 1329–1851 – Decreet of Guild Court in favour of Robert Innes against John Paterson, for obstructing vennel with middings' (15/06/1692).

North Yorkshire County Record Office, Northallerton

DC/SCB/II/1: Scarborough Corporation Minute and Order Book, 1621–1649.

Northumberland Record Office, Woodhorn

PHU/C2: Hexham Dunghill Deed.

Perth and Kinross Archives, Perth

B66/20/5: Perth Burgh Council Record, 1659–1680.
B59/16/1–2: Acts of Town Council, 1601–1635.

Scottish Borders Archive, Hawick

TDS/1/2: Hawick Town Court Book, 1640–1681.

Sheffield Archives, Sheffield

CB/161: Sheffield Church Burgesses' Account Book, 1574–1727.
ACM/S/116: A Book of Pains and Amerciaments, Sheffield Court Leet, 1578.

Stirling Archives, Stirling

B66/20/2: Stirling Council Record, 1597–1609.
B66/20/5: Stirling Council Record, 1659–1680.

The National Archives, Kew, London

C 2/Eliz/N2/36: Court of Chancery: Edmund Nicholson and Thomas Yates v Godfrey
    Bradshawe (1558–1603, exact date unknown).
C 6/192/35: Court of Chancery, Carlisle Dean and Chapter v Erasmus Towerson, gent.
DL 30/883, Bundle 2: Clare, Suffolk, Court Leet, Court Baron and General Court Rolls,
    1698–1761.
E101/545/16: Scottish Marches: Accounts of repairs at Carlisle, 1577–1602.
SC 2/315/11: Court Leet of the Borough of Macclesfield.

Tyne and Wear Archives, Newcastle upon Tyne

BC.RV/1/2: River Tyne Court Book, 1647–1650.

York City Archives, York

CB5–28: York Chamberlains' account books, 1559–1697.
C66–79: Receivers' rolls, 1627–1695 [collected rents and fines for chamberlain]
B23–40: Corporation House or Minute Books, 1560–1706.

Printed primary

Anon., *Reprints of Rare Tracts and Imprints of Ancient Manuscripts Chiefly Illustrative of
    the History of the Northern Counties*, 3 vols (1847).

Ayr Burgh Accounts, 1534–1624, ed. G. Pryde (Edinburgh: Scottish Historical Society, third series, 1937).

Belhaven, J., Baron, *An Advice to the Farmers in East Lothian how to Labour and Improve their Ground or The Countrey-man's Rudiments* (1699).

Blome, R., *Britannia* (London, 1673).

Brereton, W., Sir, *Journal of Sir William Brereton* (1635), ed. J. C. Hodgson, *North Country Diaries*, second series, 124 (Durham: Surtees Society, 1914), pp. 1–50.

Brown, P. (ed.), *Scotland Before 1700, from Contemporary Documents* (Edinburgh: David Douglas, 1893).

Calendar of Assize Records. Surrey Indictments. Elizabeth I., ed. J. Cockburn (London: Public Record Office, 1980).

Camden, W., *Britannia* (London, 1586).

Charters and Documents relating to the Burgh of Peebles, with Extracts from the Records of the Burgh, AD 1165–1710, ed. W. Chambers (Edinburgh: Scottish Burgh Record Society, 1872).

Court Leet Records, 1603–1624, ed. F. Hearnshaw and D. Hearnshaw (Southampton: Southampton Record Society, 1907).

Coventry Constables' Presentments, 1629–1742, ed. L. Fox (Stratford upon Avon: Dugdale Society, 1986).

Dalyell, J. (ed.), *Fragments of Scottish History*, 2 vols (Edinburgh: Printed for Archibald Constable at the Cross, 1798).

Defoe, D., *A Tour through the Whole Island of Great Britain* (1724), ed. P. Rogers (London: Penguin, 1971).

Denton, T., *A Perambulation of Cumberland* (1687–88), ed. A. Winchester and M. Wane (Durham: Surtees Society, 207, 2003).

Extracts from the Burgh Records of Dunfermline in the Sixteenth and Seventeenth Centuries, ed. A. Shearer (Dunfermline: Carnegie Dunfermline Trust, 1951).

Extracts from the Council Register of the Burgh of Aberdeen 1398–1625, 2 vols, ed. J. Stuart (Aberdeen: Spalding Club, 1844–1848)

Extracts from the Council Register of the Burgh of Aberdeen, 1625–1747, 2 vols, ed. J. Stuart (Edinburgh: Scottish Burgh Record Society, 1871–1872).

Extracts from the Newcastle-Upon-Tyne Council Minute Book, 1639–1656, ed. M. Hope Dodds (Newcastle upon Tyne: Publications of the Newcastle upon Tyne Record Society, 1920).

Extracts from the Records of the Burgh of Edinburgh, 1403–1589, vols 1–4, ed. J. Marwick (Edinburgh: Scottish Burgh Record Society, 1869–1882).

Extracts from the Records of the Burgh of Edinburgh, 1589–1718, vols 5–13, ed. M. Wood, R. Hannay and H. Armet (Edinburgh: Scottish Burgh Record Society, 1927–1967).

Extracts from the Records of the Burgh of Glasgow, 6 vols, ed. J. Marwick (Edinburgh: Scottish Burgh Record Society, 1876–1916).

Extracts from the Records of the Royal Burgh of Lanark: with Charters and Documents relating to the Burgh, AD 1150–1722, ed. R. Renwick (Edinburgh: Scottish Burgh Record Society, 1893).

Extracts from the Records of the Royal Burgh of Stirling, 1518–1666, 2 vols, ed. R. Renwick (Edinburgh: Scottish Burgh Record Society, 1887–1889).

Fiennes, C., *The Journeys of Celia Fiennes* (1702), ed. C. Morris (London: Cresset Press, 1947).

Franck, R., *Franck's Memoirs* (1656), ed. P. Hume, *Early Travellers in Scotland* (Edinburgh: James Thin, 1978), pp. 182–216.

Fraser, C. M. (ed.), 'Durham Quarter Sessions Rolls, 1471–1625', *The Publications of the Surtees Society*, vol. 199 (1987–1988).

Gibson, E. (ed.), *Britannia* (London, 1695).

Harrington, J., Sir, *A New Discourse of a Stale Subject, called the Metamorphosis of Ajax: Written by Misacmos, to his Friend and Cosin Philostilpnos* (London, 1596), ed. E. Story Donno (London: Routledge and Kegan Paul, 1962).

Hutchinson, W., *The History of the County of Cumberland*, 2 vols (Carlisle, 1794).

Jonson, B., *The Works of Ben Jonson* (1573–1637), 8 vols, ed. William Gifford (London, 1875).

Kirke, T., *A Modern Account of Scotland by an English Gentleman* (1679), ed. P. Brown, *Early Travellers in Scotland* (Edinburgh: James Thin, 1978), pp. 251–265.

Liverpool Town Books, 1649–1671, ed. M. Power (Liverpool: The Record Society of Lancashire and Cheshire, 136, 1998).

London Assize of Nuisance, 1301–1431, ed. H. Chew and W. Kellaway (London: London Record Society, 1973).

London Viewers and their Certificates, 1508–1558: Certificates of the sworn viewers of the City of London, ed. J. Loengard (London: London Record Society, 1989).

Monson, R., Plowden, E., Wray, C., Sir, and Manwood, J., *A Briefe Declaration for What manner of special Nusance concerning private dwelling Houses, a man may have his remedy by Assise, or other Action as the Case requires ...* (London, 1636).

Morer, T., Rev., *A Short Account of Scotland: Being a Description of the Nature of that Kingdom* (London, 1702), ed. P. Brown, *Early Travellers in Scotland* (Edinburgh: James Thin, 1978), pp. 266–290.

Pepys, S., *Diary of Samuel Pepys* (1660–1669), ed. R. Latham and W. Matthews, *The Diary of Samuel Pepys: A New and Complete Transcription*, 11 vols (London: G. Bell and Sons, 1970–1983).

Quarter Sessions Records [of Warwick], Easter 1674 to Easter 1682, ed. S. Ratcliff and H. Johnson (Warwick: L. Edgar Stephens, 1946), vol. 7.

Ray, J., *Select Remains of the Learned John Ray* (1662).

Ray, J., *A Collection of English Proverbs Digested into a Convenient Method for the Speedy Finding of Any One upon Occasions* (Cambridge, 1684).

Records of Inverness, 1556–1637, 2 vols, ed. W. Mackay, H. Cameron and G. Laing (Aberdeen: New Spalding Club, 1911–1924).

Records of Maidstone: Being Selections from Documents in the Possession of the Corporation, ed. K. Martin (Maidstone: Maidstone Borough Council, 1926).

Records of the Borough of Nottingham, being a Series of Extracts from the Archives of the Corporation of Nottingham, 7 vols, ed. Nottingham Borough Council (Nottingham: Forman, 1882–1947).

Records of the Burgery of Sheffield, commonly called the Town Trust, ed. J. Leader (London: Elliot Stock, 1897).

Records of the Convention of the Royal Burghs of Scotland with extracts from other records relating to the affairs of the Burghs of Scotland, 1295–1711, 4 vols, ed. J. Marwick (Edinburgh: Scottish Burgh Record Society, 1876–1880).

Robertson, G., *General View of the Agriculture of the County of Midlothian: with Observations on the means of its Improvement* (Edinburgh, 1795).

Seymore, R., *An Account of the Husbandry used in some parts of Dorsetshire*, Royal Agricultural Society of England, *Classified Papers*, X (Agriculture, 3), paper no. 10 (1665).

Skeldie, A., *The Only Sure Preservative against the Plague of Pestilence* (Edinburgh, 1645).

Skeyne, G., Dr, *Ane Breve Description of the Pest Quhair in the cavsis, signis and sum speciall preseruation and cure thairof ar contenit* (1568), ed. W. Skene, *Tracts by Dr. Gilbert Skeyne, medicinar to his majesty* (Edinburgh: Bannatyne Club, 6.111, 1860).

Slezer, J., *Theatrum Scotiae: Containing the Prospects of his Majesties Castles and Palaces* (London, 1874).

Somerset Assize Orders, 1629–1640, ed. T. Barnes (Frome: Butler and Frome, 1959).

Taylor, J., *Adventures* (London, 1639).

The Boke of Recorde of the Burgh of Kirkby Kendal, ed. R. Ferguson (Carlisle, 1892).

The English Reports, vols 1–178 (Edinburgh: W. Green and Sons, 1900–1932).

The London Surveys of Ralph Treswell, ed. J. Schofield (London: London Topgraphical Society, no. 135, 1987).

The Portmote or Court Leet Records of the Borough or Town and Royal Manor of Salford from the Year 1597 to the Year 1669 Inclusive, 2 vols, ed. J. Mandley (Manchester: Chetham Society, 1902).

The Register of the Privy Council of Scotland, 1545–1625, 14 vols, ed. J. Burton and D. Masson (Edinburgh: H. M. General Register House, 1877–1898).

Weldon, A., Sir, *A Perfect Description of the People and Country of Scotland* (London, 1617), ed. P. Brown, *Early Travellers in Scotland* (Edinburgh: James Thin, 1978), pp. 96–103.

Secondary works

Adams, M., 'Darlington market place: archaeological excavations' (unpublished archaeological report, Durham Sites and Monuments Record, nos. 4000, 4812, 1994).

Addyman, P., 'The archaeology of public health at York, England', *World Archaeology*, 21 (1989), pp. 244–257.

Allen-Emerson, M. (ed.), *Sanitary Reform in Victorian Britain*, 6 vols (London: Pickering and Chatto, 2012).

Archer, D., 'Kielder Water: White Elephant or White Knight?' in D. Archer (ed.), *Tyne and Tide: A Celebration of the River Tyne* (Ovingham: Daryan Press, 2000), pp. 138–156.

Baker, J. H., *An Introduction to English Legal History*, 2nd edn (London: Butterworths, 1979).

Balfour-Paul, J. P. (ed.), *The Scots Peerage*, 9 vols (Edinburgh, 1904–1914).

Barnes, T., 'The prerogative and environmental control of London building in the early seventeenth century: the lost opportunity', *California Law Review*, 58 (1970), pp. 1332–1363.

Barnwell, P., 'Workshops, industrial production and the landscape' in P. S. Barnwell et al. (eds), *The Vernacular Workshop from Craft to Industry, 1400–1900* (York: Council for British Archaeology, 2004), pp. 179–182.

Barry, J., 'Civility and civic culture in early modern England: the meanings of urban freedom', in P. Burke et al. (eds), *Civil Histories: Essays Presented to Sir Keith Thomas* (Oxford: Oxford University Press, 2000), pp. 181–197.

Beck, M. and Hill, M., 'Rubbish, relatives, and residence: the family use of middens', *Journal of Archaeological Method and Theory*, 11:3 (2004), pp. 297–333.

Biow, D., *The Culture of Cleanliness in Renaissance Italy* (London: Cornell University Press, 2006).

Borsay, P., *The English Urban Renaissance: Culture and Society in the Provincial Town, 1660–1770* (Oxford: Oxford University Press, 1989).

Borsay, P., 'Politeness and elegance: the cultural re-fashioning of eighteenth-century York' in M. Hallet and J. Rendall (eds), *Eighteenth-Century York: Culture, Space and Society* (York: Borthwick Publications, 2003), pp. 1–12.

Brenner, J., 'Nuisance law and the Industrial Revolution', *Journal of Legal Studies*, 3 (1973), pp. 403–433.

Brimblecombe, P., 'Early urban climate and atmosphere', in A. R. Hall and H. K. Kenward (eds), *Environmental Archaeology in the Urban Context* (London: Council for British Archaeology, 1982).

Brimblecombe, P., *The Big Smoke: A History of Air Pollution in London since Medieval Times* (London: Methuen, 1987).

Brooks, C. W., *Pettyfoggers and Vipers of the Commonwealth: The Lower Branch of the Legal Profession in Early Modern England* (Cambridge: Cambridge University Press, 1986).

Brooks, C. W., *Lawyers, Litigation and English Society since 1450* (London: Hambledon Press, 1998).

Brunt, L., 'Where there's muck, there's brass: the market for manure in the industrial revolution', *Economic History Review*, 60:2 (2007), pp. 333–378.

Bryson, B., *Home: A Short History of Private Life* (London: Black Swan, 2010).

Campbell-Irons, J., *Manual of the Law and Practice of the Dean of Guild Court: With Synopsis of the Law, relating to Building Restrictions, Servitudes, etc.* (Edinburgh: Green & Sons, 1895).

Capp, B., Review of *Hubbub: Filth, Noise and Stench in England*, by Cockayne, E., *Renaissance Quarterly*, 61:1 (2008), pp. 277–278.

Carter, H., *The Towns of Wales: A Study in Urban Geography* (Cardiff: University of Wales Press, 1965).

Carter, S., 'A reassessment of the origins of the St Andrews "garden soil"', *Tayside and Fife Archaeological Journal*, 7 (2001), pp. 87–92.

Cavert, W., 'The environmental policy of Charles I: coal smoke and the English monarchy, 1624–40', *Journal of British Studies*, 53:2 (2014), pp. 310–333.

Chandler, J. (ed.), *Travels through Stuart Britain: The Adventures of John Taylor, Water Poet* (Stroud: Sutton, 1999).

Clark, P. (ed.), *The Cambridge Urban History of Britain, volume II, 1540–1840* (Cambridge: Cambridge University Press, 2000).

Clark, P. and Slack, P., *English Towns in Transition 1500–1700* (London: Oxford University Press, 1976).

Clarkson, L., 'The organization of the English leather industry in the late sixteenth and seventeenth centuries', *Economic History Review*, new series, 13:2 (1960), pp. 245–256.

Classen, C., Howes, D. and Synnott, A., *Aroma: The Cultural History of Smell* (London: Routledge, 1994).

Cockayne, E., *Hubbub: Filth, Noise and Stench in England 1600–1770* (London: Yale University Press, 2007).

Colston, J., *The Incorporated Trades of Edinburgh* (Edinburgh: Colston & Co., 1891).

Comrie, J., *History of Scottish Medicine to 1860* (London: Balliere, Tindall and Cox, 1927).

Cooper, D., 'Far beyond "the early morning crowing of a cock": revisiting the place of nuisance within legal and political discourse', *Social and Legal Studies*, 11:1 (2002), pp. 5–35.

Cooper, T. P., 'The medieval highways, streets, open ditches, and sanitary conditions of the city of York', *Yorkshire Archaeological Journal*, 22 (1912), pp. 270–286.

Corbin, A., *The Foul and the Fragrant: Odour and the Social Imagination* (Cambridge, MA: Harvard University Press, 1986).

Cross, C., 'Tudor York', in P. Nuttgens (ed.), *The History of York: From Earliest Times to the Year 2000* (Pickering: Blackthorn, 2001), pp. 141–176.

Davidson, D., Dercon, G., Stewart, M. and Watson, F., 'The legacy of past urban waste disposal on local soils', *Journal of Archaeological Science*, 33:6 (2006), pp. 778–783.

Deceulaer, H., 'Implications of the street: entitlements, duties and conflicts in neighbourhoods in Ghent (17th–18th) centuries', in M. Van der Heijden, M. Elise van Nederveen, V. Griet and M. van der Burg (eds), *Serving the Urban Community. The Rise of Public Facilities in the Low Countries* (Amsterdam: Aksant Academic Publishers, 2009), pp. 194–216.

Dennison, E. P., Desbrisay, G. and Lesley Diack, H., 'Health in the two towns', in E. P. Dennison, D. Ditchburn and M. Lynch (eds), *Aberdeen Before 1800. A New History* (East Linton: Tuckwell Press, 2002), pp. 70–96.

Dennison, E. P., Ditchburn, D. and Lynch, M. (eds), *Aberdeen Before 1800. A New History* (East Linton: Tuckwell Press, 2002).

Devine, T., 'The merchant class of the larger Scottish towns in the later seventeenth and early eighteenth centuries', in G. Gordon and B. Dicks (eds), *Scottish Urban History* (Aberdeen: Aberdeen University Press, 1983), pp. 92–111.

Dickens, A., 'Tudor York', in P. Tillott (ed.), *A History of Yorkshire: The City of York* (London: Victoria County History, 1961), pp. 117–159.

Dingwall, H., 'The importance of social factors in determining the composition of the town councils of Edinburgh 1550–1650', *The Scottish Historical Review*, 65:179 (1986), pp. 17–33.

Dingwall, H., *Late Seventeenth-Century Edinburgh: A Demographic Study* (Aldershot: Scolar Press, 1994).

Dobson, M., *Contours of Death and Disease in Early Modern England* (Cambridge: Cambridge University Press, 1997).

Donaldson, G., *Edinburgh History of Scotland vol. 3: Scotland James V–James VII* (Edinburgh: Oliver & Boyd, 1976).

Dorey, M., 'Controlling corruption: regulating meat consumption as a preventative to plague in seventeenth-century London', *Urban History*, 36:1 (2009), pp. 24–41.

Douglas, M., *Purity and Danger: An Analysis of Concept of Pollution and Taboo* (London: Routledge, 2002).

Duncan, A., 'Bideford under the restored monarchy', *Transactions of the Devon Association*, 47 (1915), pp. 312–315.

Emmison, F. G., *Elizabethan Life: Home, Work and Land* (Chelmsford: Essex County Council, 1976).

Evans, D., 'A good riddance of bad rubbish? Scatalogical musings on rubbish disposal and the handling of "filth" in medieval and early post-medieval towns' in K. De Groote, D. Tys and M. Pieters (eds), *Exchanging Medieval Material Culture: Studies on Archaeology and History Presented to Frans Verhaeghe* (Brussels: Vlaams Instituut voor het Onroerend Erfgoed, 2010), pp. 267–278.

Flinn, M. (ed.), *Scottish Population History: from the Seventeenth Century to the 1930s* (Cambridge: Cambridge University Press, 1977).

Fox, R. C., 'Stirling 1550–1700: the morphology and functions of a pre-industrial Scottish burgh', in G. Gordon and B. Dicks (eds), *Scottish Urban History* (Aberdeen, 1983), pp. 52–70.

Foyster, E., 'Sensory experiences: smells, sounds and touch in early modern Scotland' in E. Foyster and C. Whatley (eds), *A History of Everyday Life in Scotland, 1600–1800* (Edinburgh: Edinburgh University Press, 2010), pp. 217–233.

Fraser, A., *The Weaker Vessel: Woman's Lot in Seventeenth-Century England*, 2nd edn (London: Orion Books, 2002).

Galley, C., *The Demography of Early Modern Towns: York in the Sixteenth and Seventeenth Centuries* (Liverpool: Liverpool University Press, 1998).

Gaunt, J., QC., and Morgan, P., QC. (eds), *Gale on the Law of Easements*, 17th edn (London: Sweet & Maxwell, 2002).

Gee, S., *Making Waste: Leftovers and the Eighteenth-Century Imagination* (Oxford: Princeton University Press, 2010).

Getzler, J., *A History of Water Rights at Common Law* (Oxford: Oxford University Press, 2004).

Girling, R., *Rubbish! Dirt on our Hands and Crisis Ahead* (London: Eden Project Books, 2005).

Green, A., 'Heartless and unhomely? Dwellings of the poor in East Anglia and North-East England', in J. McEwan and P. Sharpe (eds), *Accommodating Poverty: The Housing and Living Arrangements of the English Poor, c. 1600–1850* (Basingstoke: Palgrave MacMillan, 2010), pp. 69–101.

Greenfield, S., *The Private Life of the Brain* (London: Allen Lane, 2000).

Greig, J., 'The investigation of a medieval barrel-latrine', *Journal of Archaeological Science*, 8 (1981), pp. 265–282.

Greig, J., 'Garderobes, sewers, cesspits and latrines', *Current Archaeology*, 85 (1982), pp. 49–52.

Hallett, M. and Rendall, J. (eds), *Eighteenth-Century York: Culture, Space and Society* (York: Borthwick Publications, 2003).

Halliday, P., *Dismembering the Body Politic: Partisan Politics in England's Towns, 1650–1730* (Cambridge: Cambridge University Press, 1998).

Hamlin, C., 'Public sphere to public health: the transformation of "nuisance"', in S. Sturdy (ed.), *Medicine, Health and the Public Sphere in Britain, 1600–2000* (London: Routledge, 2002), pp. 189–204.

Harrison, C., 'Manor courts and the governance of Tudor England', in C. Brooks and M. Lobban (eds), *Communities and Courts in Britain, 1150–1900* (London: Hambledon Press, 1997), pp. 43–60.

Harrison, J., 'Public hygiene and drainage in Stirling and other early modern Scottish towns', *Review of Scottish Culture*, 11 (1998–1999), pp. 67–77.

Hartley, D., *Water in England* (London: MacDonald and Jane's, 1964).

Hartshorne, P., 'The street and the perception of public space in York, 1476–1586' (PhD dissertation, University of York, 2004).

Henderson, J., 'Public health, pollution and the problem of waste disposal in early modern Tuscany', in S. Cavaciocchi (ed.), *Le Interazioni fra economia e ambiernte biologico nell'Europa preindustriale secc. XIII–XVIII. Economic and Biological Reactions in Pre-Industrial Europe from the 13th to the 18th Centuries* (Florence, Italy: Firenze University Press, 2010), pp. 373–382.

Hey, D., *A History of Sheffield* (Lancaster: Carnegie, 1998).

Holdsworth, W. S., Sir, *A History of English Law*, vols 3 and 7, 3rd edn (London: Methuen, 1923–1925).

Hollander, M., 'Sex in two cities: the formation and regulation of sexual relationships in Edinburgh and York, 1560–1625' (PhD dissertation, University of York, 2006).

Hoskins, W., *Two Thousand Years in Exeter: An Illustrated Social History of the Mother-City of South-Western England* (Exeter: James Townsend and Sons Ltd, 1960).

Houston, R., 'Fire and filth: Edinburgh's environment, 1660–1760', *The Book of the Old Edinburgh Club*, New Series, 3 (1994), pp. 25–36.

Hudson, W. (ed.), *Leet Jurisdiction in the City of Norwich in the XIIIth and XIVth Centuries* (London: B. Quaritch, 1892).

Hunt, M., *Shakespeare's As You Like It: Late Elizabethan Culture and Literary Representation* (Basingstoke: Palgrave MacMillan, 2008).

Hutton, R., *The Restoration: A Political and Religious History of England and Wales, 1658–1667* (Oxford: Oxford University Press, 1987).

Ingram, M., 'Ridings, rough music and the reform of popular culture', *Past and Present*, 105 (1984), pp. 79–113.

Jenner, M., 'Early modern English conceptions of "cleanliness and "dirt" as reflected in the environmental regulation of London c.1530–c.1700' (D.Phil dissertation, University of Oxford, 1991).

Jenner, M., '"Another epocha"? Hartlib, John Lanyon and the improvement of London in the 1650s' in M. Greengrass et al. (eds), *Samuel Hartlib and Universal Reformation* (Cambridge: Cambridge University Press, 1994), pp. 343–356.

Jenner, M., 'The politics of London air: John Evelyn's Fumifugium and the Restoration', *Historical Journal*, 38:3 (1995), pp. 535–551.

Jenner, M., 'Overground, underground: pollution and place in urban history', *Journal of Urban Studies*, 24 (1997), pp. 97–110.

Jenner, M., 'The great dog massacre' in W. Naphy and P. Roberts (eds), *Fear in Early Modern Society* (Manchester: Manchester University Press, 1997), pp. 44–61.

Jenner, M., 'Civilization and deodorization? Smell in early modern English culture', in P. Burke et al. (eds), *Civil Histories. Essays Presented to Sir Keith Thomas* (Oxford: Oxford University Press, 2000), pp. 127–144.

Jenner, M., 'From conduit community to commercial network? Water in London, 1500–1725' in P. Griffiths and M. Jenner (eds), *Londinopolis: Essays in the Cultural and Social History of Early Modern London* (Manchester: Manchester University Press, 2000), pp. 250–272.

Jenner, M., 'The roasting of the rump: scatology and the body politic in Restoration England', *Past and Present*, 177 (2002), pp. 253–272.

Jenner, M., 'Follow your nose? Smell, smelling and their histories', *American Historical Review*, 116:2 (2011), pp. 335–351.

Jillings, K., 'Preventing plague in Post-Reformation Aberdeen', *International Review of Scottish Studies*, 30 (2005), pp. 108–134.

Jones, E. and Falkus, M., 'Urban improvement and the English economy in the seventeenth and eighteenth centuries', *Research in Economic History*, 4 (1979), pp. 193–233.

Jones, R., 'Signatures in the soil: the use of pottery in manure scatters in the identification of medieval arable farming regimes', *Archaeological Journal*, 161 (2004), pp. 159–188.

Jones, R., 'Manure and the medieval social order' in M. J. Allen, N. Sharples and T. O'Connor (eds), *Land and People: Papers in Memory of John G. Evans* (Oxford: Oxbow Books, Prehistoric Society Research Paper 2, 2009), pp. 215–225.

Jones, R., 'Why manure matters', in R. Jones (ed.), *Manure Matters: Historical, Archaeological and Ethnographic Perspectives* (Farnham: Ashgate, 2012), pp. 1–11.

Jones, R., 'Understanding medieval manure', in R. Jones (ed.), *Manure Matters: Historical, Archaeological and Ethnographic Perspectives* (Farnham: Ashgate, 2012), pp. 145–158.

Jorgensen, D., 'Co-operative sanitation: managing streets and gutters in late-medieval England and Scandanavia', *Technology and Culture*, 49:3 (2008), pp. 547–567.

Jorgensen, D., '"All good rule of the citee": sanitation and civic government in England, 1400–1600', *Journal of Urban History*, 36 (2010), pp. 300–315.

Jutte, R., *A History of the Senses from Antiquity to Cyberspace* (Cambridge: Polity, 2005).

Keene, D., 'Rubbish in medieval towns', in A. Hall and H. Kenward (eds), *Environmental Archaeology in the Urban Context* (London: Council for British Archaeology, 1982), pp. 26–30.

Kennedy, A., 'The urban community in Restoration Scotland: government, society and economy in Inverness, 1660–c.1688', *Northern Scotland*, 5 (2014), pp. 26–49.

King, W., 'How high is too high? Disposing of dung in seventeenth-century Prescot', *Sixteenth Century Journal*, 23:3 (1992), pp. 443–457.

Laing, D., 'Proposals for cleaning and lighting the city of Edinburgh in the year 1735: with explanatory remarks', *Proceedings of the Society of Antiquaries of Scotland*, 3 (1859), pp. 171–180.

Lemire, B., 'Consumerism in pre-industrial and early industrial England: the trade in second-hand clothes', *Journal of British Studies*, 27 (1988), pp. 1–24.

Lieshout, C. van, 'London's changing waterscapes: the management of water in eighteenth-century London' (PhD dissertation, King's College London, 2013).

Loengard, J., 'The Assize of Nuisance: origins of an action at common law', *California Law Journal*, 37:1 (1978), pp. 144–166.

Lynch, M., *Edinburgh and the Reformation* (Edinburgh: John Donald, 1981).

Lynch, M., 'The Scottish early modern burgh', *History Today*, 35:2 (1985), pp. 10–15.

Lynch, M. (ed.), *The Early Modern Town in Scotland* (London: Croon Helm, 1987).

MacDonald, A., *The Burghs and Parliament in Scotland, c.1550–1651* (Aldershot: Ashgate, 2007).

Macdougall, N., *James IV* (East Linton: Tuckwell Press, 1997).

MacFarlane, R., *Mountains of the Mind: A History of a Fascination* (London: Granta, 2003).

MacGibbon, D. and Ross, T., *The Castellated and Domestic Architecture of Scotland from the Twelfth to the Eighteenth Century*, 5 vols (Edinburgh: Douglas, 1887–92).

MacQueen, H. and Windram, W., 'Laws and courts in the burghs', in M. Lynch, R. Spearman and G. Stell (eds), *The Medieval Scottish Town* (Edinburgh: Donald, 1988), pp. 208–226.

Magnusson, R., *Water Technology in the Middle Ages: Cities, Monasteries and Waterworks after the Roman Empire* (Baltimore: John Hopkins University Press, 2001).

Makey, W., 'Edinburgh in mid-seventeenth century' in M. Lynch (ed.), *The Early Modern Town in Scotland* (London: Croon Helm, 1987), pp. 192–218.

McIntosh, M., *Controlling Misbehaviour in England, 1370–1600* (Oxford: Oxbow Books, 1998).

McKenzie, J., 'Manuring practices in Scotland: deep anthropogenic soils and the historical record' in B. Ballin Smith, S. Taylor and G. Williams (eds), *West Over Sea: Studies in Scandinavian Sea-Borne Expansion and Settlement before 1300* (Leiden: Brill, 2007), pp. 401–417.

McLaren, J., 'Nuisance law and the Industrial Revolution – some lessons from social history', *Oxford Journal of Legal Studies*, 3:2 (1983), pp. 155–221.

McLaughlin, T., *Dirt: A Social History as Seen Through the Uses and Abuses of Dirt* (Dorchester: Dorset Press, 1988).

Meikle, M., *The Scottish People, 1490–1625* (Raleigh, NC: Lulu, 2013).

Melosi, M., *The Sanitary City: Urban Infrastructure in America from Colonial Times to the Present* (Balitmore: John Hopkins University Press, 2000).

Melosi, M., *Garbage in the Cities: Refuse, Reform, and the Environment*, 2nd edn (Pittsburgh: University of Pittsburgh Press, 2005).

Miller, W., *The Anatomy of Disgust* (London: Harvard University Press, 1997).

Mullett, C., 'Plague policy in 16th and 17th century Scotland', *Osiris*, 9 (1950), pp. 435–456.

Oram, R., '"It cannot be decernit quha are clean and quha are foulle." Responses to epidemic disease in sixteenth- and seventeenth-century Scotland', *Renaissance and Reformation*, 30:4 (2006–2007), pp. 13–39.

Oram, R., 'Waste management and peri-urban agriculture in the early modern Scottish burgh', *Agricultural History Review*, 59:1 (2011), pp. 1–17.

Palliser, D., 'Epidemics in Tudor York', *Northern History*, 8 (1973), pp. 45–63.

Palliser, D., *Tudor York* (Oxford: Oxford University Press, 1979).

Palliser, D., 'Civic mentality and the environment in Tudor York', *Northern History Journal*, 18 (1982), pp. 78–115.

Palliser, D., 'Domesday York', *Borthwick Papers*, 78 (1990), pp. 1–31.

Palliser, D., 'The origins of British towns', in D. M. Palliser (ed.), *The Cambridge Urban History of Britain, vol. 1, 600–1540* (Cambridge: Cambridge University Press, 2000), pp. 17–24.

Palliser, D., Slater, T. and Dennison, E., 'The topography of towns, 600–1300', in D. Palliser (ed.), *The Cambridge Urban History of Britain, volume I, 600–1540* (Cambridge: Cambridge University Press, 2000), pp. 153–186.

Palmer, M., 'The workshop: type of building or method of work?' in P. Barnwell et. al (eds), *The Vernacular Workshop from Craft to Industry, 1400–1900* (York: Council for British Archaeology, 2004), pp. 1–16.

Porter, D., *Health, Civilization and the State: A History of Public Health from Ancient to Modern Times* (London: Routledge, 1999).

Pullan, B., 'Plague and perceptions of the poor in early modern Italy', in T. Ranger and P. Slack (eds), *Epidemics and Ideas: Essays on the Historical Perception of Pestilence* (Cambridge: Cambridge University Press, 1992), pp. 101–123.

Rawcliffe, C., *Urban Bodies: Communal Health in Late Medieval English Towns and Cities* (Woodbridge: Boydell and Brewer, 2013).

Reed, M., 'The urban landscape', in P. Clark (ed.), *The Cambridge Urban History of Britain, volume II, 1540–1840* (Cambridge: Cambridge University Press, 2000), pp. 289–313.

Reid, D., *Paris Sewers and Sewermen: Realities and Representations* (London: Harvard University Press, 1991).

Rennison, R., *Water to Tyneside: A History of the Newcastle & Gateshead Water Company* (Newcastle upon Tyne: Newcastle and Gateshead Water Company, 1979).

Roberts, S., 'The study of dispute: anthropological perspectives', in J. Bossy (ed.), *Disputes and Settlements: Law and Human Relations in the West* (Cambridge: Cambridge University Press, 1983), pp. 1–24.

Robson, W., *The Story of Hawick: An Introduction to the History of the Town*, 2nd edn (Hawick: R. Deans & Co., 1937).

Rodger, R., 'The evolution of Scottish town planning' in G. Gordon and B. Dicks (eds), *Scottish Urban History* (Aberdeen: Aberdeen University Press, 1983), pp. 71–91.

Sabine, E., 'Butchering in mediaeval London', *Speculum*, 8 (1933), pp. 335–353.

Sabine, E., 'Latrines and cesspools of mediaeval London', *Speculum*, 9 (1934), pp. 303–321.

Sabine, E., 'City cleaning in mediaeval London', *Speculum*, 12 (1937), pp. 19–43.

Sanderson, M., *A Kindly Place? Living in Sixteenth-Century Scotland* (East Linton: Tuckwell Press, 2002).

Schama, S., *Embarrassment of Riches: An Interpretation of Dutch Culture in the Golden Age* (New York: Knopf, 1987).

Scott-Warren, J., 'The privy politics of Sir John Harrington's *New Discourse of a Stale Subject, Called the Metamorphosis of Ajax*', *Studies in Philology*, 93:4 (1996), pp. 412–442.

Sheils, W., 'Seventeenth-century York', in P. Nuttgens (ed.), *The History of York: From Earliest Times to the Year 2000* (Pickering, 2001), pp. 177–211.

Shrewsbury, J., *A History of Bubonic Plague in the British Isles* (London: Cambridge University Press, 1971).

Skelton, L. J., 'Pursuing improvement: public hygiene in Scottish burghs, 1500–1700', *History Scotland Magazine*, 9:6 (2009), pp. 22–27.

Skelton, L. J., 'Environmental regulation in Edinburgh and York, c.1560–c.1700: with reference to several smaller Scottish Burghs and northern English towns' (PhD dissertation, Durham University, 2012).

Skelton, L. J., 'Beadles, dunghills and noisome excrements: regulating the environment in seventeenth-century Carlisle', *International Journal of Regional and Local History*, 9:1 (2014), pp. 44–62.

Slack, P., *The Impact of Plague in Early Modern England* (London: Routledge and Kegan Paul, 1985).

Slack, P., 'The response to plague in early modern England: public policies and their consequences', in J. Walter and R. Schofield (eds), *Famine, Disease and the Social Order in Early Modern Society* (Cambridge: Cambridge University Press, 1989), pp. 167–187.

Slack, P., *From Reformation to Improvement: Public Welfare in Early Modern England* (Oxford: Clarendon Press, 1999).

Smith, M., *Sensory History* (Oxford: Berg, 2007).

Smith, P., 'The foul burns of Edinburgh: public health attitudes and environmental change', *Scottish Geographical Journal*, 91:1 (1975), pp. 25–37.

Smith, V., *Clean: A History of Personal Hygiene and Purity* (Oxford: Oxford University Press, 2007).

Smout, T. C., *A History of the Scottish People, 1560–1830* (London: Fontana Press, 1969).

Smout, T. C., *Nature Contested: Environmental History in Scotland and Northern England Since 1600* (Edinburgh: Edinburgh University Press, 2000).

Steward, J. and Cowan, A., 'Introduction', in J. Steward and A. Cowan (eds), *The City and the Senses. Urban Culture since 1500* (Aldershot: Ashgate, 2007), pp. 1–24.

Stewart, L., *Urban Politics and the British Civil Wars: Edinburgh, 1617–1653* (Leiden: Brill, 2006).

Still, G. 'Housing in the two towns', in E. Dennison, D. Ditchburn and M. Lynch (eds), *Aberdeen Before 1800. A New History* (East Linton: Tuckwell Press, 2002), pp. 97–108.

Stone, L., *The Family, Sex and Marriage in England, 1500–1800* (Harmondsworth: Penguin, 1979).

Strasser, S., *Waste and Want: A Social History of Trash* (New York: Metropolitan Press, 1999).

Summerson, H., *Medieval Carlisle: The City and the Borders from the Late Eleventh to the Mid-sixteenth Century*, 2 vols (Kendal: *Transactions of the Cumberland and Westmoreland Antiquarian and Archaeological Society*, extra series, 1993).

Te Brake, W., 'Air pollution and fuel crises in pre-industrial London, 1250–1650', *Technology and Culture*, 16 (1975), pp. 337–359.

Thirsk, J., 'The farming regions of England', in J. Thirsk (ed.), *The Agrarian History of England and Wales, volume IV, 1500–1640* (Cambridge, 1967), pp. 1–112.

Thomas, J. H., *Town Government in the Sixteenth Century* (London: George Allen and Unwin Ltd, 1933).

Thomas, K., *Man and the Natural World: Changing Attitudes in England 1500–1800* (London: Penguin, 1983).

Thomas, K., 'Cleanliness and godliness in early modern England', in A. Fletcher and P. Roberts (eds), *Religion, Culture and Society in Early Modern Britain: Essays in Honour of Patrick Collinson* (Cambridge: Cambridge University Press, 1994), pp. 56–83.

Thorndike, L., 'Sanitation, baths, and street-cleaning in the Middle Ages and Renaissance', *Speculum*, 3 (1928), pp. 192–203.

Toolis, R. and Sproat, D., 'The transformation of an early post-medieval town into a major modern city: excavation and survey of the Waverley Vaults, New Street, Edinburgh, Scotland', *Post Medieval Archaeology*, 41:1 (2007), pp. 155–179.

Van Bavel, B. and Gelderblom, O., 'The economic origins of cleanliness in the Dutch Golden Age', *Past and Present*, 205:1 (2009), pp. 41–69.

Van der Heijden, M., 'New perspectives on public services in early modern Europe', *Journal of Urban History*, 36 (2010), pp. 271–284.

Van der Heijden, M., Elise van Nederveen, M., Griet, V. and van der Burg, M. (eds), *Serving the Urban Community: The Rise of Public Facilities in the Low Countries* (Amsterdam: Aksant Academic Publishers, 2009).

Vigarello, G., *Concepts of Cleanliness: Changing Attitudes in France since the Middle Ages*, trans. J. Birrel (Cambridge: Cambridge University Press, 1988).

Walker, D., *A Legal History of Scotland*, 6 vols (Edinburgh: T & T Clark, 1988–2001).

Walsham, A., *Providence in Early Modern England* (Oxford: Oxford University Press, 2000).

Webb, B., *English Local Government from the Revolution to the Municipal Corporations Act: The Manor and the Borough*, pt. 2 (London: Longmans, Green and Co., 1908).

Webb, S., *English Local Government from the Revolution to the Municipal Corporations Act: The Manor and the Borough*, pt. 1 (London: Longmans, Green and Co., 1908).

Webb, S. and Webb, B., *English Local Government from the Revolution to the Municipal Corporations Act: The Parish and the County* (London: Longmans, Green and Co, 1906).

Webb, S. and Webb, B., *English Local Government from the Revolution to the Municipal Corporations Act: The Story of the King's Highway* (London: Longmans, Green and Co, 1913).

Webb, S. and Webb, B., *English Local Government from the Revolution to the Municipal Corporations Act: Statutory Authorities for Special Purposes* (London: Longmans, Green and Co, 1922).

Wheeler, J., 'Stench in sixteenth-century Venice' in A. Cowan and J. Steward (eds), *The City and the Senses: Urban Culture Since 1500* (Aldershot, 2007), pp. 25–38.

Wilson, F., *The Plague in Shakespeare's London* (London: Oxford University Press, 1963).

Withington, P., 'Views from the bridge: revolution and restoration in seventeenth-century York', *Past and Present*, 170 (2001), pp. 121–151.

Withington, P., '"Tumbled into the dirt": wit and incivility in early modern England', *Journal of Historical Pragmatics*, vol. 12, no. 1/2 (2011), pp. 156–177.

Wood, M., 'The neighbourhood book', *The Book of the Old Edinburgh Club*, 23 (1940), pp. 82–100.

Woodward, D., '"An essay on manures": changing attitudes to fertilization in England, 1500–1800', in J. Chartres and D. Hey (eds), *English Rural Society, 1500–1800: Essays in Honour of Joan Thirsk* (Cambridge, 1990), pp. 251–278.

Woolgar, C., *The Senses in Late Medieval England* (London: Yale University Press, 2006).

Wright, L., *Clean and Decent: The Fascinating History of the Bathroom and the Water Closet* (London: Routledge and Kegan Paul, 1960).

Wrightson, K., 'Two concepts of order: justices, constables and jurymen in seventeenth-century England', in J. Brewer and J. Styles (eds), *An Ungovernable People? The English and their Law in the Seventeenth and Eighteenth Centuries* (London: Hutchinson, 1980), pp. 21–46.

Wrightson, K., 'The "Decline of Neighbourliness" revisited', in N. Jones and D. Woolf (eds), *Local Identities in Late Medieval and Early Modern England* (Basingstoke: Palgrave MacMillan, 2007), pp. 19–49.

Wrigley, E., 'A simple model of London's importance in changing English society and economy, 1650–1750', *Past and Present*, 37:1 (1967), pp. 44–70.

Wrigley, E. and Schofield, R., *The Population History of England, 1541–1871: A Reconstruction* (London: Edward Arnold, 1981).

Zupko, R. and Laures, R., *Straws in the Wind: Medieval Urban Environmental Law: The Case of Northern Italy* (Oxford: Westview, 1996).

Index

For Product Safety Concerns and Information please contact our EU
representative GPSR@taylorandfrancis.com Taylor & Francis Verlag GmbH,
Kaufingerstraße 24, 80331 München, Germany

Printed and bound by CPI Group (UK) Ltd, Croydon, CR0 4YY
01/05/2025
01858359-0002